who the F★★★ wants to be
PRESIDENT?!
my year of living politically

JJ WALCUTT
WITH SAE SCHATZ

Copyright © 2020 by JJ Walcutt and Sae Schatz

All rights reserved. No part of this book may be reproduced in any form of by any means, electronic or mechanical, including photocopying, recording, or by any information storage and retrieval system, without written permission of the publisher.

Designed by Sae Schatz

Produced with support from Girl Friday Productions

Cataloging-in-Publication Data

Library of Congress Control Number: 2020906802

Names: Walcutt, JJ, author. | Schatz, Sae, author.

Title: Who the f*** wants to be president: my year of living politically / JJ Walcutt and Sae Schatz

Description: Orlando, Florida | Summary: Memoir of one woman's exploration of the US federal government and presidential politics during the 2020 election.

Identifiers: ISBN: 9781734670608 (paperback) | ISBN: 9781734670615 (e-book)

Subjects: Biography & Autobiography—Political | Political Science—Women in Politics | Humor—Topic—Politics | Political Science—Political Process—Campaigns & Elections | Political Science—American Government—National | Political Science—Civics & Citizenship.

PRAISE FOR WHO THE F*** WANTS TO BE PRESIDENT?!

"A picture of American politics, with a cheerful Americana tone. Love it."

David Jolly, retired politician and former Member of the US House of Representatives

"An extraordinarily insightful and often funny journey through the halls of government, across the presidential campaign trail, and in the (bright red) shoes of a real—fed-up—American woman."

Bonnie Hagemann, C-Suite Advisor and CEO of EDA, Inc.

"JJ Walcutt, doctor of philosophy, veteran research psychologist, former director of innovation . . . and US presidential candidate. She's got bona fide beltway cred, tremendous insight, and a front row seat. I highly recommend JJ's written exploration of our government from a trusted insider."

Greg Williams, human behavior expert and director of training and innovation for Arcadia Cognerati

"Who the f*ck wouldn't want to read this book? JJ Walcutt is a tour de force, channeling her world-class experiences, wit, and levity to provide a road map to solutions and hope of a better tomorrow. This is a book to engage the novice political reader and political expert alike. A must read."

Al Light, Cirque du Soleil

CONTENTS

Introduction 1

American Warrior Nerd Princess 5

It's Sort of Not that Hard (to Sign up) 15

It's My Political Party, and I'll Cry if I Want To 23

Only Crazy People Run for President 31

Hi, I'm JJ, and I'm Running for President 39

But First, a Word from Our Sponsors 49

#Tour50 55

Money Is the Root of All Politics 67

At Least I Can Handle the Shit! 75

The Great American Salad Bowl 85

Neither Healthy, Caring, nor a System 95

Who's Who in the Political Zoo? 109

The Little Red Hen Strategy 117

More than a Faster Horse 131

'Ohana 145

A Dummy's Guide to Fundraising (Badly) 157

How Are We Still Talking about Money?! 169

Black Swans and Little Green Men 189

The Last Mile 207

Pieces of the Patriotic Puzzle 219

Postscript 229

Notes 231

AUTHOR'S NOTE

This book shows some dark corners of the political machine, along with some quirky stories and a little snark. I affirm everything written here describes true experiences to the fullest extent humanly possible. In a few places, my editor has inserted dialogue (she swears it reads better that way), and those conversations are paraphrased based on my memory. Also, I've changed the names of some people described in the story: Sometimes to protect them, sometimes to protect me, and sometimes because they still work on the inside—the silent civil servants making our government run.

ACKNOWLEDGMENTS

No meaningful project is done alone. I can't squeeze in the names of everyone who deserves it, but here's an attempt. First, thank you to my family and the Geek Team for making the #Tour50 possible. In particular, thanks to my husband, Chris, for managing the home front while I was away, and thanks to Robert Ramus for the time sacrificed to help coordinate the campaign tour. Also, a special thanks to Shelbi Kuhlmann-Pratt, Hank Ohnstad, Nick Armendariz, Gail Ohnstad, Bonnie Hagemann, and our editorial committee: Jen Murphy, Sydney Burton, Yasir Saleem, Karen Fray, David Fautua, Aaron and Biljana Presnall, and Joe Nolan. And, finally, a big thank you to all of the experts and everyday Americans who willingly donated their time, ideas, and passion—you provided the true story we hope to tell.

DEDICATION

For my daughter, Sarah, who gave me the courage to fly . . .

Introduction

"These can't be the best people in America."

It was 2016, and presidential hopefuls Hillary Clinton and Donald Trump (with their chorus of also-rans) were having playground fistfights on the campaign trail. Meanwhile, my son, Mitchell, seventeen years old at the time, was analyzing the race for his high school civics course. "Mom, how does this even make sense?! They're worrying about all the wrong things." This diatribe went on for a while—with a degree of irritability only achievable by the very ancient or very teenaged.

I'm a scientist by training, a developmental psychologist to be precise. That means, in my house, we don't brook idle grumbling. If you name a problem, you also need to recommend solutions. So I challenged him, "What would a good candidate look like?"

Over the course of the evening, he rattled off a series of qualifications—strategic but practical, polished but genuine, deep-thinking but pithy.

When he got to the end, I joked, "Mitchell, you just described me."

"Yeah, Mom, you want the job?" he quipped.

"Fuck no!" I sputtered, as we both laughed.

Over the intervening weeks, my family teased me about my "presidential run." They'd misquote me around the dinner table and taunt, "Fake news!" or ask me sound-bite questions in caricatures of the debates. I played along, giving feigned stately responses, and gradually the tone shifted. They forgot to tease and instead became legitimately engrossed in serious questions and meaningful answers. It started feeling less like a game and more like an audition, and I began to reconsider my original outlook.

Of course, the idea of waking up one day and running for president is ludicrous, but I also felt curious. My son's question from before also nagged at me. I wanted to see the process from the inside, to better understand why the current system seems tinged with dysfunction. And, I had to admit, it was time *I* stopped grumbling and started looking for solutions, even if that meant plunging into the dark heart of politics to find them.

Before setting foot upon that perilous yellow-brick road, I grappled with the magnitude of the decision. Even running as a write-in candidate for the sake of experience and experimentation held serious risk. The political spotlight invites public ridicule, distrust, and baggage—and not a lot of upside. What ultimately pushed my decision forward began as a simple conversation at my job.

For over a decade, I've worked with the Department of Defense in some capacity, and in this case my watercooler colleague was a former Marine, now employed as a military civilian. We were talking about his time in Fallujah, one of the bloodiest places in the recent Iraqi conflicts. Originally, he'd deployed there as a Marine and later returned a second time, out of uniform, as a civilian. During this second expedition, a bomb had exploded. He recalled his initial reaction—move to the commotion, get ready to help—before remembering he was no longer on active duty. Then he made the joke: "JJ, do you know the difference between a Marine and a civilian? Marines run toward fire; civilians hightail it the other way!"

My deep admiration for my associate mingled with an undercurrent of disappointment—not at him or his quip, but at myself. If my coworkers could risk life and limb serving our country, then how dare I shy away to protect my own ego? Still, I wasn't so naïve as to believe I was ready to run. I needed to learn more about politics and elections, particularly their unwritten rules, and I needed to learn whether my ideas (which had won critical acclaim around my dinner table) could withstand real political critique.

I made politics my new hobby. I learned to navigate the labyrinth of regulatory paperwork and grew more confident using videos and social media to share my political message. (Do you realize how anxiety-provoking it can be to edit hours of video of yourself, talking about your innermost beliefs, then tee them up for strangers on the internet to dissect?) Thankfully, my platform resonated. My ideas withstood the Twitterverse and YouTube comments section, and a few serious political operatives even took notice. But while my experimental run had given me a growing feel for our country's political apparatus, I realized there was a lot left to discover. In the end, I made it onto the 2016 ballot in thirteen states as an independent write-in candidate and earned about two votes, along with a treasure trove of experience.

Hungry for more answers, I started from the inside. I earned a special fellowship with the Office of Personnel Management (or OPM, essentially the human resources agency for our federal government) and was sworn-in on November 15, a week after the election. As an OPM Human Innovation Fellow, working as a civil servant in the Department of Defense, I saw so many inspiring, encouraging, perplexing, and downright infuriating things. I had the privilege to work with our NATO allies and to walk the Pentagon's history-clad halls next to some of the smartest, most dedicated people I've ever met. I also learned, through great personal suffering, the mind-numbing depths of inefficiency government bureaucracy can attain.

When I wasn't at work, I signed up for every political group I could find—Republican and Democrat. I attended President Trump's inauguration and the Women's March the next day. I went to political stump speeches, fundraising events, and community board meetings. I watched hundreds of how-to videos about politics and dove into educational programs offered by groups like Emily's List, Ruth's List, VoteRunLead, and 314 Action. I immersed myself, and at least initially, my goal wasn't necessarily to revive my prior presidential experiment but to be a citizen-scientist examining the foundations and forces of our political system.

Nonetheless, as the 2020 election cycle neared, I pondered my options. I had learned so much since 2016 and felt increasingly confident in my knowledge and strategies. My personal tool kit—my academic training, life experiences, and ways of thinking—are rather atypical. I'm a psychologist by schooling, have worked as a research scientist with special-needs children and military personnel, and have studied some of the inner-workings of government, which I literally wrote the book about (not this book but other drier scholarly publications). I've been a university professor, small-business contributor, and government civilian, and I'm a proud mama who's survived divorce, four children, and a funeral. And I've worked my ass off to grow from modest beginnings to where I am today.

Still, like any sane person who might consider running for president, I asked myself, "Why do you think you're worth it?" It's hard to simultaneously remain humble and embrace confidence, and any reasonable individual questions her own self-assurance. Do I have a blind spot? Could someone else do this better? If "the impossible" were to happen, would I make things better?

So many people—some of whom I've personally met and who have unashamedly said this to my face—believe only rich, crazy, or egomaniacal people run for president. (What a sad commentary on our system!) Yet it is possible to find a sliver of middle ground where someone reasonable can say, "I'm confident, capable, and willing to give it a shot for my country." Not all politicians are cocky and ego-driven, and it's OK to have personal convictions and a sense of inner worth. In fact, I'd argue that humility to the point of meekness is a greater shame than realistic self-confidence.

So in 2018, facing the murky uncertainty of a 2020 presidential bid, I thought, *What the hell?*

And that was the moment—the moment when "idea" clicked into "decision." I felt the weight of trepidation fall away. For better or worse, I'd do it. I'd trade my safe, rewarding federal job for an improbable and unpredictable presidential run. It felt terrifying and exhilarating, yet at my core I also felt a sense of peace, knowing I had the courage to embrace the challenge and test my convictions.

It took several more months to put the pieces into place. I needed approvals and licenses, online platforms and volunteers, and I needed to strengthen my policy platforms. I also needed a national tour, a grassroots campaign run outside of the political machine. A plan began to take shape that combined my love of America with my passion for science: I'd travel the nation, visiting all fifty states while also seeking out experts in topics like environment and health care to help inform and refine my ideas.

This is that story. It's the story of my year on the campaign trail, living as a dark-horse presidential candidate, and it's the story of all the things I uncovered during that experience—from deep-fried Oreos and unexpected wisdom at state fairs, to the hidden rules of politics and ideas for reforming our system. And just maybe, this is also the story of how we can change the world—at least a little.

CHAPTER ONE

American Warrior Nerd Princess

How do you train to be the president or, more precisely, to be a presidential candidate? Most obviously, it's helpful to know the political process, civics, government, leadership, and strategy—the job stuff. You also need the tacit rules, those secret handshakes for actually getting work done. And, finally, there's the human element: You, personally, need the inner strength to withstand the political gauntlet and grueling media circus.

America has plenty of smart, qualified people who understand government, business, or community and who care deeply about our nation, but only a handful are willing to bear the personal costs of running for the highest office. I'm convinced this human toll is the biggest barrier to political entry. It discourages a lot of good people and is why the candidates who make it on stage aren't necessarily the best our nation has to offer. They're just the best options out of those willing to pay the high price of admission into the race. I had to make sure I was ready.

For the three years leading up to my 2020 campaign decision, I studied both the explicit and implicit political system, and like a pro athlete, I crafted a regime to prepare. I called it my "American Warrior Nerd Princess" training. With *American* encompassing the job training, *warrior* representing strength and scrappiness, *nerd* for my academic approach to problems (this one included), and *princess* to remind myself that femininity and political savvy aren't mutually exclusive.

I've already described some of my techniques for studying government. I trained through civics groups, political events, educational programs, and a federal job. In a way, "American" training was the least complicated part of this preparation. It wasn't easy—it took time, mental energy, and vigilance—but it was difficult like moving a pile of bricks: hard work but straightforward.

The "warrior" drills were another matter. How do you prepare for the human toll? I needed to learn to manage my stamina, maintain energy and focus, and keep cool in the face of criticism. I had to train my body to live on less sleep and my brain to stay in the zone. I also had to learn to summon brilliance on demand.

As a card-carrying nerd, I already felt comfortable working in the realm of ideas, but this was different. Politicians are expected to have answers to an encyclopedic range of topics at the drop of a hat: What's your opinion on South Sudan, how do we save the black-footed ferrets, and where's the solution to the opioid crisis? You mustn't lie, shouldn't bullshit, and oughtn't deflect. And pausing to think is like blood in the water; it's misperceived as ignorance or insincerity. You have to respond rapidly, ideally with something relevant and short enough to air on the six o'clock news. As a scientist, it's difficult for me to answer without explaining all the details, citing sources, and giving caveats. (Nerdiness is cumbersome.) So, I had to grow comfortable giving wave-top statements, balancing my desire to answer substantively with the necessity of speaking in punchlines. That took a lot of work!

Next came the "princess" training. I've always considered myself a bona fide lab rat, accustomed to research spaces and bookworm style. I covet my jeans and witty T-shirts. I like to feel comfortable, with my hair tied back in braids and feet in white athletic socks, hugged by old, broken-in shoes. While that level of stylish ambivalence may fly at a university or in a company's back office, I realized it was a bit underdressed for the public spotlight.

I didn't come to that realization by myself, though; an event catalyzed it. I was at a project review with about fifty other military scientists. The scene wasn't notable: Folding tables, lined up in rows, with the attendees, mostly men, sitting in those office chairs with the little wheels splayed out at the bottom. For the first day of the meeting, I wore something nondescript that passed muster as professional attire, but I barely spared my wardrobe a second thought. The next day, though, I wore a dress a friend had bought for me. At that time, wearing a dress was uncharacteristic, but it had stretchy fabric and a flattering pattern, so I gave it a try.

As I arrived, a colleague, a Navy captain, did a double take and wryly asked, "What in the hell happened to you, JJ? Yesterday you were playing dress up out of your grandma's closet, and today you look like you're going to the Kennedy awards. You feeling OK?"

Oops.

So I guess people did notice fashion, even if I was oblivious. Looking good is nice, but even more, I wanted to look the part—I mean, the part where I'm a confident professional not an apparel fruitcake. It wouldn't do to distract people or to send the wrong message because of what I wore. But what message did I want to send?

I often find myself in airports, and during my fashion revelation, I began looking at the women depicted on books and magazines at those omnipresent in-terminal bookstores. Inevitably, one of them will feature an alpha woman—dressed in a power suit with arms crossed assertively—on its cover, usually with something like "fight" or "power" in the title. No doubt these women have blazed a trail, but along with capturing their strength those images always seem a bit angry, as if female empowerment is only achieved through seriousness and aggression. I struggled with the idea and honestly wondered whether the next rung on the professional ladder demanded that kind of outward persona, or could I climb toward success while still holding on to my cool, quirky, casual self?

Fashion doesn't come naturally to me but research does. So, I developed a data collection protocol and formed a review committee. In other words, I spent a few months scrolling through pictures of professional women online and texting my friends. After the first hour of this highly controlled investigation, I was already bored looking at the neutral colors, shapeless dresses, and soulless corporate suits. There was no way I could survive in a suit! Eventually, though, I settled on a role model: Audrey Hepburn. OK, not particularly original but she's an icon for a reason. She had personality and grace accented by femininity and a coy smile.

Once I found "the look," then I had to learn how to shop for clothes that looked the part without sacrificing comfort or personality. For several months, my bedroom became a dressing room. I tried on a collection of cuts and shapes and sent pictures to my review board for feedback. Eventually, through this methodological process, and unaided by any personal panache, I cultivated my style: a modernized version of the dresses from Audrey Hepburn's era but with my own sassy nerdiness peeking through.

I felt like I had gained a level as an adult. Good job: +1 professionalism.

On November 14, 2016, I found myself in the airport again, this time on my way to Washington, DC, to be sworn in as a civil servant—hopefully, with my personality and newfound style intact. I arrived the next day at the Office of Personnel Management, an imposing building constructed of concrete and hard angles, situated in the heart of DC. As I settled in for onboarding, I was unsurprised to see all of the other new hires wearing the "beltway uniform." They were a flock of somber black and navy suits—with me, the pink flamingo, conspicuously perched in the middle.

I felt like people were looking at me, maybe wondering where I'd come from, and definitely judging. For men, or for women who haven't worked in these kinds of suit-and-tie professions, you may not be familiar with the implicit office dress code. There's a particular needle women need to thread: You want to look put together but not *too* striking. Don't look like you just rolled out of bed, but don't come across like you're trying too hard. And, for god's sake, don't look like you're putting effort into being attractive. People will mentally subtract points from your IQ and wonder just what you did to land that management role.

Maybe it was all in my head, but after a few days of standing out in my colorful dresses, I started to think I had, just maybe, made a wardrobe blunder. Maybe I should rein in the personality a little, starting with my attire. (Even my stubborn ego isn't immune to peer pressure.) Yet, of all people, it was a general officer at the Pentagon who convinced me otherwise.

I had gathered with a crowd of coworkers, filing into the auditorium for a directorate all-hands meeting. Still only days into the job, I barely recognized anyone, and the woman shuffling through the doors next to me was no exception. She had no makeup and wore the severe bun and serious expression of a senior military leader; she also had two stars on her uniform's lapel. Even though she stood barely five feet tall, the major general had the aura of a giant. She radiated calm authority, so much so that even gregarious-me felt too nervous to greet her. I could feel her eyes on me too and wondered what she was thinking. Then, just like that, all my fears evaporated, as she leaned over and whispered, "Love the shoes!" referring to my now-signature candy-apple red pumps. I still haven't learned her name, but her nod of approval that day became a small turning point. That seemingly trivial gesture gave me the extra armor I needed to stand up to the disapproving glances and muttered expressions. It reminded me that I could—and would—let me be me.

Of course, my time in government involved so much more than sartorial drama. While I worked as a civil servant, I also kept my eyes open to how the government operates. Although I had learned the basics in school, something didn't add up between what politicians say, what the law defines, and what the news reports. If all of those sources were correct and complete, then why wasn't government more functional? Many assume the missing piece is corruption. Others figure it's simple incompetence, including, perhaps, that the government is a "jobs program" for the slowest of workers. But none of those answers seemed to fully explain things. I needed to find out for myself, from the inside; I wanted to absorb all of those small truths that can't be learned vicariously.

What I found wasn't that surprising. The sand in the gears of government is largely named "bureaucracy" and "miscommunication." Picture this: I sometimes traveled overseas for work. For that kind of business trip, I needed to get my boss's and my boss's boss's approval, and also the OK from my employing agency's chain of command. (Let that sink in. These senior executives, some of whom require Senate approval just to hold their offices, are triplicate reviewing my travel plans. And that's just the exposition of this little story.) Anyhow, after getting approval, I inserted the trip into one of the most disparaged software applications in existence: the Defense Travel System. As the name implies, it itemizes travel and expenses. In this case, the trip cost about four thousand dollars and involved a long transatlantic flight. I had selected one with just two legs. This, however, was denied. Instead, the bureaucratic machine required me to select a less expensive flight that added another layover and eight more billable hours—all to save five dollars on airline tickets. (Yes, literally five freaking dollars.) This is just one example where well-meaning processes have grown into a Dilbert-esque parody.

Don't get me wrong: Controls, approvals, and even red tape serve a purpose. They slow rash decisions and create checks and balances. But like weeds in a derelict garden, reasonable organizational bureaucracy can grow into a jumbled monster at the worker level, and rules can (and often do) take on a life of their own outside the bounds of logic.

The bureaucracy creates more than bottlenecks; it can also inadvertently skew incentives. A vast majority of civil servants, in my experience, work tirelessly for the mission, but as in any office, some people are rewards oriented. You know the type: the saleswoman who pushes herself to become the top earner in the division or the restaurant manager who drives his team to get the best turnover rates across the franchise. They want to *win*. And, in general, both the hard-chargers and their organizations benefit from that determination. In government, though, there aren't as many outlets for Type-A personalities, and it's difficult to judge whether any particular worker is "winning" or "losing." The only yardstick of personal success, in many cases, is the size of the program manager's budget. If you oversee more money, then you have more points on the scoreboard—regardless of what the money buys. It's like kids at Halloween; some just want the most candy, even if they never plan to eat it. They see it as a sign of achievement, and for the government sharks that means scheming, playing office politics, and exploiting every sneaky-but-legal trick they can to win more budgetary control. That's not to imply everyone acts so Machiavellian, but it's important to understand the unspoken game, even if only a few people are playing it. On the plus side, all of this gave me plenty of opportunities for "warrior" exercises, like getting comfortable with a target on my back, bobbing and weaving political sucker-punches, and learning how to stay afloat despite a seemingly endless sea of barriers.

But my warrior training involved more than office politics. It also meant sharpening my body and mind. I'm a strong believer in *energy*—not the kind crystal-clad psychics use—but physical, mental, and emotional resources in a practical sense. For instance, I had to find ways to manage my stamina, both for my civil service work and, even more, if I hoped to someday run a whistle-stop election campaign. So, I started monitoring my calories, eating times, and blood sugar; like an athlete, I tweaked my nutrition to maximize my focus and fortitude.

Even more than physical endurance, I had to improve my emotional resilience. Politicians face a relentless assault of scorn and insults, and they can't let attacks get under their skin. But how do you insulate yourself to criticism while remaining open to constructive input? How do you steel yourself to the disapproving tone and judgy scrutiny?

I once saw a picture of Britney Spears and Kevin Federline sitting and talking at the beach. (One of the *it* couples of my generation.) Except, instead of the typical seaside tabloid pic, the photographer had snapped the couple from behind, capturing dozens of other camera-wielding paparazzi in the picture's background. It struck me in a visceral way. I tried to imagine how it felt to have that continuous swarm of cameras and feel pressure to be always "on." Although not celebrities, per se, politicians—and certainly presidents—face something similar. They can never put their guard down or let their cool demeanor crack. They can never run to the corner café in pajamas, inadvertently raise their voice on a bad day, or go outside without a proper bra. That has to be exhausting!

That sense of being exposed and fear of public failure almost made me call off my 2020 run. The anxiety I felt at the prospect of public humiliation is difficult to sum up in words. What if I got onto the national stage as a laughingstock? What if this crazy presidential gambit, played out across network TV and internet sites, made me into a pariah—or some terrible new meme? What if I made such a fool of myself that no one would hire me again in an average job? What if I completely lost my way of life? It was scary as hell, and sometimes, when my thoughts touched that vein of apprehension, I could feel my heart start to run and my head sway. I kept asking myself, *Can you handle it?* And for a while, I wasn't sure.

I tried following the advice, "Staying alive means always moving" (not a Zen-inspired quote but something I often heard infantrymen say). I practiced taking in negative feedback without letting it seep into my conviction. I reminded myself: Just keep moving forward. Take in information and then step forward. Fire and forget. Because if you dwell, it will sap your emotional energy, sleep, and confidence, and once you begin to teeter off balance, you'll derail.

Cardio helped too. I made an upbeat playlist and would speed walk around the neighborhood to power-up songs, like Elle King's "America's Sweetheart." That proved a better energy boost than caffeine and soon these 'round-the-block laps became a keystone of my routine.

My walking time was also my thinking time. While I looped the black-asphalt path around my neighborhood, I'd scrutinize the angles of my platform. As my confidence grew, I started practicing impromptu responses to envisioned media questions, clipping my answers to thirty-second, two-minute, or five-minute sound bites. I practiced answering out loud, which based on my neighbors' stares at the time must have looked kind of crazy.

I tried a lot of ridiculous warrior exercises. I printed out pictures of TV cameras and taped them to the walls around my treadmill, so I could practice talking into a throng of lenses. In another exercise, which I mentally dubbed "glossing," I'd practice maneuvering through groups at social events like conferences, trying to briefly engage with everyone without getting bogged down in any particular group. I also worked my "resting-pleasant face" after seeing some candid photos of myself at a convention. In every one, my mouth looked like I was trying to catch flies, and my creased brow and weird posture said that (while I might be engrossed in the topic) I was clearly unaware of my audience. I thought back to Britney and Kevin on the beach and tried to remind myself to pay more attention—in the shower, in the car, on the street—stand up straight, unscrunch your face, and smile, smile, smile. I even asked some of my hometown friends to play low-budget paparazzi. They'd snap smartphone photos of me in the coffee line or idling at a red light, trying to catch me daydreaming and making ugly thinking faces. Whenever they did, they'd text, "Found you again . . . ," with the unflattering picture attached. You should try it. It's a good way to check your ego.

I tried to build routines for every little thing. I wanted to be ready for what was to come—at least those things I could control or predict. Part of that preparation also meant studying. Like a giant nerd, I scoured all the major public documents I could find on topics like education, health care, environment, economy, security, and foreign relations. I built an unwieldy spreadsheet of summaries, along with highlighted talking points for every theme. I also studied popular religions, reviewing the Bible, Torah, Book of Mormon, Quran, and Book of Buddha as if I were training for a graduate exam. It was the least I could do. If I wanted to represent the people of America, I needed to go beyond the surface to better understand how the lenses of these religions affect their followers' worldviews.

Like my walking-and-talking exercises, I shamelessly carried piles of legislative reports and religious tomes around, and I engrossed myself in them whenever and wherever time allowed. This sparked a number of interesting interactions. More than once, perplexed business travelers approached me curiously as I read a stack of holy books at the airport bar, and frequently my reading list was a conversation starter in the air. One notable encounter in this vein happened during a return flight from Norway.

I was buckled into an economy seat, my pink computer bag wedged under my feet, and my laptop awkwardly balanced on my tray table. Taking care to avoid my neighbor's personal space, I pulled out the Bible and began highlighting phrases and taking notes in my spreadsheet. It was impossible to miss my seatmate's side-eye, but she stayed politely mute and instead pulled out her own research supplies: A three-ring binder adorned with obsessively organized post-it notes. Clinically speaking, that level of sticky-note-itis is a sure sign someone's a nerd, so sensing my own kind, I broached the curious silence. My instincts proved right. She was a graduate student, finishing her doctorate in climate science from Princeton. Her assessment of me, on the other hand, was a little off. After warming up through conversation, she admitted she had thought I was the most organized missionary she'd ever seen! (Serendipitously, this chance connection later proved instrumental for my environmental strategy, but we'll get to that later.)

As I trained as an American Warrior Nerd Princess, I thought long and hard about the qualities a successful president needs, and it struck me how different presidential skills are from those presidential *candidates* require. An effective commander in chief (at least on paper) is smart and strategic, with strong foundations built on selflessness and bipartisanship. He—or she—is well versed in policy, embraces teamwork, listens openly to advisors, uses creative problem solving and complex thinking, and focuses on long-term outcomes.

Candidates, on the other hand, are incentivized to build strong partisan ties and focus on amassing financial wealth (either directly or through their political organizations). It's critical they dress well, speak well, and look the part. They're good at bobbing and weaving in response to questions, converting intricate answers into prepackaged platitudes, and delivering zingers on camera. Successful candidates have also "done their time"—they've navigated the political machine from the ground up and played their roles in the institutional circus.

After months of homemade presidential training, it finally dawned on me: If I wanted to move forward, I needed more than executive skills—those American Warrior Nerd Princess qualities I personally valued. I also needed to build candidate skills, which may—or may not—be quite so palatable.

CHAPTER TWO

It's Sort of Not that Hard (to Sign up)

At first, I tried to be a good little candidate and dutifully follow the "way it's always been done." I joined the Florida Democrats and began attending their events. Every state has a Democratic (and a Republican) committee, and they sponsor rallies, training programs, and similar things. Once a year, for instance, the Florida Democrats put on a conference. During the day, it includes free seminars, and for a fair amount of money, candidates from across the state can purchase small booth spaces (imagine tables at a science fair) where they can speak and get feedback from attendees. There are also caucus meetings, essentially communities of practice around specific issues, such as the environmental caucus, black caucus, and disability caucus. Candidates can request two-minute speaking opportunities at each of these.

More serious political hopefuls can also pay for five-minute spots on the main stage during the gala dinner. There's even a package option that includes a gala dinner table, five minutes on stage, and the chance to air a two-minute video—what a deal! The political pundits who opt for this package usually come with an entourage, and during the day their volunteers (walking billboards clad in matching T-shirts bearing their candidate's name) roam the conference halls. Sometimes they'll answer questions about the campaign; other times, they just chant and cheer for their candidate—like cheerleaders at a pep rally.

Aside from the networking (undeniably the critical function), these sorts of events largely serve as a place to teach budding politicians how to dress acceptably, speak publicly, and tell a story. They're a way to indoctrinate newbies into the "in group." A few of the Democratic National Committee training events also cover practical topics like social media and fundraising—but only in the context of local races. None of the events emphasized strategic thinking, real policy debates, or national perspectives. I think there's an assumption at the national level that you've already grown up from the inside. In other words, the system itself encourages candidates to start at the entry-level rung.

Watching stump speeches across several years of these events, I grew indifferent to the conventional formula. Take the annual Florida Democrats convention, for example. I watched mayoral candidates, who seemed like delegates from the Borg Collective. All of the speakers who took the main stage gave the same talk: They thanked the audience, told them "you're valuable," affirmed their belief in the Democratic Party platform (education, environment, and helping people), and then re-thanked attendees for the honor to serve. Every. Single. Time. No one varied from the script, unless you count those occasions where a candidate brought his wife on stage to stand like a smiling mannequin behind him. (I never saw a female or LGBTQ+ speaker use a similar "spouse prop," but my experience is limited to the Florida conference, where Southern values still encourage old-school traditions. However, I've instructed my husband to work on his mannequin look; maybe we'll break that mold next year!)

The two-minute caucus talks were even worse (if that's possible). With so many different candidates giving those pitches, you might expect a wider range of diversity. But every performance was identical. I mean, each candidate repeated the same talk to each of the caucuses, only swapping out the "Mad Lib" text field with the caucus's name: "Thank you for inviting me; it was the environment . . . or black caucus, or disability caucus . . . that inspired me to run." More than that, all of the different candidates gave the same cookie-cutter speeches, time and time and time again.

But not everyone seemed to notice. In fact, it felt like I was staring at the proverbial emperor strolling nude down the parade route—was I missing something? Despite (what I considered to be) lackluster and superficial pitches, the audience was definitely into it. Light on substance but full of emotion, they cheered their favorite gladiators. I felt like an outsider.

For most people, these sorts of events are the points of entry into politics. I remember watching one young man struggling on stage like it was a freshman job fair. Later, I had the opportunity to talk with his mother and father. They were an older couple dressed in business causal and wearing small political buttons. Although they didn't announce themselves as his relatives, their body language spoke volumes. They beamed like proud parents at their little boy's piano recital. Naturally, I had to strike up a conversation.

"We're here to see our son in his first run for office," they explained. "And we brought our friends to support him." There was no way that raw young man had a credible shot at one of the highest seats in Florida—at least, not until he gained a lot more experience. But that was the thing, his parents were getting him that experience. They had literally bought their son's ticket into the political arena. It was part of their family's legacy.

There's a stratum of the political community comprised of this kind of political elite, people whose parents tutor them from birth to have social acumen and leverage relationships. They enter the race with so many doors already open. If politics were a marathon, these lucky few start at mile fifteen and with the best equipment, fitness coaches, and cheerleaders to boot.

All of that stands in sharp contrast to my own upbringing. I grew up in the unsophisticated suburbs of Orlando, Florida, one of three daughters of a janitor and a high school bookkeeper. When I was young, my parents pushed me to study hard and build a strong resume; this would be my ticket into the middle class. After high school, I carried that mentality to Colgate University, an elite school in upstate New York. Nearly all of my classmates came from wealthy "who's who" families; they matriculated through connections and privilege. I, on the other hand, qualified through the combination of high academic scores and low socioeconomic status.

I thought the same work ethic that earned me a place at college would help me succeed there—and in life afterward. So, at first, I looked down on my dorm mates who blew off studying in lieu of Friday-night soirées, and I felt a twinge of self-satisfaction volunteering for extracurricular assignments when my peers couldn't be bothered. Over time, though, it became clear that despite my hard work and academic successes, my classmates were winning the real game. Their first priority wasn't studying hard or building extramural resumes. My peers were building connections. The friends they made at parties and tailgates would become the next generation of professional elites, and those networks—not bloated resumes or impressive GPAs—open the doors to future success.

Don't misunderstand: Studying hard has definitely benefited me, but I was so focused on that objective that I missed the bigger picture. *Who* you know is often more important than *what* you know. That's one of the unwritten rules of wealthier society. While at school, I came to realize that people raised in those high-class circles assume everyone knows this game. My classmates were surprised I thought hard work and job experience were the keys to success. They were confused that I didn't know the unwritten rules and were amazed I considered the rules "unwritten" in the first place. Doesn't everyone know connections, influence, legacy, money, and social standing make the world work?

In a similar way, the privileged class views politics differently. In regular families, like mine, running for office isn't something your relatives cheer about or, really, even pay attention to. It's a personal thing, like your nine-to-five job. Your family might give you a high five for accomplishing something, but they're not going door to door asking their friends to donate. In contrast, families among the political elite (or at least, more politically savvy) encourage their burgeoning candidates, arming them with an active support network and proverbial training wheels while they learn the ropes.

One reason for the difference stems from motivation. Regular families aren't advantaged by political clout in the same way upper-class families are. It may sound cynical, but wealthier families who hold real estate, own businesses, or control investments have a larger stake in how taxes are spent and laws are written. These families benefit from having someone in public office—someone with a hand on the controls of financial and regulatory power. Nurturing their children into politics literally becomes part of their diversified investment portfolio.

Of course, not everyone has politically inclined children; fortunately, for the politically privileged, there are plenty of naïve hopefuls to nurture. In the Florida Democratic circles, I saw some elites who would seek out fresh-faced supporters to mold in their own image. In particular, I noticed some political groups favored a certain archetype: Underpaid women who were intelligent, but not *too* smart, and also a little anxious—people who would willingly follow their so-called elders' direction and be satisfied by earning accolades and self-confidence in return.

Not everyone is so self-serving, of course. A second path into politics starts outside of the establishment circles. It's the rocky road trod by true believers, the activism-motivated candidates who care so deeply about a particular issue that it motivates them to climb the political mountain. They usually start at the grassroots and brute-force their way through the process, often starting from mile zero and without the secret rulebook. Sometimes their doggedness wins out, and what they lack in savvy, they make up for in determination and earnestness. Oftentimes, though, the secret handshakes trip them up. Consider this lesson about getting onto the ballot.

For state elections in Florida, candidates can qualify to get onto the ballot in two ways. They can work harder or smarter. They can either collect signatures or find money. People with less money (usually the bleeding-heart types) pound the pavement to get signatures. The other group will apply money to the race. For local races, this can be relatively inexpensive, say around two thousand dollars—a small investment compared to the pain of begging strangers on the street corner for two thousand signatures under the unforgiving Florida sun.

I met a woman once at a training convention, emanating fresh bitterness following her unsuccessful run in a legislative primary. She resentfully explained how her campaign had enjoyed a sizable proletariat following. As it progressed over weeks, she steadily collected small donations from the community and was poised to win the Democratic nomination, only to be beaten last minute by a "vile woman" (in her words) who came from nowhere and had only a single, large campaign donation. Even in retrospect, the woman couldn't understand why her opponent had won. She didn't recognize the lesson, but I could see the outlines of those hidden rules. The winner had played the game: Rather than working hard to drum up support and pad her political resume, she had found the right person to endorse her, the right benefactor to give her money, and the right pathway to success. She had played the real game, the hidden game with the invisible rules.

I'm not very good at being a Stepford wife, and as a fortysomething professional, I couldn't stomach starting from the proverbial mail room. So I needed to learn the ropes a different way. I decided the best way forward was through the middle, to learn by doing.

I switched from spending my time at training conferences to volunteering on campaigns. Naively, I thought my knowledge and experience would be valued, but I quickly learned campaign organizations are only interested in your money or your labor—legwork like holding signs, collecting signatures, or acting as a human robo-caller. I tried contributing my other skills, offering to help pen policy concepts or strategize on campaign positions, but not a single candidate wanted that kind of assistance. Some would feign interest and give me hackneyed replies, followed predictably by, "Let's get you involved!"—meaning, let's get you involved in the bread making or signature harvesting. A few of the more jaded ones straight-up told me, "It doesn't matter what ideas anyone has; it's all about money."

Not easily deterred, I thought about starting my own campaign, but there was a hiccup: The Hatch Act. The law, which "prevents pernicious political activities" (exactly what it says), bans government employees from running for elected office. Originally passed in 1939, it's since grown into a jumble of legislative and judicial rulings, policies, and norms. And as a federal employee at the time, the Hatch Act tied my hands; I had to work with my Office of General Counsel—essentially government ethics lawyers—to make sure I followed its labyrinthine rules. The lawyers advised that while running for office and pushing a partisan agenda were off limits, I could form a nonpartisan, nonprofit political corporation.

Technically, this sort of organization is called a 501(c)(4), a reference to the federal tax code that defines them. They're similar to traditional 501(c)(3) nonprofit businesses but with an added "social welfare" element. Usually, 501(c)(4) organizations can endorse candidates and engage in partisan activities, although mine couldn't because of the Hatch Act. Instead, the attorneys advised me to focus on educational pursuits, for instance, contrasting Republicans and Democrats from a scholarly perspective. (By my analysis, the overlap between those parties' platforms is about seventy-nine percent, by the way.) My 501(c)(4) was called UNIFY USA. It became my vehicle to explore the political process, independently and legally, from the inside—albeit while eschewing some partisan norms. I had created my own on-ramp, outside of the entry-level pipeline or establishment circles.

On nights and weekends, under the auspices of my newborn corporation, I was determined to learn the political ropes. But without training camps or mentorship, how does someone learn the system? I figured the internet would know. The US government is required to make all nonsensitive information accessible and understandable to its citizens, and in my search, I found the Federal Election Commission (or FEC) offered a wealth of resources. The FEC's YouTube channel literally has videos on how to run for president. I listened to them in the shower and studied them on my phone while my family watched Saturday night movies. I warn you, though, these aren't high-budget films—they're comically dull. Still, I learned a lot from them, and more than that, I knew when I had questions, I could call the agency directly. You can do that too—I don't have special access. I'm just very tenacious.

You have to be tenacious to run for president, especially without an army of volunteers. There are so many little forms and regulations to monitor. For example, each state has different rules for getting onto the ballot. It's a logistical obstacle course, but if you don't let that deter you, there is a silver lining. The civil servants and volunteers who support elections will help. No matter how much funding your campaign has (or doesn't have), they'll treat you like any bona fide, serious candidate. In 2016 when I ran my experimental campaign, state workers phoned to follow-up on overnighted paperwork or to confirm faxes in the face of looming deadlines. One even took the time to walk me through the legalities of proxy signatures.

Then there were the election workers in Arizona. To get onto that ballot, you need signatures from the state party delegates (a requirement in many states). I was only running a pseudo-campaign from my kitchen table, so couldn't drop everything to fly to Arizona, and I couldn't access the delegates from my kitchen. Instead, through word of mouth and kind strangers online, I managed to reach them—and they signed! Then, at the eleventh hour, we found one final requirement: I had to wet-ink my signature on the same page as theirs. With the deadline looming, I didn't have enough time to make it happen. Undeterred, the election volunteers didn't give up. They figured out a creative solution, where I granted power of attorney to a political marketing group, who signed the form and argued my case to the Arizona Secretary of State's office—who ultimately still didn't let me be onto the ballot. *C'est la vie.* Still, I gained an enormous respect for the people in these offices, people who take their jobs seriously and who give even the most unlikely candidates their effort and respect.

From the FEC and other election workers, I learned how to file the paperwork, fundraise legally, and report on finance activities. Yet, there were still the "other" rules. How do you get accepted by the political activists? Where do you find a good accountant? Who do you talk with to land a major endorsement? How do you get onto the ballot without using the conventional entry points? I still had a lot more to learn.

CHAPTER THREE

It's My Political Party, and I'll Cry if I Want To

Since my 2016 run, I'd been collecting a Rolodex of civically minded thinkers. Conservatives and liberals, Democrats and Republicans, spiritualists and atheists who share a talent for problem solving and passion to make things better. These are my nerdy political friends, people I can trust and listen to. Too often, I think, politicians are missing this kind of support network. They're surrounded by minions and brownnosers—people who will agree on-demand—and gradually, the politicians lose touch with reality. They can't find the truth through all the noise and vitriol of social media and mainstream news; meanwhile, their closest associates are feeding them spoonfuls of sugar that rot their egos. Yuck.

Instead of that fate, I had built a motley crew of people willing to question assumptions, test unwritten rules, and tell me when I got egg on my face. As our cohort grew, we'd spend time in the usual ways. We chatted on video calls and threw dinner parties, and when friends visited from out of town, we'd grab a drink together. But all of those encounters had an added twist: The conversation always concentrated on politics and government—albeit from the lens of problem solving, not partisanship.

One long weekend, before UNIFY USA was established, we got together at my place in Florida. I'd laid out oversized sheets of newsprint and colorful notepads next to the obligatory sodas, snacks, and Twizzlers. When my friends arrived, we chatted and brainstormed: What would a different approach to politics look like? What makes a good executive different from a good legislator? Universally, what are the most important things for a society—looking beyond party agendas? For hours, the whole thing ran like a fervent corporate retreat. People scrawled ideas on sticky notes, which we lumped and split into piles around the living room. We drew diagrams and made lists across the scattered papers. After a few hours and several boxes of pizza, we started connecting the dots: What's redundant? What concepts group together? Which ideas affect one another?

We considered everything—immigration, religion, Constitution, transportation, even national happiness. The conversation spilled enthusiastically across topics with no holds barred as we iterated, debated, and ate too much dessert. By the end of that weekend, we'd developed a framework, a sort of Maslow's hierarchy of national needs.

Picture a pyramid-shaped model. At its base, we placed defense, health care, and environment—the essential elements required to maintain a secure and vital society. On the next tier, we inserted education and economy; these are the enablers a functional society uses to build prosperity. At the pinnacle of the triangle there's innovation, which represents the process and passion needed to solve problems throughout the rest of the framework.

Working on that model helped me visualize the interconnectedness of society. When the government changes education, for instance, it can affect people's health. Changes to defense can impact the environment. Society works like a giant Rubik's Cube; it's not a series of disconnected issues but a single, multifaceted challenge. From that perspective, the complexity grows exponentially but our solution space does, too. If you're not only asking, "How can Health and Human Services improve our well-being?" but also open the aperture to ask, "Can the Defense Department expand its pool of eligible recruits while also improving the health of our society?" you create more options. If you understand the big picture, how all the little pieces fit into the whole, you suddenly have a multiplicity of resources. Each move of the Rubik's Cube can reap double or triple rewards. The key is to make as few moves as possible, and if we do that—if we look at the whole rather than the separate tiled parts—it becomes clear we have all the resources we need. We just need to twist the cube more strategically.

My nerdy and brilliant crew (affectionately named the Geek Team), not only helped me understand Rubik's Cube decision making, they also joined me on the UNIFY USA adventure. Unlike our all-night brainstorming parties, though, our work with UNIFY USA didn't focus on specific solutions or even particular subjects. Instead, UNIFY USA became our sandbox for figuring out the basic logistics of politics: How do you throw a rally? How much lead time do you need for invitations or posters? What's the right way to do social media?

Under the auspices of UNIFY USA, we ran a sort of simulated campaign, albeit without the partisan politics. We started by mimicking what other campaigns did: We threw a party. The Geek Team came, of course, and we also invited acquaintances from the community active on all sides of the political spectrum. This marked my first, cautious step into the political spotlight with people outside my trusted circle of friends.

I had hoped people would donate to UNIFY USA. They did not. I had set out activity stations around the house, like whiteboards where partygoers could collectively construct policy ideas. (I mean, that sounded like fun to me!) They looked but didn't engage. Instead, like any typical house party, people just stood around drinking and talking. After an initial pang of frustration, I conceded that even these discussions counted as a small victory. Few people like to argue with friends, and many people—even politically active types—have an aversion to debating politics. But the untouched activities and overall atmosphere created a safe space where people felt comfortable sharing their opinions.

So, I listened.

The conversations that night highlighted new facets of different political ideas, but even those different perspectives came from people with fairly similar lives and backgrounds. I still needed to find other voices—people who could help diversify my thoughts on economics, environment, urban development, and other policy issues. So, I started attending more marches and rallies. I asked questions and listened to anyone who would talk, which certainly included establishment partisans and political activists but not only those types. I talked to everyone: Neighbors, students, die-hards, radicals, moderates, and politically undecideds.

This is when the seeds of thought took root, which would eventually grow into the plans for my fifty-state tour. What if I spoke to people throughout America? What if I could find *the* experts in different policy areas and also interview wildly different people from across our nation? Running for office or not, that experience would be life-shaping. As 2018 slipped from summer into autumn, I knew my heart was made up, but it took several more weeks for my head to agree. By November 2018, I was certain. I'd do it. I'd make the next year a civic tour. I'd experience our nation for myself, from every corner of the union, and I'd dedicate my next year to living politically.

I felt a sense of growing anticipation, but before I could turn my sights to the future, I had to finish my federal job. I couldn't run for office and remain a civil servant; that's against the rules. I announced my departure in November but still needed several months to close out my projects. In particular, I had to finish editing two full-length books: the first, a report on government innovation (don't laugh; that's not an oxymoron!) and the second, a blueprint for modernizing the

US education system.

The book on education was an edited volume; in other words, other people wrote most of the chapters, while my co-editor and I worked on refining their writing and stitching their ideas together. This may sound relatively easy, but working with scientists and academics can be like herding cats. Every one of us has multiple opinions on any given topic. (If the adage about opinions and assholes were true, academic-types would have some seriously messed-up anatomy!) Academic writers also think deeply about ideas, which makes us particularly sensitive about our written work. Any time I sent a new draft to the authors, many would grow emotional about the feedback. Even happy-to-glad edits required word-by-word negotiation. This "interrogating minutiae" phase happens in every academic project—it's often the frustratingly welcome sign a project is nearing its completion—but with so many authors, this process became exhausting, not so much academically but socially. It almost felt like couples counseling at times. And with more than eighty contributors, my therapy couch was in high demand.

Another challenge with having so many authors—and in particular, authors working around government—is the mountain of red tape they each needed to navigate. I counted around two hundred separate approvals required to complete the book. Every contributor needed to sign-off on his or her part, and typically their bosses did too. For the government contributors, many also had to send their writing through independent security reviews (to ensure no one gave away state secrets) and to public affairs offices (who watch for potential embarrassments). Of course, the overall manuscript, in its final glorious form, also needed approval from the boss, the security office, the public affairs staff, and, finally, the Office of General Counsel.

One of my favorite movies is *Zootopia*, an animated flick where all the characters are anamorphic creatures, like talking bunnies. There's a scene where the main characters go to the DMV (that's the Department of Mammal Vehicles). The DMV clerk—a sloth, of course—moves at a painfully slow pace, making the audience cringe along with the protagonists. That image, of the affable but listless bureaucrat, is the picture a lot of people must have of government workers. That wasn't my experience, though.

Instead, imagine a workforce hamstrung by three-generations-old technology and decades of accumulated red tape. I've seen projects stymied because managers couldn't figure out where to find approval paperwork—not because the approvals weren't granted but because they literally couldn't figure out how to file the right administrative forms. I've personally had to run around the Pentagon (my bright red heels clickety-clacking down the white terrazzo halls), knocking on the sealed metal doors to find the one office who would sign-off on an approval package.

Our government is, necessarily, risk adverse, and government employees—those average day-to-day workers in the bowels of the bureaucracy—rarely get incentivized to push for success. Instead, they're mostly motivated through negative means: Punishments come swiftly whenever a misstep is made. So, people learn to avoid personal risk, scan for traps, and proceed with caution. Take approval processes, for instance. Too few people are willing to accept responsibility for a decision. Instead, they want to pass the buck all around—get the next-level boss to approve, ask the lawyers to sign on the line, and have the public affairs specialists do another review. Even when quintuple reviews aren't called for, they're often requested. It gums up the gears of government but means each decision maker safely spreads responsibility across a crowd.

When I first joined the Office of Personnel Management, my supervisor asked me to document my experiences there. That was a part of the fellowship they hired me under, a program meant to expose private-sector professionals to federal jobs for two- to three-year stints. I wanted to capture my thoughts as a weekly blog, but, of course, that needed approval. When I called to ask for the attorneys' blessing, I almost came to tears. They aggressively warned me: Keep your head down, don't publish anything, and keep your thoughts to yourself. Their measure of success was the elimination of risk, and the less I said, the better. This was a common response, no matter the topic. The government had hired me as a subject-matter expert, ostensibly to provide expert opinion, but whenever I wanted to share those opinions publicly, I was told to bite my tongue. Even for topics as innocuous as educational theory (part of my official duties), there was pressure for me to stay mute—not out of disagreement but purely out of risk aversion.

Still, no matter how antagonistic the red tape became, I always found people with the courage to take a stand and the propensity to bend over backward to help. For instance, despite the initial rebuff, I eventually found an attorney willing to say, "Let's see if we can find a workaround for that blog." It just takes a lot of persistence and a willingness to scour the maze of rules—both the written and unspoken ones—to find a pathway to yes.

Too many people lack the time, energy, or stubbornness to fight against the bureaucracy, though. As a result, so much goodness gets left on the cutting-room floor, and even projects that see the light of day take orders of magnitude longer to complete. That's how I ended up at Christmastime, with my family and I on "vacation" in our rural Georgia cabin and me cloistered in a makeshift home office. I had grossly underestimated how long it would take to finish my work before I left federal service. But you don't get points for how many things you start; only projects you finish end-up on the scoreboard. So it became a sprint to finish the books before my tenure as a civil servant ended.

Each morning, during my holiday break, I'd fill the largest mug we had with green tea and spend my time writing and editing, negotiating with the book contributors, and finding ways to navigate the mounting red tape. Then I'd switch to Mountain Dew and Twizzlers for the afternoon.

My warrior training paid dividends. I'd been practicing focus, learning how to manage my physical and mental energy despite long working hours and insufficient sleep. I had figured out how to balance my diet to compensate (yes, Twizzlers are part of a balanced diet) and had learned to listen to my inner energy to know when I needed to switch from a deep-thinking task to a social one and when I needed to take a break entirely. It may sound like an exaggeration but maintaining focus for so many hours a day becomes grueling. I once read an ESPN article about grandmaster chess players.[1] Sitting at a tournament, they can burn up to six thousand calories a day just from their mental efforts, at a level of exertion similar to pro-athletes. While I wasn't on their level, I was certainly burning my candle at all ends—left, right, and across the middle.

Threaded throughout the work, I also tried to spend time with my family. Maddie, my youngest, was just seven years old, and Christmas still held all of its magic for her. Like all families, though, mine brings chaos in addition to love and comfort. Christmas Day was no exception. I began the day at my computer, before the sunrise. Meanwhile, my son Mitch, a college freshman in New York, and my daughter Monica, who attended boarding school in Baltimore, were en route to the cabin. My mom was flying in from Florida. Meanwhile my husband, just one flight shy of diamond status on his airline of choice, decided to also spend his day in the air, flying round trip to Albuquerque to earn those precious frequent-flyer points before the new year.

For most of Christmas Day, it was just Maddie and me, with everyone else checking in online. We all celebrated together the next day, but I still wanted to make Christmas special for my youngest daughter. So, after she rolled groggily out of bed (my cue to stop working), we decided to spend some quality mommy-daughter time baking a cake. Now, anyone who knows me understands I'm a danger to humanity in the kitchen. I've started microwave fires while reheating leftovers and suffered several incidents with cutting knives. Even without causing bodily harm, my cooking tends toward inedible. Despite these innate cooking skills, though, I'm pretty good at following directions.

We found a step-by-step video online for a pineapple upside-down cake and, together, fumbled our way through its creation. We used all the bowls, too many cups, and half the spoons in the house. The messy cookware littered the sink (after we licked the bowls, of course), but like a Christmas miracle, our cake turned out. We positioned it on the kitchen island and snapped a glamor shot, with the unwashed plates carefully cropped out of frame, and then posted it on Facebook for the rest of my distributed family to enjoy. Still in our jammies, Maddie and I snuggled on the living room couch, framed by a pile of presents and the pine-scented Christmas tree with its discount ornaments. Behind us, the cabin's picture window overlooked a bucolic landscape dusted with snow and our neighbor's less-than-picturesque single-wide. Cozy under a blanket, with two big pieces of cake, we watched every Barbie movie we could find. For the next several days, all the red tape, approval forms, and politicking melted away, buried under the warmth of family and holiday times. Although I didn't fully appreciate it then, those tender memories would become the emotional fuel I'd soon need for the roller-coaster journey to come.

CHAPTER FOUR

Only Crazy People Run for President

As the new year dawned, it was almost time for my coming-out party, but first I needed some professional help. I started by calling political consultants, either recommended to me by friends or whom I had met at Democratic events. Largely, the calls went like this: I'd express interest in running, and the consultant would get excited. They'd butter me up, saying I made a great candidate and commenting on my federal experience, but then they'd warn that government experience isn't the same as campaign savvy. So, I needed to rely on them, these sage guides, who could steer me through the political jungle. They'd offer to help me craft my message, take campaign photos, and make a website—all of which would look and sound pretty much like everyone else's. There was a little room for personality, of course. I could choose one major issue to champion and one personality trait to show; anything more would confuse or bore voters. But, they explained, if I listened to them—and if I followed this trusted formula—I'd be sure to win.

While all the consultants readily agreed the 2016 presidential election had changed the rules of the politics game, they were similarly quick to scoff at out-of-the-box campaign ideas. Inevitably, one of their first pieces of advice would be "start small." Focus on local, entry-level positions, and build your resume. (They generally assumed would-be candidates couldn't possibly have relevant experience from outside of politics. It felt like an episode of *The Twilight Zone*, where somehow I'd been transported back twenty years into a first-level version of myself.)

"I'm interested in something bigger," I'd explain, and the consultant would try to dissuade me. Then I'd introduce my plan.

As soon as I mentioned running for president, their tone would change. It took on a distinct air of "oh, you're one of *those*." Then they'd skeptically ask, "How much money, and how many friends do you have?"

When I admitted to only having skills and experience, they'd tiredly explain, as if to a small child, "You're qualified, and we'd love to help, but without those resources, you're not going anywhere." Then the call would end.

There's a common belief only crazy or crooked people run for president;

particularly if the candidate hasn't spent a lifetime in elected office. Why do we discourage people from running and, in particular, ridicule nontraditionals? Americans often complain we don't have enough qualified candidates, but we also imply those who do run are delusional, egotistical, or corrupt. "Don't do this," our society seems to say, "or we'll think you're a bad person."

That's on us, everyday Americans. Every time we tell well-meaning presidential hopefuls they're crazy or on an ego trip, we're spreading a subtle message that only narcissists or lifelong insiders run for higher office.

When I first announced my plans on social media, one childhood acquaintance replied with a shotgun of questions, many of which read like accusations punctuated with question marks. At the end she wrote, "Why are you doing this? It seems like a vanity project to me."

I replied, with as much grace as I could muster, and gave her my spiel about wanting to understand and, eventually, support our government.

"If that's really true," she responded, "then do something here. Work at the local level."

That's another preconception I've tediously encountered time and time again. Although my middle-school classmate wasn't wrong about needing good leaders locally, she was incorrect in the unspoken assumption that political offices are fungible. City- and state-level government isn't inferior to the federal level, but they are fundamentally different. Local-level politics is tangible, fast, and often has immediate results. The military would call those tactical effects. National-level politics, on the other hand, is bafflingly multifaceted, longer term, and often focuses on outcomes difficult to immediately visualize. National-level politics operates at the strategic level. To have a functioning system, we need both—strategic and tactical, national and local, the big gear and the small ones turning in harmony. More than that, politicians need different skill sets for each. It takes meticulous organizational skills, for instance, to run Buffalo's annual snow-fighting operations, and it takes equally impressive—but wholly different—skills to negotiate an environmental plan across intersecting regions, diverse sectors, and competing interests. My abilities and experience tend toward the federal-level skill sets, much more than the local ones, and I wasn't ready to jettison those talents just yet.

I couldn't fight those biases head-on, though, so in my meet-and-greet calls with the professionals, I soon learned to avoid the p-word. I focused first on more general questions and nudged their thinking with subtle comments. Eventually this roundabout approach paid off. It happened during my call with a consultancy in Central Florida. Rather than lead with my unconventional POTUS plan, I instead asked how their constituents would feel about a nontraditional politician running at a national level.

"That's a good question," the consultant responded. "I'm honestly not sure, but we can schedule some focus groups. They always surprise you with their perspectives. Why don't you stop by to discuss things further?"

Yes! After weeks of dead-end calls, I'd finally unlocked the door. But before I could walk through it, I still had to pass the firm's litmus test. His name, it turns out, was Spenser.

Spenser is a high-end lawyer. Physically, he's fairly unremarkable, an average-looking guy in his fifties, but his demeanor is powerful. He has an intensity, a hypervigilance. You can feel his calculating eyes sizing you up, watching every gesture, and hanging on every word to see behind the social mask. As I walked into our meeting, an hour-long cross-examination where he'd determine my worthiness, I instantly felt his whip-like attention focus. He grilled me, and I didn't try to bluff. Spenser wouldn't have been impressed by deflections or double-talk, so instead, I let him in on my presidential plans, even though that line of discussion risked bringing an early end to our conversation. Spenser listened, poised in an easy stance, leaning back in his chair with his legs crossed at the knee. Then he leaned forward.

"You know you can't win, so what's your real game?" he probed.

I explained my process, my decision making, and how I thought an outsider was needed. I shared my ideas about the changing character of national politics and about how a catch-22 had quietly formed: Those attributes typically used to judge someone's worthiness for national office—political experience, deep pockets, and little black books full of well-connected friends—are becoming the very qualities voters reject. Average Americans have a growing distrust of the usual suspects, those career politicians with shady ties to money and robotic responses to questions. I think Americans want something different—someone from the outside but who's not completely devoid of government experience, someone who thinks strategically but also connects locally, someone who everyday people can relate to but who can still hold her own on a debate stage. In other words, I explained to Spenser, the American public wants something fresh (an American Warrior Nerd Princess, if you will), and the time is ripe for me to fill that role.

He leaned back in his chair, clearly past the examination phase and now more relaxed and thoughtful. "That's an interesting plan," he said after a beat. "I've got some ideas that might help . . . but you're still not going to win."

Spenser wasn't the first operative to tell me I didn't stand a chance, and he was far from the last. Still, all the consultants I spoke with, even the most skeptical ones, taught me something. One of those eureka moments came from an opposition researcher who was recommended to me by some friends. That call started differently than the others. The consultant had already been told the gist of my plan and my aspirations for federal office, but she still agreed to talk. (Baby steps of progress!)

During our conversation she questioned me, "Why do you want to run?"

As usual, I explained my process, my interest in national-level strategic thinking, and my belief our country was open for change.

"That's a good answer," she replied, in her brisk, no-nonsense tone. "I didn't expect that."

"What did you expect?" I wondered aloud.

"Well," she explained, "to be honest, most people want to run for federal office because they think it'd be nice to be called 'Senator.'"

So let me get this straight, I thought. *People expose themselves (and their families) to all that public drama, devote gobs of energy, and spend small fortunes to achieve federal office—all for a cool title?* I had no reason to doubt her, though.

As an opposition researcher, she deals with humanity's baser instincts and is accustomed to many ugly truths—the shallowness of some politicians probably least surprising among them. I guess I was still too unjaded, though, because I found her observations troubling. Throughout the call, I kept thinking, *We're in way worse shape than I imagined.*

She went on to explain that opposition researchers essentially dig up dirt on opposing candidates. They usually start by searching through public records and then progressively use more clandestine methods to find places where someone has made poor decisions, like taking a homestead deduction twice in a year or wearing an inappropriate Halloween costume in college. They're looking for mistakes to exploit.

Of course, some candidates are genuine bad actors, with a history of dishonesty or faulty decisions. Those flaws should be aired. But candidates are also human, and a lot of humans make mistakes. The best of us learn from those mistakes and grow into wiser, more empathetic versions of ourselves. I think most Americans are willing to forgive someone's occasional flaws, particularly if they happened in the past, and most people say they're uncomfortable with mudslinging campaigns. Yet, despite its indignity, voters respond to dirt, and political marketing teams continue to advocate for negative politics. As the consultants say, "You don't have to prove you're a good candidate; you just have to prove the other guy's less acceptable." It's all part of the grotesque underbelly of politics, and it works so damn well, a lot of candidates and consultants can't let it go.[1]

Certainly, not everyone in politics takes a *realpolitik* approach. Millions of people also fill the opposite end of the spectrum, exhibiting a guileless optimism that's often equally disconcerting. I once encountered that sense of obstinate naivety at a Bernie Sanders assembly.

It happened during the Run Bernie Run rally, before he had officially announced his candidacy for the 2020 election. The online buzz implied Sanders would make his decision to run based on the grassroots response, so his supporters planned a massive rally, with thousands of people across hundreds of locations to send him a message. Participants could gather for "house parties" in restaurants and offices across the country, or they could sign-on independently to the real-time stream on Facebook Live. Curiosity piqued, I decided to attend, along with my friend Robert Ramus, one of the most dedicated players on my Geek Team.

We picked a site in Orlando, held at one of those community flex spaces where companies can rent storefronts designed to look like façades in an outdoor market. As we approached the folding table that served as a registration desk, I was struck by how homegrown the whole thing felt. The rally didn't seem fancy or even professionally organized. It wasn't like something you'd see on TV or expect from a presidential event.

We were ushered into a room with maybe ten to fifteen other people who all seemed cut from a similar cloth, with hipster beards, environmental T-shirts, and hippy skirts. In front of us, on a rolling whiteboard someone had written, "Brown Girls Can," which, we soon learned, was the activist group responsible for the local gathering.

After the organizers welcomed our small group, the live stream began with the video projected onto one of the walls. It was impressively amateurish. The picture quality was bad, the sound quality was bad, and the organization was crude. But it didn't matter. The organizers' authenticity and genuine enthusiasm carried the day. Apparently, a compelling message can still mobilize people, even without million-dollar glitz and K-Street sophistication.

The rally was, more or less, a series of real-time testimonials for Sanders. An assortment of supporters joined in, each one responding on live webcam to the question, "When did you first feel the Bern?" One woman called in from her car. Wearing earbuds and a winter coat, she looked like she had just pulled over in the middle of her grocery run—even though she was on the national stage. Another supporter connected from her home office and spent (what felt like) hours adjusting her camera, seemingly without concern for her own lack of technological preparation.

The testimonial that stood out most came from a New York grade-school teacher. It looked like she had called in from a mudroom, with children's backpacks hanging behind her, but the backdrop didn't make this call unique. Her testimonial was evangelical. She was tearful, passionate, and clearly in anguish. She spoke about the difficulty of teaching in underserved areas, where kids lack options, and she pleaded for hope for their futures. She wanted her students to have opportunity and for them to escape the poverty they were born into, but, she sobbed, they could only have those options if they had free postsecondary education. And without that, then why even bother? In 2016, when Sanders didn't win the Democratic nomination, it had sent her into a spiral of depression. She had had to break the bad news to her kids: They wouldn't be going to college. They wouldn't have happy lives. They didn't have any hope. She had felt devastated.

That teacher's fervent emotionality made supporting Sanders seem almost spiritual. In fact, the whole rally felt like a religious revival. Even the question about "feeling the Bern" evoked parallels to "feeling the call," the spiritual epiphany that transforms someone's life. Those parallels are concerning. When religiousness and politics begin to mix, it blurs reality. No matter the party or platform, it's dangerous to view any politician as superhuman. That kind of demagoguery lends itself to hyperbole and utopian thinking, and it short-circuits our brains. We stop seeing politicians as capable-but-fallible leaders, and instead, our support for them morphs into a matter of faith, and agreement with their opinions becomes a test of devotion.

That rally, like so many events in recent years, also had an undercurrent of desperation. Supporters at Run Bernie Run seemed to believe if Sanders became president their troubles would end. None of this is a critique of Sanders (who didn't organize or even attend the rally) or his politics. Ultimately, it's not even a critique of his supporters, who seemed to have their hearts in the right place and who aren't alone in displaying that sort of sentiment. Maybe it's our zeitgeist. People across the country seem desperate for a messiah, not just a president. How did our system get to the point where so many people are looking for a savior?

Sadly, that's not how the executive branch works, though. Even if a picture-perfect president unwaveringly focused on achieving all of his campaign promises, he wouldn't have the power to, let's say, mandate free college for all. The legislative branch controls the purse strings, and the states control public colleges and universities. Only Congress, not the president, can eliminate postsecondary tuition costs. And that's not even considering whether we still want a 1950s-era model of education or how we'd manage all of the second- and third-order effects created by making four-year degrees free—the Rubik's Cube of unintended consequences.

While most Americans are familiar with the "separation of powers" concept, many of us haven't given it much thought. We often think of national government as a monolithic mass—a big, swampy melting pot—and we judge candidates on whether they'll bring more of the flavor we prefer into that federal stew. We rarely try to evaluate their practical skills or consider whether candidates are suited for particular roles, and during campaigns, we seldom give thought to the span of control different offices possess.

As a result, despite the job mismatch, presidential candidates typically campaign on a litany of policy proposals, even though they're running for an executive—not legislative—role. As much as our recent presidents have expanded the limits of executive power, presidents still can't rule by fiat, hire and fire whomever they please, or move money without congressional approval. Presidents wield significant power, but not the legislative kind usually emphasized in campaigns. So, when presidential hopefuls campaign on their policy proposals, it's either disingenuous or an indicator of inexperience. They're either pandering to voters' hopes and relying on their ignorance of the federal system or they're demonstrating their own ignorance of how to achieve outcomes within our governmental structures.

Certainly, you can argue that modern presidents act as strategic leaders for their party in Congress, and presidents can influence the legislative policy agenda. In that way, presidents are like a sort of concept artist-cum-salesperson. Imagine a president painting a beautiful picture of a castle, which represents a rich and idealistic policy goal. The president says, "Let's build this shining palace," and takes the elegant painting, that utopian policy concept, to a disagreeable Congress. The president works with the legislature, selling the design, cajoling and compromising, scaling it down, bargaining-off those carefully considered pieces—like the moat and portcullis—to make the sale. And in the end, the president is left with little more than a lean-to, which everyone refers to as a castle, either out of an enduring sense of optimism or with a cynical expectation the public will ignore or misapprehend its flaws.

Voting for presidential candidates based on their policy proposals is like searching for better concept artists. Too many people seem to think, "If only we had a prettier picture, the world would be better." They pin their ardent dreams on their next favorite painter, but when those artists—those presidential candidates—are successfully elected, they disappoint. Because no matter how elegant their painting, no matter how skilled their salesmanship, they can't build the illustrated castle. *That's not their role; that's not their position's power.* And, so, the process sows distrust. Voters grow frustrated. Eventually, they begin looking for something different; they vote for someone different. They vote for change and disruption, and even try candidates who eschew paintings and castles in favor of breaking down the system.

But what we need isn't a better painter—or a better art dealer, salesman, or orator. We don't need another candidate who can present increasingly finer policy concepts nor even one who rails against the portraits and palaces paintings. We need a wholly different approach.

CHAPTER FIVE

Hi, I'm JJ, and I'm Running for President

As winter crept toward spring, I said a somber farewell to my federal job and a pensive hello to being a full-time political hopeful. It was time to start my campaign—and my fifty-state tour—in earnest. My grandparents, longtime weekend wanderers with a fifth-wheel camper, inspired me to do the fifty-state tour by motor home. First, though, I needed one. That may seem straightforward, but if (like me) you've never owned a recreational vehicle before (and have questionable automotive skills), it's a daunting prospect. And expensive. And there are more options than flavors of jelly beans. Good grief! Eventually I found one that drove well, fit all my kids, and didn't break the bank. Comically, the model is called the "J Ride." Perhaps it was meant to be!

Next, I needed to turn the RV into a proper election mobile. I wanted to wrap the exterior in a design promoting my campaign, and step one was to create that artwork. For a fleeting moment, I oh-so-cleverly envisioned the RV branded as a "she shed" on wheels or, more precisely, my great "American She Shed." That thought, however, died a swift and ignoble death as my husband gleefully pointed out the inevitable acronym. Clearly, I was better off sending this task to the professionals.

In working with creative-types, I've found it best to give general goals and then let their ingenuity run. So when I sat down with the graphic design team, I outlined my ideas in broad strokes: Make it campaign focused, patriotic, and retro inspired (as a nod to my grandparents). Sometimes, though, removing constraints encourages people to fall into conventional ways of thinking. The first draft looked like it came from a mainstream consultant's playbook: It had a classic red-white-and-blue motif and a huge American flag. It looked fantastic but missed my personality, quirkiness, and alternative political approach. *Of course*, I thought, *they can't see inside my head and couldn't be expected to know I wanted something different.* We had to go back to the drawing board.

Together, the designers and I scoured hundreds of pictures until we landed on the mid-century turquoise look. That became our palette, but what to put on it?

The design needed to tell a story, a story focused on our country. Was there a way to make the campaign about everyday Americans, to incorporate people into it? I thought the slogan "Ready Nation National Tour" should feature prominently, because that focuses on the interdependence of our citizenry. We found dry-erase vinyl too, so people could write notes on the RV—it could become America's whiteboard. Now, this was starting to feel inspired! Before we locked-in the second go-round, though, the designers reminded me to also feature myself, and I indifferently agreed. They took our newly invigorated ideas back to their design software, and I waited eagerly to see what they would produce.

The next draft had my slogan, the dry-erase background—and a billboard-sized close-up of my face. I noped out of that! I couldn't imagine staring at my giant mug, plastered on the side of my home, for months. More than that, I didn't want to showcase those same characterless headshots and tired refrains most politicians use. The design should show I'm a real person, with different facets, and running a different kind of campaign.

Ultimately, we ended up using a smattering of pictures, ranging from informal (my family and me casually in the kitchen) to more traditional (me behind a tabletop flag at a NATO meeting). The designers superimposed these on a US map and also added "Team JJ USA." Finally, with a little bit of cheekiness, one designer threw in a Hollywood-like star on the door, with "Dr. JJ" in the middle. It was a good joke, marking my movie-star door that would shield me from the (nonexistent) throngs of adoring fans and mobs of (photocopied) paparazzi cameras (like ones taped around my treadmill).

At last complete, I showed the final design to my Geek Team—who were horrified. I'd forgotten the website, all the social media links, and even an American flag! How did we miss that?! The designers and I had gotten so into the weeds, we had missed the most essential thing. (It was an important metaphorical lesson to remember.) But in the end, with my team's help, we were able to complete and successfully wrap a beautiful, distinctive, and flag-adorned design. Then it was time to roll out, albeit not too far just yet.

Our next task involved an overnight test run at the local RV park. I enlisted my family for this part: Husband, three kids, and our dog. As we neared the park, the afternoon sky filled with black-gray clouds, and it started raining. Not sprinkling, mind you, but a full biblical downpour like you only get in Florida. The ground turned to mud, and I started to wonder how far the RV—with its now seemingly tiny wheels—would sink.

Once we found our reserved spot, the real fun began. In the pouring rain, we had to hook up all the cables: Power, water, and sewer. Remember, connect the blue line to potable water not the white one—you do not want to drink that! Picture my son holding an umbrella over me, mud-soaked in the rainstorm, while I'm trying to figure out which cable to connect where. The vinyl wrapping had covered the labels for the clean-water and black-water ports. I looked online for instructions to no avail. There are too many similar but not-quite-the-same versions of that RV model. (And make no mistake, this was a high-pressure decision. While searching online, I watched a half dozen horror-story videos of people mixing-up these lines—imagine poop spraying across the living space when the sink turns on. Yikes!)

Fortunately, I'm a compulsive planner. I had filmed the salesman at the RV lot showing us how to connect the lines. So, huddled under the umbrella, we pulled up the video and walked step by step through the connection process. Job done, we splashed back inside and tentatively tried the sink. A small triumph: clean water and no living-room shit storm that day! If only the rest of my political escapade could be so auspicious.

Several weeks before picking-up the RV, I met with a business associate visiting Florida. John, a Pentagon executive, was down from DC for a seminar on innovation, and at dinner that night, we struck up a friendly conversation about innovation in education.

"There's a lot of distrust across the country right now," he observed, "but education is one of those places everyone agrees, at least as an end state. Everyone agrees a good education is a good thing."

Although clearly an enthusiast of education in my own life, I pushed back. "A lot of people actually don't support education, at least not after high school. Around four in ten think going to college biases you toward liberal thinking, and they're not fans." That wasn't my opinion; I had just read a Pew Research report[1] and was eager (OK, maybe a little overeager) to geek out with him over its data. We bantered back and forth for a while, and eventually he conceded.

"It's interesting," he admitted. "My in-laws live in the Midwest, and their beliefs are entirely unlike mine. I've never understood why they think so differently, why they criticize education . . . " His words sounded thoughtful, acquiescent even, but his body language still reiterated, " . . . but only if they knew better, they'd agree."

I gave John credit for listening, but he couldn't seem to internalize the alternative viewpoint. It's not always natural to see other angles, let alone empathize with them. That's part of the reason why I had to travel the country. You can't learn how it feels to be hungry by visiting one soup kitchen, and you can't understand America by barnstorming a handful of cities. You've got to spend time in flyover country. You have to visit the population centers and small towns in between. You've got to take a selfie with the giant prairie chicken in Rothsay, pay homage to Smokey Bear in Dover, and have a margarita at the Hub of the Universe in Marion.

Politics and government have become deeply divisive. But why? Why do so many reasonable Americans have diametrically opposed views? You can't truly understand the different angles, grok all the perspectives, from printed polls. You can't just memorize state trivia and read political blogs. You have to talk with real people, see how they live their lives, and engage them in their own worlds. You have to climb into each person's distinct American experience and look out from that worldview.

Make no mistake, people have so many worldviews, and each state has distinct perspectives. During my tour, I began to truly appreciate those differences. Some are obvious as soon as you cross the border, like the crops neighboring states grow, the quality of their roads, or orderliness of their buildings. People differ across state lines too, although that transition happens more gradually. As you get closer to the heart of a state, little cultural quirks begin to surface in things like hairstyles, pace, and formality. Dig a little, and you'll find the differences run deeper, manifesting as regional mores, values, and political stances.

I've sometimes thought about how different communities develop their personalities. Do cities and towns nurture common viewpoints thanks to generations of long-term residents, or do people with similar views get drawn to the same place? When people move around the country, do they transport their hometown culture, cross-pollinating their beliefs around our nation? Or are people more apt to flock to birds of their own feather, encouraging islands of like-minded thinking to develop across America?

Regardless of the reason, it's clear our country is a diverse tapestry. Although that's such a cliché, it's difficult to appreciate, and it gets said so often, it's been diluted into triviality. In political circles too, it's common for seemingly world-weary pundits to toss around the phrase "all politics is local." People mean a variety of things with that saying, including that every region—every electoral district—cares about different things. But I don't think most fully appreciate the sentiment or even understand at a deep level what that means. The idea of diversity, of distinct perspectives and regional personalities, gets twisted. Like so many things in politics, the nuance gets lost, and political pundits end up following that initial truth to misguided conclusions.

Let me share an example. As part of my Politics 101 preparation, I once met a friend of a friend who works as a professional analyst on high-profile campaigns. That conversation with (let's call her) Isabella was eye-opening, although not in the way she had intended. Isabella had dark, close-cropped curls, which framed her black-rimmed eyeglasses and vexed expression. Like many consultants before her, she was aghast at my plans. During an initially pleasant Sunday brunch, between croissants and mimosas she had condescendingly explained why my campaign approach could never work. I can sum up her hour-long scolding in about a paragraph.

"On our campaign during the last election," she had lectured, "we ran three shifts of analysts—24/7 leading up to the vote. Every time the candidate went to a new place, we'd canvass it for weeks beforehand to find out those voters' issues and perspectives. Then we'd crunch the numbers and make new talking points for each city. It takes millions and millions of dollars, but that's the level of precision you need to run a competitive campaign."

As the brunch atmosphere soured into awkwardness, she had doubled down on her position. "You can't run a serious campaign without hundreds, or thousands, of people, and they're not cheap. You need money, and you need data, and you need a political machine."

Isabella made me feel like I'd personally offended her. Then again, I also found her whole approach appalling. It seemed disingenuous to change the message at every stop, not to mention a complete waste of resources. Of course, the polar-opposite approach isn't ideal either. Any time politicians take a one-size-fits-all perspective, they necessarily leave out someone's concerns. The better approach is to look at the whole system and have an authentic message that acknowledges different facets and necessary trade-offs in a way that's explainable to different people—in a way that highlights the good but also explains the bad. Politicians probably avoid this approach out of fear of its complexity. As the mainstream consultants like to say, just pick one idea, one message—anything more bores or confuses voters.

I think the best politicians, and the best leaders in general, can hold conflicting truths in mind and find a way to thread the needle between them. They can acknowledge, for instance, that firearms have a long-established role in many rural communities and also recognize that gun laws have grown hazardously untenable. They can value multiple angles on a single issue.

Part of America's strategic advantage is the diversity of our backgrounds, viewpoints, and experiences. We're stronger because of the heterogeneity of our fifty states but only if we acknowledge the value of those different views along with the creativity and exceptional outcomes they can collectively produce. We're also stronger when politicians treat people as "capable entities," able to come together on complex challenges, versus "cogs in a wheel" to pander to.

I've often wondered, what makes America exceptional or, at least, distinct from competitive and adversarial nations like China, Russia, Iran, and North Korea. China has a greater population, and although the US still tops the charts in terms of GDP, other countries are closing the gap in competitiveness on various indicators.[2] Our technological prowess once made America unique, and the US military classically relied on that advantage to provide (what they call) military overmatch against adversarial nations. But, today, the big tech companies are mostly global—not American—and off-the-shelf technologies are creating increasing scientific parity. While I'm a fan of global development. It does makes me wonder, *What will make the American brand, so to speak, continue to stand out on an international stage?*

My fifty-state road trip reinforced an idea that had been percolating for a while: The US is unique because of our people. OK, that sounds like another saccharine platitude but hear me out. There are at least three, specific characteristics that make us unique. First, as you might have already guessed, is diversity.[3] Research repeatedly shows more diverse teams make better decisions. They bring wider knowledge, can play different roles, and can collectively build more creative solutions—but only if the team has functional, inclusive diversity.[4] Infighting and contempt discourage productive outcomes, no matter the situation. So, it's diversity—with coordination, mutual respect, and appreciation for differences—that's key.

The second characteristic derives, in part, from our diversity: innovation. As a nation, America often exhibits unique creativity and out-of-the-box thinking. We have a culture that (when it's at its best) cheers new ideas and willingly tries new trends. We laud creatives and entrepreneurs, and we encourage each other to try new things, fail fast, and get up again.[5]

Finally, the last ingredient is trust. Even with the growing undercurrent of discontent in America, we're still a nation that generally believes in one another. I don't necessarily mean trust in our government or trust in our political leaders, but trust in ourselves, trust in each other as neighbors and people. Nations without that internal trust fall into chaos; they're ruled by gangs or strongmen. People spend too much time looking over their shoulders, and constantly trapped in a prisoner's dilemma, they struggle to form the bonds and interconnections needed to collectively progress. Sustainable development is fueled by trust, with a belief in the rule of law and a confidence in the logic and reliability of systems. Trust is the enabler.

To be fair, the US doesn't top the list in diversity, innovation, or trust, but if you look up the research, we're pretty close to the top in each category.[6] More than that, it's the combination of the three that makes things interesting. Collectively those three attributes are more than the sum of their parts—just like Americans. When we come together, we're so much more than some three-hundred million individuals. But we have to *come together* to earn that gestalt. When we're disorganized or distrusting, disenfranchised or broken down, we lose the magic that makes us all, collectively, exceptional.

People often call the US a melting pot, but that's a bad metaphor. A melting pot implies we all gradually become the same. We meld into the same broth, with everyone regressing toward the mean, toward the generic average. Rather than a melting pot, picture the US as a salad bowl. We each keep our unique flavors, bringing different tastes and textures to the plate. That's the American experience, and it's why we can't paint a single picture that works for everyone. Nonetheless, the response to that diversity shouldn't involve a 24/7 team of custom speechwriters. We need political ideas that reflect the nation, which, unfortunately for the mainstream consultants, often means multifaceted solutions. Instead of pitching different policies and changing the message at every whistle-stop, politicians need to work with the American people. Government shouldn't be something done *to* its people; it should be done *by, with, and through* them.[7]

My daughter Monica played national-level lacrosse while she was growing up. I was surprised to discover that university coaches began watching fledgling athletes as young as thirteen. I don't have a lot of sports experience, personally, so I found the whole activity fascinating—like an anthropologist studying a newly discovered culture. My first research question was, *What the heck are these coaches looking for in eighth graders?* How can they predict how the girls will act as juniors in college or even how these youngsters will perform next year? I started observing the top coaches during games, trying to see what caught their attention, and importantly, how the expert coaches compared to some of their less effective peers.

Over several years, I came to realize that the star athletes in middle school—mostly the tall and hard-hitting players—were often surpassed by their smaller-but-tenacious teammates as they all matured. By high school, the smaller scrappy ones (who had had to work harder through the younger grades) frequently outperformed their middle school rivals. Despite my realization of this, I noticed the less effective coaches often honed-in on the most aggressive players—the best players here and now—and seemed to assume their earlier successes would continue as they aged. The Tier-I coaches looked for different skills, and more than that, they looked for personality traits. Plus, they weren't just looking at single players; they looked at how different players complemented one another and how they integrated with the team. I was particularly impressed by the top-quality coaches at smaller colleges, the ones with smaller budgets who can't afford to recruit the seemingly best athletes. It was like watching a teenage version of *Moneyball*; those coaches put together assemblies of second-string players, combining them into top-tier teams. It's not about collecting a team of experts; it's about cultivating an expert team.

Of course, as I pondered these things over countless afternoons on the sideline bleachers, I couldn't help but see lacrosse as an analogy for our country. As a nation—as a government—it's not about having more money or finding individual all-stars, it's about building a composite team that can win together.

Sports metaphors already litter political discussions, of course, although football tends to be a more popular comparison. For instance, people often draw parallels between presidents and quarterbacks. A quarterback handles the ball and makes game-time decisions. They're seen as the centers of gravity of their teams, leading through the heart of each scrimmage and calling the shots on every play. The symbolism of an all-star Oval Office quarterback makes for a satisfying analogy, but I think it misses the mark. We need a presidential model that more closely resembles those clever lacrosse coaches—someone on the sidelines, who's watching the plays, working with the athletes, and integrating winning teams. And when I say "teams," I'm not just referring to the president's cabinet or elected politicians; I mean the whole country. The entire United States—every contributor to this nation—is a member of the team; although, we're currently missing the coordinated playbook.

A president isn't only a coach in chief, of course, but that's a good place to begin. Imagine electing a president not based on his running speed or her passing percentage, but instead based on their coaching skills. Imagine electing a president who's expert at assembling a champion team, crafting plays to their strengths, strategizing for the future, and bringing the nation together. Rather than judge presidents on their individual star-athlete qualities, what if we looked for something different? What if we looked for something innovative?

CHAPTER SIX

But First, a Word from Our Sponsors...

Innovation means using the resources at hand in new and creative ways. It's not the same as *invention* or creating something wholly new. Innovation is an evolution, not a revolution. As I began my presidential campaign, I wanted it to be innovative—but that didn't mean wholesale disruption of the usual process. Instead, I had to learn which parts to keep, modify, or discard.

For obvious reasons, my countrywide tour was slated to begin in Florida. Not only did I conveniently live there, but I had already built inroads with the political community. As I readied myself to launch that tour, though, it was those well-meaning local consultants who nearly derailed my plans. For weeks, I had heard a steady drip-drip-drip of patronization, discouragement, and cajoling. Many people meant well, but they couldn't understand what I was trying to do or picture an alternative—an innovative—way to participate in national-level politics. Anyway, I'm not so foolhardy as to immediately believe I know more than the experts (at least, not until those experts give me reason to doubt them), so I listened, percolated, and eventually decided to at least give their approach consideration.

My Florida political contacts, like whip-smart lawyer Spenser, had spent the last several months coaxing me to change plans and, specifically, to run for the Florida State Senate. "You'll be a shoo-in," they'd flatter, or they'd admonish, "If you start nationally, you'll alienate people. Plus, it just won't work." The consultants also reminded me that they often convince would-be candidates to change their initial aspirations, to move away from their original plans in favor of more winnable races. *They are the experts,* I thought, *so let me at least see what they're selling.*

Pleased with my willingness to listen, my professional colleagues jumped at the chance to prepare me for a state-wide run. Cue the montage music, and picture them springing into action setting up calls with state ringleaders, priming me for meetings, and sketching out campaign ideas. There are a handful of movers and shakers in Florida, they explained, and you need to get connected to them. First, there's a guy down south. We think he'll love you! And if he loves you, he'll make things happen. He goes by the name The Duke.

On a postcard-perfect afternoon, Robert and I found ourselves at one of those prolific main street cafes popular in beach towns. The seating spilled out from the main restaurant onto a shaded patio through a picture-window wall that had been opened to let in the springtime air. But we weren't there to enjoy the beach; we had come to have lunch with the Duke of South Florida.

My first thought on seeing him was that the Duke looked like "Florida Retiree #1" out of central casting. He sported a beach-bum look that bordered on stereotypical, complete with a white tank top and unkempt hair under an old, floppy hat. He seemed mid-sixties-ish and had the leathery skin iconic of sun-worshiping seniors. In addition to him, Robert, and me, two consultants, his assistant, and a couple of his "children" joined us at the table. The latter two appeared around twentysomething; both looked put-together and seemed kind, although a bit starry-eyed.

After we gave the waitress our orders, the Duke began peppering me with questions. That seemed right. I had already assumed he'd want to interview me to get a sense of my political leanings and ways of thinking. He needed to know whether or not I was worthy of his patronage. Something seemed off, though. He wasn't really listening to the answers, and the questions were growing increasingly bizarre.

"I'm breaking up with my girlfriend," he explained, as we cut into our salads. "She's a twin, and she's moving out of the house. I used to date her sister, what do you think?"

This has got to be a test, I thought. He wants to see how I roll with things. So, I bantered with him. But, no, he kept his eyes on his lunch or let them slide around the table idly, and he'd interject with non sequiturs as soon as I paused my response. His divergences also grew more inappropriate each time. He asked about my stance on public nudity and then told a story about getting banned from a particular forum because of something to do with racism and nakedness.

After about the third exchange like this, I understood I had made a mistake. He was testing me, but not for my answers. His wasn't asking about politics, governance, or the country. He didn't want to hear my observations or see whether

I was a good problem solver. He just wanted to gauge my agreeableness—which I had failed with each interchange. He wanted to judge whether I'd be malleable to his direction, like an apprentice with her master or a compliant devotee with a cult leader. Once I understood the game, the conversation changed.

Finally, after I had let the man drone on, playing the one-up power broker role for a while, the Duke paused, half complete with his meal. He looked at me, head cocked slightly and eyes peering out from under his hat's floppy brim. He put his hand to his mouth, in an exaggerated motion of thoughtfulness, and then started a new thread of discussion.

"I like you," he said bluntly, a slight accent coloring his words. "I like you, and I think you've got what it takes. I can see you doing this." He took a sip from his glass and feigned contemplation again, transparently pausing for dramatic effect.

"OK," he snapped and lightly slapped the table, as if he had just made the decision and wasn't clearly playing a role. "Let me let you in on how all of this works. You see, I don't care if you have a big-D or a big-R next to your name. I don't care if you want to be in Tallahassee or do something more local. What I do care about, for the people I work with, is that we trust one another—explicitly. You see Elaine and Raphael, here?" he gestured to his "children" with his fork still in hand. "They're part of the family."

I nodded, a bit confused. Clearly, his children were family. What did he mean?

He pressed on, not noticing or, at least, not acknowledging my masked confusion. "You see, everyone I take on becomes part of the family—my sons and daughters. I find young professionals with a whole lot of potential, and I bring them into the fold. I teach them. I help them."

As he continued to talk, his underlying process became uncomfortably clear: He combed the state for bright, eager young adults—often very young, like early twenties. He'd invite them to join his so-called family and would even ask their parents to relinquish control. Then he'd raise them in his image. He would mold them to believe and act on his vision for South Florida. This, of course, involved actively supporting policies in his business interest.

As the discussion stretched out, now well past the meal, I excused myself to the restroom. When I returned, he took an exaggerated look at my derriere. "Dang, you didn't tell me you had those assets," he quipped, needlessly stressing the first syllable. "You could rule the whole Florida Senate!"

★ ★ ★

As you might expect, my lunch with the Duke didn't have the desired effect. Although far from the only empire builder (or creep, if you prefer) whom I've met during my short foray into politics, that meeting, in particular, reinforced my resolve to run an alternative national race. For one, I thought: If someone like the Duke reflects even a portion of the movers and shakers running our country, then we're in dire need of disruption. For another, meeting him made me realize just how ingrained the politics-as-usual mindset has become and that people who are already part of the political system are too close to see it. That realization also meant I would need to take all of the experts' advice with a grain of salt. Plenty of smart, well-meaning people give flawed recommendations because they lack the scope of experience, vision, or lateral thinking. Like the graphic designers with my campaign-mobile, they couldn't initially picture an unconventional design. And, in this case, the Florida consultants couldn't envision a different way to run for elected office.

Imagine a political campaign as a 26.2-mile race. That phrase—26.2 miles—immediately evokes visions of a marathon, a grueling footrace with lithe runners who wind their way en masse through an urban backdrop lined with cheering crowds, drink stations, banners, and media. We're biased by our prior experiences to expect these races to always work the same and so assume the way to win is by placing one foot in front of the next.

But what if you could compete differently? When you look at the same problem from a different perspective, your mind opens to new possibilities. In this case, no one said the competitors had to race on foot—we presumed that rule because it's how the race has been historically run. What if, instead of an exhausting footrace, we could build a flying machine to soar above the runners? Keep the same finish line but travel the distance in a different way. The flying machine would take longer to build, and the runners would have an advantage for the first fifteen miles while we constructed it. But once airborne, our flying machine could quickly overtake the tradition-bound runners.

If not already obvious, the footrace represents the classical approach of slogging step-by-painful-step from entry-level politics through each conventional milestone. Everyone expects the runners to wage this sort of traditional race, and even well-meaning marathon supporters can't imagine a flying machine joining the mix. More than that, many less savory characters will actively work against any disruption to the status quo. Countless people, like the Duke, are actively invested in the terrestrial marathon. By way of analogy, imagine the marathon sponsors, race-side vendors, and running coaches. They make money from the current model, and they've established lines of control throughout it. How would they feel if a flying machine changed the game?

The spectators watching from the sidelines aren't necessarily ready for a flying machine either. The television cameras and track-side audience all focus on the ground level. They measure competitors' success by comparing runners' progress at each mile. Meanwhile, the flying machine is slowly being constructed at the starting line, but the onlookers (if they even notice) assume it's hopelessly left behind.

It's unsurprising the Florida consultants and volunteers were dubious of a flying machine in their footrace, but I had a strong hypothesis it would work. And if my choices were to run a conventional race through the power brokers and gatekeepers of traditional politics like the Duke, or to make a crazy gamble, learn a thousand lessons, and shoot for "the impossible" on at the national level, then there was no competition. If I was right about the flying machine, about competing differently outside of the brittle convention system, then even if I lost, that demonstration alone could benefit the country. Someone has to blaze the trail, but few people can see the unmarked path and few among those are willing. So, shame on me if I didn't even try.

Mind made up, it was time. Go out and daringly do it: run the race but on my own terms.

CHAPTER SEVEN

#Tour50

May 2019

After so many delays, setbacks, and complications, the time had come to roll out for real! It was time to launch my national tour, and what better place to start than at my alma mater, Florida State University. The classic brick buildings, clustered in the city center of the state capital, made a picturesque backdrop. Imagine my turquoise campaign-mobile, parked in front of a red-brick lecture hall with the springtime sun peeking through the palm trees as an eager crowd forms. Well, I was hoping a crowd would form. Students are still interested in civics, right? Wait, and how much does it cost to rent space on campus?

I was reminded of the quip from *Zootopia*: " . . . it's great to dream . . . just as long as you don't believe in them too much." Where else could I host a (potentially sparsely attended) rally? The community center charged an arm and a leg, the downtown park wasn't available, and I sorely hoped more people would come than could fit into my living room.

The local American Legion saved me. They let me use their space for free—but only if the rally stayed nonpartisan. No problem. I had grown comfortable with nonpartisanship through UNIFY USA and, truth be told, it felt better focusing on collective national readiness rather than my own candidacy. To further emphasize that nonpartisan diversity, I had also asked around a dozen people join me on stage at the rally. They represented activists, subject-matter experts, and pundits from across the spectrum—a Democrat, a Republican, an Independent, someone representing the Green Party, and one guy who just hates politics. In the audience, around seventy people showed up to support, and for the first time, with my big Team JJ USA banner and a packed house full of rapt faces, I felt like a real candidate.

I only talked for about ten minutes, and then others spoke. In between each, I emceed to highlight how each fit into the bigger picture and how we could collectively work together—across parties and partisan axioms. It felt good. The fifty-state tour was starting on the right foot.

A successful local rally is one thing, but how could I build on that momentum? How does someone with nearly zero funds, an unknown name, and no partisan backing get started with an alternative campaign? I had considered hosting town halls or knocking on doors across the country, but those traditional methods didn't seem right. Instead, I had decided to design my fifty-state tour like a social science study. As I traveled, I hoped to find experts willing to be interviewed; they would collectively help craft solutions and participate in co-talks with me. In part, I wanted to shift the political discussion away from *funding* specific programs and toward more integrated problem solving. I also wanted to make space for people, both subject-matter experts and average citizens, to participate in those solutions. And, I hoped, the interview videos and public co-talks would attract attention.

I decided to focus the expert discussions around topics from the hierarchy of national needs my Geek Team and I had crafted: environment, health care, defense, education, economy, and innovation. It gave me a framework to structure my thinking and schedule. We teed up environment first. I had arranged nearly two-dozen experts to interview as my campaign trundled up the eastern coast, and that number would eventually swell into the triple digits. The morning after my campaign kickoff at the American Legion, I left my home in Orlando and drove a couple hours up the coast to Jacksonville. I had lined-up my first expert interview with Tony Vecchio, executive director of the Jacksonville Zoo and Gardens. Unfortunately, Murphy's law was in full effect.

We started early, but already the day felt like a sauna. Too hot and sticky for makeup and heels, I instead threw on a T-shirt and red tennis shoes. As the family packed into the RV, the atmosphere reverberated with tension. Admittedly, I felt rather frantic too. It was really happening. I was pulling away from my house and headed to an on-camera interview with a VIP whom I didn't know. What exactly was I going to ask him? Was I encroaching on his time? What kind of release permissions did I need for the video? How did the recording equipment work again? My brain buzzed on and on.

Only an hour down the road, my husband's voice interrupted my frenetic mental planning. "I think Robert just stopped," he observed with concern in his voice.

Robert had volunteered to join me on the tour. We'd first met in high school but, like most childhood acquaintances, had drifted apart during the intervening years. As my Geek Team began to mobilize, though, he had reengaged, first out of curiosity about our political system and, as the campaign grew more serious, as an opportunity to model activism for his teenage daughter. Robert sported his own truck-towed camper, and sure enough, it had pulled over onto the highway's shoulder. We soon found out he had blown a tire, but already running late, we agreed to press on and rendezvous later.

My family and I arrived at the zoo with only minutes to spare, and then squandered that time looking for a place to park—RVs aren't garage friendly! OK, now I only had three minutes before my appointment with Tony. I still needed to get dressed, put on makeup, shove my frazzled nerves into a façade of calm, and then—there was a knock on the door of my RV. Tony had arrived.

Tony wore a gray Jacksonville Zoo polo shirt that matched his heavily hooded eyes and horseshoe ring of hair. He squinted at me through the door's window as I mouthed, "One minute!" and did the bare minimum to make myself presentable. Then I opened the door to Tony and the sweltering midday sun. (At least no one would notice my rushed makeup and informal clothes if I melted into a puddle!) Tony escorted me, my husband, and our three children through a nearby entrance. As we walked, he and I chatted about the environment, conservation, and endangered species. My family trailed behind, including my bubbling seven-year-old who excitedly skipped along singing to herself.

The conversation morphed into a genuine interview once we reached Tony's office and set-up the camera. I felt nervous but not about being filmed—I had long ago made peace with looking foolish in public. I desperately wanted the interview to go well for Tony, though. He clearly had such passion for the zoo and for his work.

"Most people just think of a zoo as animals," he explained. "But I don't think our mission has anything to do with animals. I think our mission has to do with making our community a better place. It just happens our expertise is in animals and conservation."

I asked Tony about that conservation.

"I can remember one time in the zoo business just a few decades ago, we really focused on individual species. We'd want to save, let's say, the lions. We'd focus on lions. It's all about lions. But it's not that simple. You can't save lions in a vacuum. Everything's connected and interconnected. You have to look at things in a much bigger picture."

He went on to explain about the Association of Zoos and Aquariums, a nonprofit organization dedicated to conservation, education, and research. Professionals join it so they can share information and so they can work holistically—not just one species at a time but across the larger ecosystem. As humans, though, we naturally want to simplify, and in the government that urge multiplies. People want quick fixes; they want to solve problems by distilling solutions into sound bites and budget lines. It's easier to declare, "Save the lions!" than to develop complex, interdependent plans at the ecosystem level. *How do you get people (including politicians) to embrace the necessary complexity?* I wondered.

"I don't know that there's anything we can teach—any specific behavior or action or even level of awareness—that's going to make as much difference as simply inspiring people and reaching them on an emotional level," Tony answered. Conservationists can't force people to change, and no amount of money or policy will solve that problem. Instead, he advised, focus on inspiring people to think environmentally.

He's right, I thought. Motivation is the gatekeeper to human behavior. When people want to do something, they find a way, but if they're unmotivated no amount of reward or punishment will make a lasting difference. Inspired and intrinsically motivated people do amazing things, though. More than that, as a whole, inspired people become active change-agents, each individually seeking and implementing solutions rather than acting as nameless members of a crowd halfheartedly following someone else's direction. Tony's philosophy of inspiration applies to so much more than just conservation, and it's a role the government can (and should) play. Unfortunately, we don't usually see that; the government rarely takes on the mandate to inspire people, despite the critical role collective motivation plays in many policy outcomes.

After the interview, Tony thanked me for the opportunity to share his message. I accepted his gratitude and returned the compliment, the whole time thinking, *I'm the one who should be thanking you!* He had given me so much to consider. He even gave my youngest daughter something, a souvenir from the zoo: a stuffed plush rat that immediately became her beloved treasure. He had one final gift for me, as well.

"You remind me of Jimmy Carter," he remarked as we were saying our goodbyes. "Everyone said he had no chance because he didn't have the traditional credentials. But he went out and connected to people and learned the process. You can do that too. Go meet people, hear what the nation needs, and then get yourself elected. You can do this."

After the interview, we linked back up with teammate Robert. The molten-hot highway had caused one of the tires on his secondhand trailer to blow, not only temporarily stranding him but also throwing rubber shrapnel into the camper's undercarriage. (Pro tip: When you buy a used camper, make sure to always replace the tires.) Fortunately, Robert was able to limp his trailer to the campground where we planned to stay that night.

If you've never had the opportunity to visit an RV park, you're missing out. Some of the parks are true five-star destinations, with all manner of family recreation, like waterslides, bars, and karaoke. The people at RV parks also make them special with their interesting stories and neighborly hospitality.

At this particular site, we met a retired Army veteran, there with his family on vacation. Robert and my husband, Chris, started chatting with him at the bar, and before I knew it, they had collectively decided to repair Robert's camper. Like MacGyver, the three assembled their resources—mainly duct tape and a blue utility tarp—and developed an elaborate solution for the demolished camper floor.

Ironically, the former Solider was a die-hard Trump supporter, but that didn't stop him from volunteering to help. It just goes to show: It doesn't matter which party any of us supports. When there's a problem, Americans come together to fix it.

The next morning, we hit the road. As we crossed from Florida into Georgia, the landscape changed. Cotton fields began lining the highway, and the trees hung heavy with moss. More houses featured front porches, and the people we met would reply with "yes ma'am" or "no sir" in a Southern drawl.

In Savannah, we had scheduled an interview with Dr. Joe Pfaller, research director of the Caretta Research Project, a science and conservation program for loggerhead turtles. Joe seems younger than his age. He's fit and gregarious and has warm dark eyes and an easy demeanor. I think anyone would be hard pressed to dislike him. And he's incredibly geeky! He's all about science and data, and he clearly loves to share his knowledge of sea turtles. We spoke about the local loggerheads and their immediate environment. We also talked about the project's outreach through eco-vacations.

The Caretta Research Project hosts weeklong educational retreats for anyone interested in conservation, turtles, or nature. People pay a nominal fee for room and board and, in turn, get to work with the biologists and even watch the hatchlings emerge (at the right time of year). The Caretta researchers get additional helping hands, and the extra bit of money they earn from participant fees goes into a scholarship fund for underserved children. The scholarship pays for high schoolers to have eco-vacations and take part in a program where they learn about becoming scientists.

"But we've had a hard time getting kids to sign up," Joe told me regretfully.

People love turtles, he explained. They're great ambassadors for the environment and for professions like marine biology. When he recruits for the scholarship program, the kids show a lot of excitement, but when it comes time for them to actually participate—to leave their families and try something radically different by themselves—they get cold feet.

"Unfortunately," Joe sighed, "we made the program and found the money, but students still won't get involved."

Joe's scholarship predicament highlighted one of the hidden barriers to change: creating opportunity isn't enough. People won't always take advantage of available options, maybe out of fear of the unknown or a sense they're not truly welcome. Or maybe they have other concerns, such as a job they can't take-off from or a family member relying on them. Nonetheless, well-meaning policymakers often assume providing opportunity—and putting money into human-centric problems—is enough.

What's more, it's natural to think, *If people want better opportunities in life, they will take advantage of opportunities available.* Unfortunately, it doesn't always work this way. People are more complex and fear of the unknown can drive the best of us to pause. Joe's struggle, though, highlighted those other invisible impediments to participation and helped opened my eyes to a larger, more general set of challenges. It helped me understand that people need to be inspired (as Tony said) and also encouraged to play an active role in solutions. It's not enough to simply open the door, we have to actively encourage people to walk through it.

★ ★ ★

After Savannah we traveled to Charleston, South Carolina. We had hoped to talk with a scientist from the South Carolina Aquarium, but no one responded to our e-mails. Undeterred, we had decided to visit the aquarium directly and try to make a connection. In person, the aquarium staff were more receptive. They explained their hesitancy to reply to a politician's e-mail, but as they talked with me and learned I also had a scientific background, they began to warm up.

Essentially, the aquarium staff put me through an examination. First, two women asked me basic questions: What's your academic background? Why do you want to interview someone? What questions will you ask? Once I answered those sufficiently, the next gatekeeper took over. He probed my judgment and integrity: Where will you use this information? Are you going to cut segments out of context? Will you twist it? I ultimately passed his tests too.

The screening I experienced at the South Carolina Aquarium would happen again and again, in many different places. I wasn't offended people wanted to vet me, even though those gatekeepers often expressed apologies. Frankly, I thought their caution was smart. Still, it took an emotional toll.

Scientists and researchers often have incredible passion for their work. They want to share their knowledge and, frequently, want to inspire others with it. That desire to share clashes with our current climate, though. Sensationalist media, fake news, and disreputable influencers have soured a lot of people, and now, rather than jumping at the chance to talk, researchers' first reaction is suspicion. On a personal level, I also found the mistrust unsettling. In my professional career before attempting to run for office, I had grown accustomed to a certain level of baseline trust and respect. I hadn't realized it at the time, but working in scholarly circles, where my professional standing and formal credentials preceded me, had been a luxury. Now, like a shocking plunge into cold water, I had suddenly transformed from trusted scientist into suspicious politician. Of all the challenges I faced transitioning to the political world, this was one of the hardest to swallow. I was suddenly a pariah, having done nothing to deserve that treatment or presumed reputation.

Even after the first three aquarium staffers warmed up to me, I still had to convince (let's call her) Shannon, the conservation expert I hoped to interview, that I wouldn't misuse her words or spin her platform. After many assurances, she finally agreed. I felt honored. Shannon had an important message, and I think it was her dedication to sharing it that ultimately pushed her to say yes to the interview. She worried about our nation's declining connections to nature and wanted to talk about some of the ways the aquarium encourages people to get more involved.

"We're looking for ways to engage the public in litter sweeps and understanding sea level rise and flooding," she told me, "and we have a pretty robust citizen science program." Shannon explained how the aquarium has even developed a mobile app, where average people can monitor environmental trends; for instance, it has a litter journal where people can record their observations.

"When we get people to input litter data into this app, they're able to find out the most problematic types of debris and then find solutions," she explained. "It's open-source data, so everyone who's a member of this app can download the data, analyze it, and use it."

When I asked her who looks at the data, she replied, "It's communities. It's community leaders, town halls, and city council folks—it's people passionate about protecting their children."

That was Shannon's ultimate message: Every one of us, in our own communities, can make an impact. Each person can contribute in so many ways. The information, conservation programs, and even ready-made smartphone applications are there. We don't need to invent something new; we just need to commit to using what's already available.

After Charleston, we continued up Interstate 26. In North Carolina, it felt like we drove for ages and through a half-dozen different terrains. We increasingly shared the road with pickup trucks (often sporting NASCAR stickers), and a rural working-class practicality slowly replaced the stately charm of the more southern Carolina.

We stopped in Charlotte, where I had scheduled a visit to the local chapter of the League of Women Voters, a nonpartisan political action organization founded around the time of women's suffrage. The group met at a sort of community center, a squat brown-brick structure along one of the suburban streets. Inside, the meeting space looked much like you'd imagine. The white corporate walls were rimmed with stacks of conference chairs, lined-up like soldiers around the edges of the room. A hodgepodge of government swag lined the walls: Empower Voters posters, pictures of smiling volunteers, and certificates of community appreciation. A smudged whiteboard hung across the front with an old-school projector screen haphazardly obscuring part of it.

In the center of the room, a handful of older women sat at plastic folding tables, leaning over manila folders and small stacks of paperwork. Their meeting agenda included discussions on the regional environment and applied problem solving for those local issues.

We arrived a few minutes late, thanks to my ongoing struggle to find RV parking. Maddie, clutching her stuffed rat from the Jacksonville Zoo, joined me. As we walked in, the ladies greeted us pleasantly and then waited expectantly. I made brief introductions. Then we stared at each other awkwardly for a long moment.

"So, what's your plan?" One of the women prompted.

Although I was only there to observe, these women all assumed I was there to speak. They expected a visiting politician to tell versus listen, to push out her wisdom versus pull in their ideas. Not wanting to act rudely, I addressed the woman's initial question but then countered, "I know you want to hear my environmental plan, but I don't have one yet. How could I have a plan if I haven't heard from you? What's working in your community? What's not working? What do you wish people in Raleigh or DC knew about your issues?"

After that, the conversation mellowed. These ladies had dozens of ideas, all focused at the pragmatic local level. They had energy and motivation too, as shown by their willingness to fill out paperwork and discuss city ordinances on an otherwise beautiful Thursday afternoon. Surprisingly, though, when I asked them about applying for government grants or collaborating with the many nongovernmental environmental groups, they grew more timid. They didn't seem familiar with these opportunities, and when I tried to share my knowledge about federal funding for citizen projects, they politely changed the subject.

It's incredibly common for people—even active civic groups—to lack awareness of available state and federal opportunities. Sadly, government's inscrutability also discourages people from even trying to find out. They may worry, "What if we file the wrong form or misstep on some arbitrary rule?" or "How hard will it be to find the necessary information?" or "How many attorneys and accountants will we need to even try?"

Easier and safer to focus on other options and cede these avenues to insiders already comfortable with the system.

All told, I interviewed more than a dozen experts, scoured reports and policy papers, and chatted with countless everyday citizens, from the ladies at the Women's League to the Princeton student I had met on a plane so many months before. I even chatted with biologist Christine Figgener, famous for starting the anti-plastic movement when her video of a sea turtle suffering from a straw in its nose went viral. I wanted to integrate what I had learned into a strategy, but I needed to avoid the disingenuous trap of making a legislative proposal. So I set some parameters to keep the plan appropriately presidential: First, the actions it recommends needed to fall within the purview of the executive branch. Second, similar to the first rule, it couldn't depend upon any new laws—legislation falls into Congress's swim lane. Finally, it couldn't require any additional funds. People already have a heavy tax burden and, besides, apportioning funds once again falls under Congress's authorities.

Fortunately, I came to realize through my investigation, we don't necessarily need more money or additional legislative actions. We already have a wealth of environmental ideas, programs, and passion. We're just missing a few small things—just a few deft twists of the Rubik's Cube to align all the pieces.

In the end, I developed an environmental strategy focused around three principles: Innovation, activation, and inspiration. (OK, don't roll your eyes at me, I know it sounds hyperbolic but people like sound bites.) There is a depth under the superficial packaging.

First, innovation, because we can't solve environmental problems with money alone—if we could have, they'd already be solved. Local and federal governments, countless charities, and many individual philanthropists already pour money into environmental causes. We don't need more resources. We need to use the resources at hand in different and more coordinated ways. We need to help people find and use existing tools, like the aquarium's citizen science app, and we need to connect people like Joe Pfaller, who already have resourced solutions, to groups like the Women's League, who can bring those solutions to local communities and help clear barriers to their integration. We don't need more federal programs. Rather, the government can help by using some programs differently. It can play orchestra conductor to existing efforts, helping to uncover and scale-up effective local solutions and interconnect complementary projects so that they multiply (rather than duplicate) each other's efforts.

Second, activation, because as Tony Vecchio highlighted, many problems are too complex to resolve through policy or programs, alone, and if you try to address complex issues with simplified answers ("Save the Lions!"), you'll unbalance the ecosystem. Environmental solutions need a societal ecosystem approach; in other words, we need everyone—from governments and nonprofits to individuals and corporations—to contribute. And that can't be achieved through top-down control. Instead we have to start encouraging people to act, and we need to make smarter use of their efforts. A whole heaping helping of good-hearted Americans, many with bleeding hearts and boundless enthusiasm already want to help, but too many would-be contributors are spinning their wheels on stationary bikes. While the government can't solve complex problems alone, it still has a unique role to play. The government can help direct individuals' energy toward coherent solutions, and as Joe showed me, it can help identify and remove barriers to citizen participation so that people feel confident, invited, and able to meaningfully contribute.

Finally, inspiration, because we need both body (activation) and mind. More precisely, environmental solutions demand a shift away from a scarcity mindset and toward one of abundance. People in scarcity conditions act from a short-term survival perspective and live in a world of limitation. They make decisions based upon what's immediately available and act out of fear of missing out. A scarcity mindset also encourages learned helplessness—a sense of "there's nothing I can do so why even try?" In contrast, people in abundance conditions make decisions from a place of calm security and optimism. They problem solve—not only for whatever suffices in the moment but for the long term. When people act out of scarcity, for example, they use the plastic straws at hand because they're there. Besides, what else can be done? But, from an abundance perspective, people embrace creativity and naturally yearn to solve problems—to make newfangled cups or eco-friendly straws, for instance. An abundance mindset opens up possibilities, and it encourages reflection on a better tomorrow. Put another way, it's not enough for people to be educated in facts or have pathways to actively contribute, they need to be inspired to think differently, to reach for creative solutions. And they can, with just a little nudging.

Overall, we have everything we need to address our environmental challenges. We have the puzzle pieces in abundance. We're just missing a little coordination. It's like what Kris Cole from the Carolina Raptor Center told me when I interviewed her: "I don't think there's a single problem on this planet right now that humans can't fix, including the ones that we've caused. So let's innovate. We can do this!"

CHAPTER EIGHT

Money Is the Root of All Politics

So you want to get into national politics? Are you independently wealthy? Can you hustle? Without a ton of dough, you can't pass go. There's no path forward. (Trust me. I've tried.) You can only play in this arena if you have a lot of money or a big name that brings in a lot of money. Nothing else matters—not qualifications, not experience—just money.

I'm not outright offended by the idea of fundraising. Campaigns have plenty of reasonable expenses, especially when candidates run the traditional way (the marathon footrace approach). They need to pay for administrative staff, travel, rallies, logistics, surveys, data, and speechwriters—all more or less legitimate requirements. They also need cash for marketing, videos and mailers, catchy campaign jingles, and Facebook ads. Sometimes the sponsored publicity stunts slip into questionable territory, like smarmy attack ads, and of course, candidates have to shell out greenbacks for opposition research to dig up that dirt. Still, even if not always palatable, dirty campaign tricks are an understandable cost. All of these reasonable expenditures, however, pale in comparison to the other campaign costs.

First, candidates spend a good chunk of their scratch marketing for more money. My consultants estimated presidential campaigns spend about seventy-five dollars just to collect one dollar from someone new. You read that correctly. Campaigns take a huge loss just to find fresh donors, largely because some ballot qualifications require a certain number of unique contributors and often donors from different geographical regions. So candidates with two or three large benefactors use those patrons' sizable donations to go after smaller one dollar and five dollar grassroots contributions, often under the pretense of running a grassroots operation. Campaigns spend thousands on social media and direct marketing to get those small sums, not to mention the Benjamins spent buying voter lists so they know who to spam for donations. There are hundreds of lists to buy (per state, per region), and unless you're already part of the political establishment, it takes even more coin to research, aggregate, and use those lists effectively.

Next, part of the money also goes to, essentially, buying off political power brokers. Candidates pay other politicians to endorse them publicly or to bury opposition research against them. They can also pay politicians or fellow candidates to act as campaign surrogates. For instance, if a presidential candidate can't visit, say, Alaska on a regular basis, he might send funds to an Alaskan congressperson who, in turn, speaks for the candidate on stage and stands in at fundraising events. Politicians are rarely stumping for one another out of an ideological sense of camaraderie. Instead, most form factions around money.

Another reason candidates build fiscal factions is to collect larger donations than individual contribution limits allow. Simply put, factions help people skirt the Federal Election Commission's fundraising regulations. While sometimes ethically questionable, it's still perfectly legal through Political Action Committees or, as they're more commonly known, PACs.

Essentially, PACs are regulated slush funds. Their rules are impregnably complex, creating plenty of dark corners and legal loopholes, and FEC enforcement of them is roughly nonexistent. PACs come in different shapes and sizes, and they can operate at the national or state levels. They enroll as tax-exempt organizations (527s in finance-speak) and register with the FEC. After that, the various flavors of PACs each follow different guidelines, but in general, they all accept money and then spend it for political outcomes like advocacy for certain issues or support for particular candidates.

At first glance, PACs don't seem that bad. At the state level, a typical PAC follows rules similar to the FEC fundraising guidelines for politicians: They can only accept so much money from a given contributor, and the types of donors are regulated. For example, people without US citizenship can't donate. There's a similar kind of traditional PAC at the national level. They follow rules similar to those for federal campaign committees, except that PACs can represent several candidates, and corporations or labor unions, which can't traditionally donate to individual candidates, can establish special PACs around ideologies. Still, typical FEC rules largely apply to these general PACs.

There are two other types of PACs (well, three types, if you count their hybrid combination). But before I explain them, grab your favorite adult beverage, and if you're operating a motor vehicle right now, you may want to pull over, because this is where things get infuriating.

The next kind of PAC is a super PAC, made possible by the *Citizens United* Supreme Court case. Super PACs are so-called independent expenditure-only funds, which means they can only spend money on political activities undertaken, *ahem,* independently. That means activities taken without direct coordination with candidates or their campaigns. (Although, there's no rule a super PAC can't be run by, say, a candidate's best friend who *independently* takes all sorts of helpful actions for her political bestie.) Provided a super PAC meets that broad requirement and a few other rules, like not blatantly taking foreign contributions, it can accept unlimited donations. Oh, and don't worry, my eager global despots, there's an easy built-in loophole to avoid those pesky rules. Unqualified potential donors can contribute funds to third-party groups outside of FEC oversight, like social welfare nonprofits. Since those go-betweens aren't required to report their donation sources, super PACs can mainline dark money from their coffers.[1]

Super PACs can spend their ducats on pretty much anything, so long as it doesn't directly fund a candidate's own FEC-regulated campaign committee and hasn't been coordinated (*wink, wink*) with the campaign. They can buy marketing to sway voters about a referendum or an election. They can spend money on polling, opposition research, and other political activities. Super PACs can even spend their money on fundraising for more money, so they can perpetually grow in wealth and influence. And, of course, super PACs can throw fundraising shindigs where they invite distinguished speakers—for instance, certain candidates—who mingle and present talks on whatever topics they please.

The next breed of PAC is the leadership PAC, designed for established politicians and other prominent political figures. Similar to super PACs, leadership PACs have few restrictions on their spending, so people use them to cover expenses that their campaigns (or their elected offices) aren't otherwise allowed to fund, like travel to political rallies while holding elected office, meals and alcohol, wardrobe makeovers, international resort vacations, and country club fees. (You know, the campaign essentials.) Under the guise of fundraising, around half of all leadership PAC funds go toward luxury items.[2] Admittedly, some of those fundraising activities can help raise the politician's profile. For instance, picture a US senator who's just won reelection. She might still have three hundred thousand dollars in her leadership PAC after the race, and she can continue to collect more at any time. Then, over the next six years, she can spread those funds across her home state, hosting pledge drives at elite golf courses and throwing fundraising galas for her donors—all the while promoting herself in preparation for the next election and continuing to refuel her leadership PAC. Those kinds of tactics give incumbents a major advantage. *Grassroots popularity my ass!*

But wait, it gets better. Individual campaigns have contribution limits. For example, our hypothetical US senator could accept around fifty-six hundred dollars from a particular donor during an election cycle (half for the primary and half for the general election), but she can also accept roughly six times that—from nearly every domestic source—over the next six years for her leadership PAC.[3] Once in the leadership PAC, whatever funds not applied to laying the groundwork for reelection or used to subsidize her lifestyle, can go to other politicians. In other words, politicians can use leadership PACs to pay off their peers and buy their way to the top—to encourage their fellow lawmakers to open spots on important committees or to vote them into leadership posts.[4] Leadership PACs let political power brokers spread their wealth, secure fealty through funding, and solidify their footholds in Washington.

Finally, in case your blood hasn't reached a full rolling boil, I'll add that many wealthy businesses feel squeezed to contribute to leadership PACs. In his book, *Extortion: How Politicians Extract Your Money, Buy Votes, and Line Their Own Pockets,* Peter Schweizer (president of the Government Accountability Institute) quoted business executives, from companies like Microsoft, calling leadership PACs mafia-like and saying politicians will "go after you" if your business doesn't donate. Politicians create "milker bills," as an example. These are policy proposals that dramatically raise taxes on a certain sector or threaten some sort of apocalyptic business regulations. Then the politicians watch the funds roll in, and when their cash cow is suitably milked, they withdraw the proposed legislation.[5]

Well, that's more than enough about PACs, but we're still not done. Even after presidential candidates have sufficiently greased all the PAC palms, they still need more money, this time for entrance fees. It's neither cheap nor easy getting onto the ballots. Presidential candidates have to register in every single state, and the methods vary across the country.

Of course, the most common route onto the ballot is through each state's political parties. Basically, the party leaders submit lists of designated candidates. Easy peasy for those willing to slog through the marathon footrace of conventional politics. For those candidates operating outside the established partisan machine, there are other (albeit more costly and time consuming) pathways. Some states, like New Hampshire, simply require paperwork and a filing fee. Other states require petitions, with signatures collected from qualified local voters. In Alabama, for instance, candidates who collect a few hundred signatures from across the state can get onto the ballot. Another way is through a combination of news media and state political parties. Michigan is a good example. In Michigan, the state parties identify potential candidates and the secretary of state also compiles a list of candidates named in the national news media. Basically, candidates who've achieved some attention in national polls make it onto one (or both) lists. If that doesn't work, a candidate can petition for inclusion, after collecting several thousand voter signatures.[6]

Rather than further bore you with all of the minutiae, let me simply point out how much control the national political parties have over which names make it onto the primary ballot. State party leaders who "like" candidates (and what's more likable than a well-resourced friend?) can fast-track their names onto the ballot. Candidates without that advantage are forced to spend substantial time navigating the byzantine state rules, hand collecting signatures (usually from each region across a state), and paying other filing fees. The system does not encourage unconventional participation.

When people say, "It's all about the money," that's not just a glib expression. It's a statement of fact and, perhaps, even an *under*statement. Small wonder candidates (and even elected politicians) spend much of their time fundraising.

A few years ago, *60 Minutes* released an exposé called "Dialing for Dollars." In it, then-Florida Representative David Jolly shared his experience as a freshman congressman. When he first arrived in Washington, his fellow Republicans explained that fundraising was his first responsibility. He was introduced to the donation call centers, essentially telemarketing sweatshops, which party members can use—for a fee, of course. Congressman Jolly's colleague, Democratic Representative Rick Nolan, also took part in the documentary. He added that Republicans and Democrats have similar fundraising practices, and both parties advise their junior members to spend about thirty hours each week fundraising.[7] (You read that correctly: As elected and actively practicing politicians, they're supposed to spend roughly thirty hours during their workweek chasing gold.)

Meanwhile, as hopeful candidates and elected politicians spend their time digging for gold, what aren't they doing? They barely have time for their regular duties or to meet with constituents, let alone time for genuine problem solving, self-improvement, or strategic thinking. And, since money is the touchstone of modern politics, we can only assume that many of those who've advanced through the conventional ranks have done so largely thanks to their fundraising prowess, money, connections, and ability to schmooze. Are these really the skill sets we value in our leaders? Do we want leaders who are skilled telemarketers and charismatic beggars, or do we want qualified executives and policymakers?

After all the costs associated with running a campaign, paying off the partisan system, and getting onto the ballot, it should surprise precisely no one that the primary qualification to participate in the official Democratic Party debate involves a dollar sign. To win a spot in the first presidential debate of the 2020 election cycle, candidates needed to show donations of sixty-five thousand dollars from more than four thousand unique donors. Subsequent debates raised the bar on that financing amount, but the general principle remained the same.[8] (Other requirements related to national polling later came into play, but money, as you might expect, also greatly influences those figures.) Candidates are essentially begging for dollars to perform on stage.

I couldn't bring myself to watch the first debate in real time. I had a strong suspicion it would be cringeworthy, so I ended up watching a few days after it aired, and only made it through thanks to the accelerated playback option and several glasses of chardonnay.

The Democrats were so clearly performing the politics-as-usual movie script. It looked like the *Hunger Games*: Ten tributes entered the arena. They lined up behind old-school lecterns, each poised on his or her starting block. Then the gong chimed, and the bloodbath began—each competitor cutting the others down with sensational quips and carefully laid traps, fighting against the rest for that precious cornucopia of screen time.

All of this may make for entertaining TV, but these gladiators aren't vying for roles in a primetime drama. They're petitioning for a real, serious-minded job. What's more, even though the Democratic Party had organized the debates, ostensibly for their own benefit and for the benefit of these candidates, it still felt like a death match. The questions didn't encourage cooperation or help reveal genuine solutions. Instead, the debate seemed designed for entertainment value and to provide openings for quotable sound bites. It was designed for the candidates to metaphorically destroy each other, so only one would be left standing.

But what if there was a different way? Could that airtime be used for something that revealed candidates' applied skills, rather than their clever insults and witticisms? Could it be used to showcase things that uplift the party—and the nation? For example, what if the candidates held a session on national TV where they worked with citizens and subject-matter experts to address timely issues? Something like *Queer Eye* or *American Ninja Warrior,* albeit with more problem solving and less post-production scripting. Rather than redesigning a contestant's wardrobe, the candidates could clean out our policy closet, and instead of leaping across ropes and platforms, they could face a presidential obstacle course with timed challenges on real-world problems. Maybe it's a bit silly, but it couldn't be worse than the current gauntlet. It's one thing for the news media to set up gladiatorial events and encourage directionless sensationalism. We need the political parties and other serious politicians to do better. Sadly, today, the only option for individuals is to annihilate their colleagues—their fellow tributes. How is that a good strategy for America?

What makes someone qualified for federal office? Is it name recognition, fundraising skills, or on-air charisma? Is it financial acumen or wealthy friends? Or is it simply tenacity during the long, mudslinging campaign trail and their ability to give and take zingers along the way?

The characteristics that make someone a good candidate seem to have little in common with the skills actually needed to govern. I suppose the ideal person would have both candidate skills and a wholly different set of executive skills, and he or she could swap between them at a moment's notice. At times, this political "Dr. Jekyll" would speak comfortably in punchlines and charm donations from wealthy patrons. Then, behind closed doors, he or she would think strategically and delve into complex issues with discerning zeal. Unfortunately, the kind of extravert who's comfortable with schmoozing and repartee in the limelight isn't likely the kind of person who likes to (and knows when to) dive into the problem-solving weeds. The combination of those characteristics is rare, which unduly limits the field, and even those unicorns able to play both roles face serious hurdles. The system is stacked against them, constantly threatening to disrupt the delicate balance between Dr. Jekyll and Mr. Hyde.

Political hopefuls may begin with virtuous intent but then lose their scruples as they run the political gauntlet. Politics not only attracts swindlers and narcissists; it also creates them. Put people into situations that constantly urge attention-seeking behaviors and then force them to prostitute for money, and it should come as no surprise when they begin to act badly. Instead, those handful of politicians who've eschewed leadership PACs and rejected dark money are truly the surprising ones.

Our political system has written and staged its own dark comedy, so it's only natural when the actors follow that storyline. It's easy to throw rotten tomatoes from the audience and boo the protagonists when they fall from grace, but until we rewrite the script, the same story will continue to play. It's not enough to levy critiques at the playwrights or walk out of the theater in disgust. We have to stand up from the audience, get onto that stage, and rewrite the script from the inside. Only those participating in a system can reform it. Until then, we have to learn the rules and find some way to play by them, and for now, at least, that means money, money, money.

CHAPTER NINE

At Least I Can Handle the Shit!

Traveling by RV isn't all glamorous karaoke bars and roadside takeout. It's hard work steering a multi-ton block of metal at highway speeds. (Hats off to truckers and my fellow camper captains.) Added to all of that, I wasn't just taking a leisurely road trip. I also had to plan my campaign stops, make online posts and edit videos, work on my national strategies, and interact with all sorts of people along the way.

I've lost count of the number of times people stopped me to chat in campgrounds, quizzed me on politics at gas stations, or honked at me on the interstate. (My trundling turquoise campaign mobile attracts all sorts of attention.) Although it happened often, I remember one particular time while driving on the highway. I had come to realize that about four hours was my on-road limit. The noise, vibrations, and vigilance take a toll. Anyway, on this particular day, I had already driven over three hours and was biting the inside of my cheek to stay alert. On the drivers' side, I could sense another car just keeping pace. Intuitively, I knew these folks wanted to catch my eye, but feeling drained, I stubbornly ignored the sedan in the left lane. This continued for over a minute, until social pressure finally wore me down, and I turned to acknowledge my highway companions.

In the car beside me sat two grandmotherly figures, with their gray hair styled in the tight curls so often favored by women of a certain age. They were looking and gesturing at me with open encouragement, and both wore huge shit-eating grins. Despite my haggard state, I couldn't help but beam back. "Hi, ladies!" I mouthed and gave a brief wave. After that, from my periphery, I saw them laugh and wave and then, finally satiated, speed ahead of my lumbering bus.

Another time, while parked at a campsite, my neighbor greeted me in the early morning. I was wearing yoga pants and unruly bedhead and had just climbed down from my RV for a sunrise jog. With two rambunctious dogs in tow, my neighbor had apparently had a similar idea. He had a mumble-mouth way of talking, with sloppy enunciation and guileless diction, but his ideas came through clearly enough. The man worked as a concrete mason for construction sites, and although he claimed to have never graduated high school, he was quick to announce his commitment to staying informed on current events.

We exchanged the usual pleasantries, and when I mentioned my campaign, he blurted, "You know what the government's problem is?"

I shook my head and encouraged him to continue.

"It's the same problem I see all the time, that I see in my business. The people who design the layout haven't ever poured concrete before. That's the politicians' problem. You know, they make this blueprint, but they're not the ones who have to put it into place. They don't get their hands dirty. So they don't know what it takes to make all them things work in the real world."

I couldn't have said it better myself.

Of course, these routine interactions weren't limited to waving roadmates and parking-lot encounters. Eagerly and sometimes shamelessly, people have approached me under all sorts of circumstances. One zealous acquaintance even greeted me while I was emptying my toilet. It happened at an RV park along the East Coast. Only a few minutes before, I had parked my camper and was beginning to set up for the night. By this time in the tour, I had learned which water lines to connect where, and, as glorious as it sounds, I had also grown expert at emptying refuse from the RV. Clad in thick rubber gloves, I was busy pumping waste out of its tank when my campground neighbor decided to say hi.

The man, a somewhat portly fellow who seemed to be fast approaching senior-citizen status, gestured a greeting and asked, "Whatcha got there?"

"I'm trying to pump the septic," I explained dully, hoping he'd leave me in peace while I finished the unenviable task. Undeterred (and apparently oblivious to social cues), he nodded toward my official-looking picture on the side of the RV.

"No, I mean *that*."

More curtly than usual, I explained, "I'm running for president. I used to work in government—as a civil servant not a politician—but a lot of us civilians are getting tired how of things are going. So I thought I'd switch things up, try the political side, and find out if we can fix the system or if we're really just screwed."

After a cynical snort, he assured me, "Oh, we're screwed, all right," then began listing the reasons why our government is irredeemable.

When he paused long enough for me to interject, I countered, "Well, I can tell you the problem isn't average folks. Every place I've been, people want to do something and want to listen, but they're also disgruntled. The process is a mess. We need someone willing to roll up her sleeves and get her hands dirty to fix it." I held up my hands, still encased in industrial gloves. "And we know, at least, I can handle the shit." It was a lame joke, but we both laughed all the same.

Over the course of my time in politics, I've met so many people—from all walks of life, from across our entire country, and from every political faction. I've talked to award-winning doctors and high-school dropouts, hardcore conservatives and far-left progressives. To a person, they've shown interest and engagement. Some have had blind spots when it comes to political practices or current events, a few have even deliberately eschewed the news, viewing it as emotional poison. Still, I've never met anyone completely out of touch, too lazy to care, or entirely disengaged. As my fifty-state tour progressed, my doubt in the conventional wisdom intensified. I wasn't finding an America full of flippant and feebleminded voters, unable to parse more than a single simplified message (as the political consultants had ardently predicted). I was, however, finding fed-up people frustrated with the system, people who were concerned or sickened by the state of things, but still hopeful—still eager for a solution to our ugly, growing set of political problems.

After visiting Asheville, Charlotte, and Raleigh, our caravan lumbered onward into Virginia. We stopped in Norfolk, home to the largest Naval base in the world, US Joint Staff offices, and one of the NATO Strategic Commands. The area also boasts plenty of nonmilitary charm, from nearby Virginia Beach to all of the attractions on and around the Elizabeth River.

I started by touring the Battleship Wisconsin, where the volunteer docents eagerly explained modern shipyard innovations. (Who knew shipping containers were so unironically cool?) After those interviews, Maddie and I visited the maritime science center poised on the banks of the river and grandly dubbed the *Nauticus*. As we approached, I was drawn to a group of older gentlemen congregating outside. They were clustered around some kind of maritime miniatures, and as I neared, telltale signs of their prior service stood out, like ball caps embroidered with military patches and Sailors' tattoos peeking out from short sleeves. The elder veterans were delighted to show off their models, realistic military submarines they had assembled, and it took little prompting for them to share their war stories too. We talked for some time, and when we eventually parted ways, they wished me well in my presidential run. I'm not sure they knew whether I was running as a Democrat, Republican, or something else, but they were excited to hear about a young person (in their eyes) trying to do something for our nation.

As our trip continued, we passed through Richmond and Harrisonburg, conducting interviews and visiting more historic sites along the route. Virginia has a long memory when it comes to the Civil War, and we took the opportunity to stop at the American Civil War Museum in the state's capital. Richmond was once the epicenter of the Confederacy. It also had a massive slave market, and during the Civil War, it operated the largest arms factory. Some of those wounds still haven't healed, even so many generations later, and the museum's exhibits (now housed in the remnants of that old artillery works) create a powerful reminder of the sacrifice righteousness so often requires and that the arc of the moral universe can be painfully long.[1]

After Richmond, we drove northeast into the DMV—that's what residents call the larger metropolitan nexus of DC, Maryland, and northern Virginia. I've spent a lot of time there, both for work and with friends, and have a full Rolodex for the area. So we hadn't had difficulty filling my interview dance card, at least, not at first.

I had planned to use our time in the nation's capital to record talks with federal insiders and had lined up video shoots with civil servants from across the branches. But, at the last minute, every one of them withdrew. From their personal e-mail accounts to my personal in-box, I received nearly identical messages from several civilians, each from different agencies. The e-mails all went something like this:

> The department is getting really crazy right now, even crazier than usual. People are getting escorted out of the building without notice. The rules are changing almost daily, and people are getting nervous. I can't be on camera right now. Talking publicly about anything could mean my job. I'm still happy to meet over a beer and talk informally. I'll get the first round as an apology.

Clearly, even in the six months since I had resigned from the civil service, the situation had worsened. When I later talked with my friends and colleagues (off the record, of course), they confirmed the government was becoming an increasingly antagonistic workplace. People were afraid, and not only afraid of failure or of making mistakes. They were afraid of getting noticed at all, even for good work. "The wisest course of action is to fly under the radar," one colleague advised. "Stay in your office and hopefully be forgotten."

To appreciate these dynamics, it's important to have some understanding of the general administration of our federal government. It doesn't operate like a normal business or even like typical local or state governments. At the federal level, the workforce is made up of several types of employees. First, there are your elected politicians and their (typically young and underpaid) staffers who do the lion's share of routine political work. Next, you have the uniformed military personnel, who (if you count them as federal employees) make up about a third of the workforce.[2] Although technically federal employees, like service members, postal workers are usually considered a special category and partitioned out. So, that leaves about two million regular, full-time staff. Among those, there are career civil servants, which is what I used to be. These are government workers hired to do a particular job and qualified based on their knowledge and expertise. In other words, career civil servants have "normal" jobs, except they do that work for the government. Finally, there are the political appointees.

Appointees come and go with the presidential administration, and it's kind of shocking just how many there are. Appointees fill about four thousand of the top leadership positions across the federal government. That's a good chunk of all executives and top-level leaders (the C-suite in business jargon), including the department secretaries, along with a majority of the under secretaries, assistant secretaries, and deputy secretaries of different offices. Most of the agency heads and ambassadors are appointees too.

Essentially, political appointees serve as the layer in between the career civil servants (the technical experts, if you will) and the Oval Office. So you might think appointees would be chosen for their managerial prowess, expertise, and senior leadership experience. More often, however, appointees' foremost qualifications relate to their campaign contributions and partisan commitments, with their political clout rating a close second. That's not to imply appointees lack ability. Most are smart and hard working. Then again, so is my surgeon—but that doesn't mean I want him building my house. Some political appointees lack technical knowhow and real-world experience with anything other than political campaigns, and only a smattering have practical management experience. Even those few with the requisite knowledge and skill are still usually outsiders, largely unfamiliar with their new workplace's procedures, culture, employees, or organizational systems.[3] Just imagine any other large-scale business operating like this—swapping out scores of its top-level staff every few years only to replace them with eager-but-green newcomers. And imagine this happening not in a careful gradual way, but in periodic exoduses, and with little (if any) succession planning and meager coordination among the outgoing and incoming leaders.

To make matters worse, political appointees come into government knowing they're on a clock. On paper, they could keep their jobs for four to eight years (or even more), but in reality, most spend little more than a couple of years in a given role.[4] That doesn't really engender a sense of commitment or encourage long-term planning. Unsurprisingly, a transitory attitude permeates the appointee caste. Some move from across the country but don't sell their primary homes; others simply take a leave of absence from their "real" jobs. Then once on their political junket, they apply short-term thinking, eagerly robbing the future to pay the present. That approach creates unsustainable solutions and kicks the can down the road when it comes to solving underlying, slower moving issues. It also stifles innovation. It's tough to take intellectual risks and spend time building a future vision when your horizon ends in less than a handful of years.[5]

The issues caused by the appointee system (once upon a time called the "spoils system") aren't reserved for one particular political party. Regardless of the administration, these issues repeat, time and time again. Still, as my campaign caravan rolled into DC, I found things had grown notably worse. Not only did the appointees sense the ticking clock, but many were operating as if the sword of Damocles hung over their heads. They were expecting to be canned at any moment, they just didn't know why or when.

Even while I still worked for the government, we saw appointed executives who were let go with no notice or who quit unexpectedly when they saw the writing on the wall. At that time, most of the regular employees still thought they were safe, but clearly by the time I visited in June that was no longer true. The workplace anxiety, and maybe the genuine threat of unexpected dismissals, had spread throughout the rank-and-file workforce.

People, both career civilians and appointed leaders, were spending an inordinate amount of time taking steps to cover their asses. Many were working political angles, attempting to find "top cover" among high-ranking and powerful leaders. Others were playing more conniving games, like attempting to frame their office rivals for negative attention while they hid in the shadows. Some people were simply checking out, submitting their resumes to new jobs or turtling in place. No normal business could operate with that level of workforce dysfunction, and I worried how this hidden cancer would manifest years in the future, once its effects finally break the surface.

After a disappointing visit to our nation's capital, we traveled into Maryland, stopping in Baltimore and then Annapolis, the picturesque home of the US Naval Academy and purported capital of oyster gastronomy. Professionally, I started by interviewing a conservationist from the Maryland Oyster Restoration Center. Then we honked and waved at the Naval Academy as we drove past on our way to the historic district. (My daughter had been in the Sea Cadets, so we'd already done our time at the academy. If you haven't visited, though, it's definitely worth a tour.)

Once downtown, I joined my three kids and husband, along with teammate Robert and his children, at a sumptuous seafood buffet. It had bushels of Maryland blue crabs, whitefish, and salmon, and a whole aisle of desserts. This may seem heavenly, and if one were on vacation, it probably would have been, but I was still in work mode. So, instead of enjoying a night with family and friends, I was planning upcoming appointments, transcribing interview notes, and trying to settle the knot of concern my Washington colleagues had planted in my gut days prior.

From Annapolis, it was a short drive into Delaware, a state far more agrarian than I had anticipated. Miles of corn and plush greenery surrounded the highway. I hadn't expected so much farmland or that the state's capital, Dover, would be so incredibly small. We went to the Delaware Agricultural Museum and later stopped in Wilmington at the DuPont Environmental Education Station, an exhibition hall and urban park dedicated to the local marshland. Then we carried on, finally pulling into the campground where we'd stay that night.

Like a surprising number of the parks, this one abutted a striking landscape, with a tree-lined lake right behind my camper. The summer sun sat fat on the horizon, and combined with a soft breeze from the lake, the day felt idyllic, like sweet tea and summer holidays. Plenty of folks sat outside their own campers, drinking from koozies and chatting about nothing. As I went about the usual routine, my neighbor called some pleasantries and asked about my curiously adorned RV.

"So, who's JJ?" the older man called, gesturing at my name displayed on the side of my ride.

"That's me," I replied. One could forgive him for not recognizing me, dressed in blue jeans and a ponytail as I carried a trash bag to the dumpster.

"Huh, you running for president?" He questioned a bit incredulously. "What party?"

"Democrat."

It's funny, when you tell someone your beliefs or experiences, I find nearly everyone is quite reasonable, but when you reduce all that complexity down to a partisan title, people can get a little weird. When I tell people that I'm running as a Democrat, I usually get one of a handful of reactions. Sometimes they dubiously raise an eyebrow. Other times, they sigh with relief, and sometimes people just question, "Are you sure?"

In this case, it was my neighbor's wife who interjected, unabashedly eavesdropping from inside the doorway of their own RV. "Well, we're Republicans," she barked, "and we're not racists!"

That reaction piqued my attention. In a previous life, I had spent a fair number of hours working as a therapist. Eventually, I'd decided psychological counseling wasn't the career for me, but I still learned a lot from the experience. For instance, I've learned when people have swift, sharp reactions like that, they're not responding to you personally, and I've discovered the best way to defuse this sort of situation is with flat emotions and space for whoever it is to work out whatever it is bubbling below the surface.

"OK," I responded simply, carefully keeping dismissiveness and frustration out of my tone. I think I threw her off guard, because she just blinked at me for a few beats. I let the silence hang, and as often happens, she started talking again to fill it.

"Democrats act like everyone who's Republican is a racist. But I'm not a racist—we're not racists," she gestured to herself and her husband. "I don't like seeing Democrats on TV talking about how Republicans are supposedly all of these bad things. I don't think abortion should be legal. I don't think Medicare for All is a good idea. And I don't like the way they want to run to the country."

"OK," I replied neutrally. She took the cue to continue talking. I won't go into all she said during those minutes, but as she calmed down, her ideas grew more cogent.

"I have to admit," she sighed, "Trump does say a lot of things on Twitter that I wish he wouldn't say. He's just such a . . ." She groped for the word, "an instigator." Then she continued a bit more introspectively, "I don't personally agree when he says that stuff, but when I tell people I'm still a Trump supporter, they say I'm supporting racism." She paused again, mustering her words, "I wish he'd just shut his trap, put his phone down, and stop stirring the pot so much. I think his administration is doing good things, but he's not representing it as well as he could."

Now that her emotions had run their course, we were able to talk more rationally. And we did. We chatted for quite a while, touching on gun control, military service, and health care. At the end, she told me warmly, "I'm really glad we talked. You've given me a lot to think about."

I felt good about that discussion. The woman may not have changed her mind about any of the issues, but perhaps she shed some political baggage. There's something therapeutic about being able to talk, be heard, and not get heated. Emotionality in politics has grown to an unhealthy level, and many people have begun to expect hot-blooded responses just out of hand. But histrionics undermine discourse and, ultimately, weaken democracy, so in emotional situations where I stay calm, I'd like to think I'm helping our nation in some small way. As one of my respected colleagues (a retired vice admiral) once advised, "Whenever we do something without grace, there is collateral damage—great collateral damage." I'm trying to do my part to temper that harm.

Oftentimes people choose to stay silent on politics, to not engage or to stay in their bubbles only watching Fox News or MSNBC, safely shielded within a like-minded community. As a consequence, when you engage someone across the aisle that experience may be one of only a handful they've had. Being classy and calm matters. In contrast, when you see politicians on TV, yelling dramatically or pounding their fists, it scares people. Anyone who isn't already drinking that Kool-Aid is put off, and outside observers start to think the whole party (the whole lot of Republicans or Democrats or whatever) are delusional and emotional.

In practice, I haven't found a society of raving dogmatists, and I didn't encounter a bunch of mindless sheeple or willfully ignorant dimwits. Despite some initial bouts of emotion, I've found people are willing to listen and engage. Individual Americans have differing perspectives and varying policy ideas, but these can be navigated. More often than not, it's vitriol and rhetoric—not fundamental differences—that fuel dysfunction. Opportunistic pundits and unscrupulous politicians stoke the fires of emotional politics. Gridlock favors the status quo, after all, and in the fervor stirred by hyperbole and sensationalism, voters often lose sight of other issues. The first step forward is to simmer down, give space for discourse, and maintain our grace. The alternative is unpalatable. Ignoring the problem won't make it go away, and unless we begin moving toward calmer rationality, the only other option is to standby as this cancer eats our political system from the inside out—like a building rotting from its foundations, until one day its veneer of stability falters, and it suddenly collapses from a mere gust of wind.

CHAPTER TEN

The Great American Salad Bowl

After Delaware, we continued north into Pennsylvania. As it was a *presidential* road trip, we were cosmically obliged to stop in Philadelphia. My kids and husband joined me on a visit to the national park. We took the quintessential family photo in front of the Liberty Bell and then toured Independence Hall. Inside, it's a monument to our nation's founding, with most of the rooms preserved to look like they did in the 1700s, when our Founding Fathers penned the Declaration of Independence and later signed the Constitution there.

Part of the hall also houses presidential portraits, with all forty-five past and present leaders lined up on display. Looking at that gallery, it struck me just how outwardly similar all of our presidents seem. People laud Barack Obama for serving as America's first black president, and rightfully so, but even he sports a similar appearance to the others: clean-cut, serious men wearing ties (or cravats) and effecting a particular demeanor. They seem cut from the same cloth. Highlighting our presidents' similarities isn't meant to disparage that demographic, and I don't think most people have an explicit bias against other presidential shapes or sizes or genders. It's just that when you see all forty-five American leaders in a row, it's tough to envision a different archetype. Psychologically, that look and feel has become the template for success and, perhaps, an unintentional bias.

After Independence Hall, we ventured into East Philadelphia, the Vegas Strip of cheesesteak shacks. Neon lights flashed, luring tourists to hole-in-the-wall dives with names like King's Steaks or Hoagies Haven. We picked one of the joints and ordered a classic roll, with beefsteak and . . . Cheez Whiz? I hadn't realized that authentic cheesesteaks use cheese sprayed from a can. Go figure.

I did a few more professional activities in Philly and picked up another expert interview, and then we were off to New Jersey. In Jersey City, we stopped at an RV park on the banks of the Hudson. In contrast to so many campgrounds around the country, this one had more of a New Jersey flair. That's to say, it looked like a strip-mall parking lot minus the charm. Still, despite the cracked asphalt and sagging power lines, we could see the Statue of Liberty, and as I found almost universally, our fellow campers had an exuberance of charm and talkativeness.

We visited Trenton for a day, which I spent reviewing New Jersey's education program at the State Planetarium, interviewing a culture-change expert, and chatting up random people on various political topics. (Just imagine how much fun I bring to small talk at dinner parties!) The next morning, we took the ferry into New York City. My son, Mitchell, lives there. He's completely engrossed in classical music. Even at just twenty years old, I have to admit, the kid is way more cultured than me. In fact, all of my children seem to gravitate toward music, fashion, or theater.

My daughter, Monica, was turning eighteen. So, we took time to celebrate her birthday. We visited the Metropolitan Museum of Art and, at her birthday request, she and I saw *Hadestown* on Broadway. Then we filled up on milkshakes and loaded fries at Hard Rock after the show. Afterward, I returned to the campaign grind.

I held one of my expert interviews with a retired orchestral conductor, formerly of the National Symphony and London Philharmonic (among others). Today, he runs a consulting business, teaching teamwork to corporate workers. He uses music to evoke an emotional experience during his seminars and to make his message more memorable. He also uses musical metaphors to illuminate teamwork principles.

"In an orchestra," he explained, "each person has to play his or her own part, but each must also listen to the fellow players. If someone focuses solely on her own music, or his own job in a business context, then the concerto suffers. That's why we need conductors too. They help the musicians play in harmony. This is what I teach to businesses: how to pay attention to fellow players, for the individual workers, and how to move people to work in concert, like a conductor, for their leaders."

What an elegant analogy, I reflected, *and how applicable to society as a whole.* At its best, our nation should operate like a well-tuned orchestra, rather than as fifty separate states, or two (plus) political parties, or umpteen different subcultures.

My interview with the conductor gave me much to consider, but I couldn't spare much time for contemplation. Like so many experts, the former conductor didn't want his dialogue with a politician filmed, so I still needed to record an on-air interview to meet my self-imposed YouTube schedule. My friend, Brahm Horowitz, volunteered for that task.

I had met Brahm years prior, when my son originally moved to New York for school. While we were settling Mitchell into his freshman dorm, I had decided to take a break and stroll around Central Park. Manhattan has an electrifying energy; I could people-watch there for the rest of my life. Near the park, I had stumbled upon a group of retirees talking politics with the accents and volume characteristic of native New Yorkers. They had the archetypal bluntness too, not mincing words as they loudly proclaimed their political views to one another (and to anyone nearby with ears). Me being me, once the social vibes seemed right, I had introduced myself and complimented the group on their political concern. One of the seniors that day, as it turns out, was Brahm. Since then, we've met periodically for coffee and a chinwag when I'm in town visiting my son.

Brahm has sand-colored skin dappled with liver spots and marked with deep crescent lines around his mouth. He uses thick tortoise-rim glasses and slicks back his wispy gray hair. On this particular day, we met at one of his favorite Manhattan cafés. Sitting there amidst the bustling baristas and hectic clientele, we chatted about politics, university costs, and the Electoral College, but what stood out most was Brahm's reminiscing on his life in and around the city.

As a boy in 1950s-era New York, Brahm recalled, he hadn't really understood the distinctions of race or ethnicity. "I got introduced to racism when I went to camp. We would go on these three-day trips, and we went to Philadelphia one time. We went to go swimming, and we had a black counselor, and they wouldn't let him in. We didn't know what they were talking about. What do you mean he can't swim? Well, they tried to explain it." Brahm screwed up his face in an exaggerated mask of confusion as he acted out his memory, "We all said, 'Uh, what?! If he don't go, we don't go. That's the end of this place.' That was the first time I ran into racism."

Closer to home, Brahm hadn't experienced the same intolerance, and he had only become aware of the diversity so prevalent around New York City as he grew older.

"I wound up marrying a black woman, and we've been married forty-six years. So it worked for us," he reflected. "The community was very mixed," he continued, recalling the neighborhood where he and his wife later raised their family. "I'll give you an idea, when my daughter graduated high school in 1997, they gave the kids a survey: 'What language or languages, if any, besides English are spoken in your household?' There were sixty-seven different languages in one graduating class. And they all got along."

Later that day, as I took the return trip to New Jersey, I thought about

Brahm's stories. Around me on the subway, I counted conversations in at least eight different languages, but no one paid anyone else any mind. In unhealthy situations, I mused, people act aggressively or contemptuously to people they've decided are "other." The opposite of prejudice isn't kindness, though; it's more like indifference. (Not ignorance, mind you, but unconcerned awareness.) People striving to be tolerant are conscious of their actions. They go out of their way to act politely to those who look, sound, or pray differently. Although immeasurably better than the bigoted alternative, these overly polite mannerisms still imply, *You're different from everyone else.* In New York City, there's almost an apathy around people's differences, which seems to say, *This is normal, not exceptional.* From the outside, it may look like stereotypical New Yorker rudeness, but to me it seems to imply an authentic disinterest in those superficial characteristics.

Of course, New Yorkers still have flares of intolerance around race and ethnicity, and the city hasn't always been the pinnacle of egalitarianism. Still, I think the Big Apple, among all the places in the nation, is getting the "diversity salad" concept right. New Yorkers will squabble internally and air their differences loudly, but when pushed or threatened, they all become one high-strung, opinionated, unruly family.

We passed through Connecticut (I'll recount my embarrassing run there in a few chapters), then we traveled onward to Providence. I didn't have any formal engagements scheduled; instead, we just explored the town. We visited the Providence Athenæum library, a masterwork of architecture and literary charm, and then toured the Rhode Island School of Design. Eventually, we found ourselves downtown. The city center has an eclectic vibe that mixes a cool modern aesthetic with its classical New England foundations. As we strolled the tree-lined cobbles, I felt the aura of history all around us. Cities like Providence exude that characteristic American narrative, and when I envision American history, something like this always comes to mind.

Without a doubt, New England plays a starring role in our nation's founding, but I pondered as we wandered along, *Are the stories of native Alaskans or southwestern Latinos somehow less vivid?* I grew up with a Euro-centric view of our foundations. It's what I learned from textbooks and in my high-school civics classes, but that's just one facet of our nation's chronicle. Does it diminish that history to add more voices? Or, as that New York conductor might have argued, do the added voices instead bring depth and verve to the chorus. I decided to make it a point to seek out those other harmonies, those distinct American experiences, as we continued our national tour.

Again we pressed on, hastening northward from Providence to Cambridge.

A friend of a friend had introduced me to Dr. Aithan Shapira, whom she'd called a brainy and charismatic innovator. She insisted we connect, and at her urging, we'd scheduled an interview during my time in Massachusetts. We met at MIT, in a two-story glass-and-metal building. As I walked in, the reflected light dazzled my eyes. The open-air atrium featured clusters of seats where people congregated in small groups (no doubt solving the mysteries of the universe). Upstairs, where I met Aithan, meeting nooks lined the perimeter, with each adorned by whiteboards and colorful erasable markers—my kind of place!

Aithan looks like a youthful professor straight out of a movie, and he has a warm demeanor that's immediately likable. When we met, Aithan sported a slightly disheveled corporate look, which screamed "academic," and he spoke with the fastidious tones and exaggerated gestures iconic of college lecturers. His bio claims Aithan's work involves social equality, empowerment, and culture—but I had no idea what those buzzwords meant in practical terms. So when we met I prompted, "Wrap my head around this."

"I'm working on developing cultures that innovate," Aithan explained with practiced ease. "The first question I get is, 'What is innovation?' Everyone uses that term a lot. Innovation, to me—or creativity, which I think is often interchangeable—is the ability to change. So if we want to become more innovative, then we actually have to be more willing to change. And how do you enable a culture to be more able to change? In the simplest way, that's what I do."

Intrigued, we chatted a bit more. Then I asked, "If you look across the country, what are those things keeping people in a more rigid stance versus an evolving one?"

"The idea that comes to mind is *both-ness*. Both-ness is polarity. There are all sorts of polarities—polarities in myself and polarities between us. And they're not necessarily good or evil. Polarity just means difference. But in order for me to be right, you don't have to be wrong. That fundamental idea is something that could be worked on. The idea of both-ness is a complex thing, but I think the skills it's composed of can be developed and practiced."

If only someone could teach the Democrats and Republicans that, I thought. Aithan, can you train our politicians both-ness?

My family didn't always travel with me. They each came and went between their school, work, orchestra, sports, and other activities, but we were all together again on the Fourth of July. We celebrated America's birthday in Amherst, Massachusetts (which, by the way, the locals pronounce like "Am-erst," without the *h*). Similar to Providence, Amherst has a quintessential northeasterly vibe, with well-maintained sidewalks, golf course–like grass, and the eponymous university with classic brick buildings and white colonnades.

The weather on July Fourth couldn't have been finer, and people flocked to the city center to celebrate and bask in the mellow summer's day. With several thousand others, we made our way to the fairgrounds, where the city had erected a traveling carnival, complete with whirling rides and stalls of irresistible street food. We bought tickets and made our game plans. My husband and two eldest children raced off toward bad culinary decisions while I took Madison to the amusement rides.

Standing in line, a plump-faced child around Maddie's age ran up to her. The little girl showed telltale signs of poverty. Her alabaster skin was streaked with dirt, as were her threadbare clothes. Her corn-silk hair hung in unkempt tangles down her back, and she demonstrated an unsettling lack of social awareness, even for an eight-year-old. Unfiltered, she started talking to Maddie, a shy stranger she had never met before, as if they were longtime companions. Then she asked Maddie to join her on the ride.

By now, the girl's mom had approached, a heavyset woman with similarly stained attire. She and I nodded for our children to climb into a teacup together. Then, as the ride began to whirl, we were left standing there with nothing to do but watch our little ones spin around and to make small talk with one another.

After some initial pleasantries, she soon asked, "What do you do for a living?"

"I'm running for president," I replied and shared a truncated version of my usual spiel.

"OK," she said in return, revealing nothing of what might have been passing through her mind. We both looked ahead for a few moments, quietly watching the smiling little faces go 'round and 'round. Then she unexpectedly broke the silence, jumping past pleasantries into a more personal narrative.

"My granddaddy and my uncle both work in government. I have a few friends too: one in elected office and a couple just regular workers—all state and local, mind you, not in Washington. They really understand what's happening in government, and they're always saying how government is different from politics. Because of them, we're all pretty aware of what's going on."

I was a little surprised to hear her unexpected insight. Judging by her clothes and bearing, I wouldn't have expected the woman to be that astute or so knowledgeable about government. She didn't look or talk like my Beltway friends in the nation's capital, but as we chatted, she expressed many similar sentiments. Shame on me for nearly judging a book by its cover. I might have dismissed her, for her rural accent and unpolished attire, and I would have been poorer for it. I nearly fell into a common trap, underestimating someone who lacks the "right" pedigree or who doesn't fit the classic template of what success looks like. One of the best antidotes is, of course, to seek out experiences that force you to confront those hidden biases. That's been one of the treasures of my time touring our nation. I've found a colorful surplus of leadership potential so much broader than the forty-five portraits hanging in Independence Hall seem to imply.

After talking with the woman over several more carnival rides, Maddie and I drifted toward the junk food. It's a universal law that all county-fair attendees must eat corn dogs, deep-fried Oreos, and cotton candy (which, I strongly believe, should be blue not pink). Then you can have kettle corn, and, if possible, wash it down with fresh-squeezed lemonade. As upstanding citizens, we naturally followed these rules and ended up having a wonderful, calorie-packed, red, white, and blue–themed Independence Day.

The next day, with our bellies—and my family-packed RV—full to bursting, we left for Vermont. We stopped in Marlboro and Burlington and, in between, visited the nearby Art of Humor Gallery. It's dedicated to illustrator Skip Morrow, who among other things, made a library of satirical political comics. They're hysterical! And, rather sadly, many of his sardonic cartoons on topics like pollution and partisanism are still relevant today, even though most were drawn over twenty years ago. After the museum, we stopped for ice cream. Famously, Vermont is home to Ben & Jerry's. We visited the scoop shop in downtown Burlington and then walked its scenic Main Street, lined with flags-adorned lampposts and scores of friendly pedestrians.

The day after, we lumbered eastward toward Bangor and, the following morning, set our alarms for 4:00 a.m. to watch First Light. Acadia National Park boasts the highest peak on the Eastern Seaboard, Cadillac Mountain, and tourists flock there to watch the first rays of sun peek over the horizon. By the time we arrived at 4:30 a.m., the park was already full of early-bird sightseers and the road's shoulder congested with parked cars. Undeterred, we precariously stashed the RV on the roadside and then walked up the mountain. At the top, we found dozens of fellow visitors, some sitting on a low stone wall, and others scattered among the trees just below it. Many sported their obligatory selfie sticks.

I thought of my National Park Service colleagues, who fill several thousand spots in the federal workforce, and snapped some pictures in their honor. Perhaps not the first thing that comes to mind when you envision government, but the national parks stem directly from our federal government. These parks span a sizable swath of the nation, and the Park Service employs more workers than eBay, Hershey, or Mastercard.[1] Even our federal government is filled with more diversity than the cable-news stereotypes lead one to believe.

Traveling to places like Acadia or Burlington wasn't mere sightseeing. For me, it was about seeing Washington's policies in action and talking with people from all over the country and from all walks of life. Watching the light crest over Cadillac Mountain or eating deep-fried Oreos with unexpectedly perceptive fair-goers, these are things most politicians would miss. And without that grounding in the authentic American experience or the real-world appreciation of the impact of federal actions, I can only assume they're missing out on the larger picture.

A few years ago, the superintendent of the Air Force Academy gave a speech that went viral. In it, he chided his cadets saying, "If you can't treat someone with dignity and respect, get out." Lieutenant General Jay Silveria later explained, "Diversity is a force multiplier. We must do this together—all ranks and ages, races and religions, sexual orientations and identities—all of us."[2]

The general's words still ring true, for the military and our nation. But, really, what is diversity? Often, we reduce it down to the most visible characteristics—X or Y chromosomes, a yarmulke or hijab, the color of someone's skin. While each of those things contribute to diversity, they are not, themselves, the essence of it. Diversity involves differences in background, lifestyle, culture, belief systems, education, skill sets, capabilities, and viewpoints. It's so much broader than the easily discernible features. And, as our military knows, embracing this deep, fundamental diversity brings profound benefits. When you have those different perspectives on your team, all of the different tools in your tool kit, your ability to find the best answer increases exponentially.

I once attended a business conference where one of the speakers urged from the podium, "We need to change the visual of leadership, away from 'pale, male, and Yale.'" She's not wrong: We need space for different ethnicities, genders, and backgrounds. It's important to have role models who look and sound different, leaders whom young people can see themselves in. At the same time, we can make that space without denigrating Ivy League men. We can have both. As Aithan said, just because one thing is right, doesn't make the other wrong. More than that, the "pale, male, and Yale" kind of thinking veers precariously close to a check-the-box mentality where we distill diversity down to a handful of superficial features and celebrate success as they're ticked off a list.

I've caught myself falling into that headspace before. On one of my campaign videos, we had filled the b-roll with "diverse" stock photos: fit, clean-cut thirtysomethings, with their preppy attire and smiling faces. Some had afros or ethnic noses, some had mahogany skin, while others were alabaster. A couple sat in wheelchairs. But they all shared a similar aesthetic—like the presidential portraits in Independence Hall. Only when someone from my Geek Team pointed out the pretend diversity, did we realize the blunder. We quickly replaced the overly polished images with real-life photos I had taken during my fifty-state tour—people of different ages and sizes, different levels of prep and polish, and with so much more authenticity than the Instagram reality we'd first drafted.

In a similar way, we don't need a façade of diversity in politics. We don't specifically need a woman, or an Indian American, or a fill-in-the-blank token candidate—it's not enough to simply cover the same mold with a different veneer. We do, however, need to embrace the mosaic of American experiences in all of their kaleidoscopic intricacies. Like an orchestra, it's the differences in our experiences, the differences in our rhythm and tone, that make the richest music. For the political system, that may mean constructing different archetypes of electoral success, but it also means valuing the differences in others' views and striving for coordination across symphonic sections—across regions, demographics, and partisan perspectives.

Diversity is a hallmark of our country. It's one of our secret weapons as a nation. When played correctly, diversity and inclusion form a powerful opus, unlocking a kind of innovation only achievable through those manifold perspectives. But when mishandled, we turn into an awkward middle-school band, all playing instruments only to produce a discordant clamor. We are each a member of this orchestra, so the choice is ours to make: Which music will we play? How well will we harmonize? And what will our American symphony become?

CHAPTER ELEVEN

Neither Healthy, Caring, nor a System

Less than two months into the trip and I was starting to crack. Admittedly, I kept a grueling schedule, but added to that, I was a total novice, trying to claw my way into the political space—without a professional team and live on social media. Every day brought new challenges; I could never just coast on autopilot. As we started our southerly return from New England, true fatigue set in. I could feel my mental horsepower flagging. I started eating too much and sleeping too little.

I was, or rather *am*, also a full-time mom. My kids didn't always travel with me, but they were never far from mind or smartphone. I love my children, but it was difficult to manage their needs and run my one-woman band–style campaign. Plus, we were living in a pressure cooker, each with our own lives—campaign, college, concerts, friends—and literally living on top of each other in a small RV with only a single bathroom and, at times, no internet connectivity (truly, one of the Herculean trials of the modern era). Shifting from being a mentor to my eldest children, to a campaign maven, and then back to just-mommy for my youngest took its toll too. As did the regular interruptions of "Mom . . . ," "Hey, Mom . . . ," "Mom, could you . . . " throughout the day. (I call it the "mom chirp." Fellow parents, you know what I mean.)

I had to get a handle on things, or my tour wouldn't make it past the East Coast. I tried a trick I had learned to confront jet lag. Over the course of a few days, I shifted my schedule earlier and earlier until I eventually began waking up at three in the morning. That let me put in nearly a full day of work before the flurry of interruptions derailed my focused thought.

Staying healthy means, in part, working with your natural tendencies. For me, that meant waking up in the middle of the night and breaking my Twizzlers addiction cold turkey. The interviews helped too. They kept me focused on a steady rhythm, and each time I spoke with an ER professional or a pharmacy reform expert, I felt a jolt of inspiration that kept me moving along—like Pac-Man pellets fueling me forward on my national tour.

Around the tail end of June, we had kicked off our health-care strategy focus at the Mütter Museum while still in Philadelphia. The museum's own promo material bills it as a place to become "disturbingly informed." As promised, it features creepy displays on medical abnormalities, old surgical techniques, and real human specimens—think heads floating in fluid-filled jars. My eldest daughter loved it. For my own part, I felt grateful that people (who are not me) devote themselves to this kind of medical science.

I had also begun interviewing health-care experts. All told, I interviewed a couple of physicians and medical directors along with several professionals focused on preventative care and mental health. I talked to people familiar with Big Pharma and the Veterans Health Administration, and I intentionally sought out unique angles, looking beyond the obvious for enterprising nuggets of wisdom.

In Maine, for example, I interviewed Chris Bennett about "prevention, not pills," and in New York, I chatted with Dr. Robert Osgood about the critical role university research plays in addressing rare and yet-undiscovered diseases. I visited a Planned Parenthood center—to see what it was like, firsthand—and I interviewed a Texas oil tycoon who'd built a successful substance abuse and mental health services program after his son developed an addiction. I even talked with a (fully legal!) retailer about the benefits of CBD oil, the chemical compound in marijuana.

In upstate New York, we stopped by a historical medical college, and over lunch I chatted with Dr. Sanjay Mannan, one of the senior faculty members.

"You've worked in government research, right? So help me understand this," Sanjay prompted between bites of food. "I've been working on this line of research for over ten years, so why do I have to reapply for funding every year as if I'm an unknown quantity. It takes tons of time—and look at me, I'm not an accountant or lawyer or paperwork enthusiast."

He had a solid point. His time spent filling out forms, rather than studying medical issues, seemed less than productive. As we continued to talk, he brought up another semi-rhetorical question.

"OK, here's the second riddle for you: Rather than funding individual projects—or not funding projects—why doesn't the government try to fund solutions? I mean, the same agencies sponsor dozens of research projects. Rather than just divvying out grants to whatever labs do good work, shouldn't someone have a unifying plan or try to connect across projects toward some common goal? Let me give you an example. A lot of my work right now involves taking techniques from other disciplines and applying them toward my own line of work, but why am I the one hunting for the overlaps? The same agencies sponsor their work and mine. Couldn't they drop a hint?"

I shared Sanjay's frustration, and sadly, had no answers for him. I'd personally seen the same trends in military research and educational programs. Although exceptions exist, more often government offices evaluate research projects in isolation, grading each on its inherent merits rather than trying to optimize collectively across a portfolio.

Another, related dilemma was highlighted by my chat with Mariana Rivera, a health sciences research assistant. Mariana has licorice-colored hair and peaches-and-cream skin, which she adorns with a nose ring and retro eyeglasses. I couldn't entirely follow the details, but her work has something to do with combating hard-to-treat infections. We chatted for a bit as I tried to understand her area of study, and (although unsuccessful in that regard) I developed a healthy appreciation for the importance of her research on those bacteria.

"Do you think this line of work gets the federal attention it deserves?" I asked.

"Probably not. There's so much more we need to understand about antibiotic resistance, gut bacteria, and personalized medicine. We're just at the tippy-top of that iceberg."

I was reminded of my interview with the lead conservationist from the Atlanta Botanical Gardens. Dr. Emily Coffey had similarly complained. In her case, she'd highlighted that, while over half of endangered species are plants, only a fraction of conservation research funds goes toward them.[1] When I'd asked her why, she'd replied, "Turtles are cute."

"Maybe we need to make a movie," I'd quipped in reply. "Instead of *Life of Pets*, we need *Life of Plants!*"

Mariana laughed out loud as I retold the story. Then she dashed across the room to retrieve her own "cute" specimens from one of the benches. "Eat your heart out, Grumpy Cat," she laughed as she waggled a petri dish of wriggling maggots in my direction, "because we have these!" (Mariana, if you're reading this, please leave the meme-making to the professionals and return to your true calling: saving all our lives in your under-supported and underappreciated lab!)

As our tour lumbered forward, I continued my small-town anthropology across the eastern states. From a health-care perspective, several things stood out in sharp relief. First, there's a stark contrast between urban and rural health access. Take Lancaster, New Hampshire, for example. We stopped in a beautiful campground at the top of a conifer-lined mountain lake with RVs scattered around its banks, amidst the trees and among the houses of full-time residents.

Excited to have a full day (me to work and my children to do whatever they had planned), we quickly tethered the camper and set about our respective activities. Only to find—to our city-bred horror—the camp's advertised Wi-Fi was, by and large, nonexistent. We couldn't get a cell signal either, no matter how much we twirled and twisted and screamed at the sky. Of course, we all encounter dead zones from time to time, but this was different—the entire park had nothing: no bars, no bandwidth.

Connectivity has become my baseline. I use it to look up stupid trivia and do all manner of business. I store my files on a remote server and rely on my smartphone to stay in touch with family. (In fact, my husband, back at home at the time, was waiting on just such a call.) None of that was happening. As I looked around, it struck me how remote we really were, and as we idly strolled around the park, I tried to imagine how it must feel to live in those mountains, so secluded from the rest of the 24/7-connected world. I also wondered, *What if someone gets hurt or if you need to send an emergency message?* You can't just dial 9-1-1 from the lakeside.

Until that day, I'd associated health-care access with affordable treatment, but my time in rural New Hampshire made me realize that "access" means so much more. It means having communication channels, not only for emergencies but also for routine and ongoing care. It means having nearby clinics and medical options and, in general, a way to reach modern resources when they're needed. It's easy to tell someone about the feeling of being cutoff, of being physically and digitally detached, but until you've felt it yourself, it's difficult to fully appreciate. That was the first lesson small-town America taught me about health care. The second lesson I learned on our return trip through Pennsylvania.

We had stopped in Hershey but not to sample its chocolate bars or visit the amusement park. We were there for an "advanced planning" seminar. That's the medical euphemism for end-of-life preparation (and, obviously, the kind of roadside attraction everyone looks for). The program's goal was to help attendees step forward in their planning process, regardless of their age or situation. In my case, that could mean having a conversation with my grown children about what might happen if I were to pass unexpectedly.

The seminar was held in a senior center, and as you might expect, wrinkled faces filled the audience. A few middle-aged attendees also peppered the crowd; maybe they'd recently lost loved ones? The panelists discussed end-of-life plans and paperwork and hospice, palliative care, holistic assessments, advanced directives, and other terms I'd never heard before.

After the panel, the crowd split into groups. I joined a cohort to play an aging and dying–themed game (yes, that's a thing, apparently). It came with these question-filled booklets, and all of the players got a handful of tokens. Every time someone answered well, the others gave that player more tokens, and for each answer, the seminar organizers sweetened the pot with a piece of candy. That was just the nudge everyone needed to get talking.

The questions were icebreakers, albeit highly personal ones, meant to help us think about life and death. It worked surprisingly well. People started talking about mistakes they'd made years before, family members they'd grown distant from, and people they've held grudges against. Throughout it all, the event organizers shepherded the discussion, driving it toward self-discovery. The care and patience of these social workers shone brightly, touching myself and, I believe, all those who attended that free seminar. Although the same information could have been found online, the personal touch made a considerable difference. This was community service at its finest—authentic, practical, and delivered with genuine warmth to anyone who walked in the door. It opened my eyes to how valuable those grassroots programs can be, and it also made me reexamine my perception of social services. When done right, they're so much more than a last-resort charity for underserved populations.

We took a winding interstate into West Virginia, stopping at Morgantown, a small college town scattered across the rolling foothills of the Allegheny Mountains. There, we visited a local Democratic Socialist meeting to hear the "far-left" perspective on health care. You can picture the scene: a handful of hillbilly bohemians, with funky hairdos and worn T-shirts, gathering in the downtown library. They welcomed me warmly, and after some small talk, we launched into the main discussion. I'd expected to hear a bleeding-heart platform, heavy on platitudes and light on substance, but that's not what I discovered. They felt the argument between "take care of everyone" and "we all fend for ourselves" was a pointless dichotomy. While they thought health-care debates should have more compassion, they also wanted practical answers that fit with the modern era. Never once did someone mention Bernie Sanders, Elizabeth Warren, or President Trump. The entire meeting focused on devising solutions, debating ideas, and conceiving of ways to better inform the public; there wasn't room for partisan personalities.

Afterward, as we left the library, an apparently homeless man approached our group. He wore tattered layers of clothes, all covered with grime, and had a rank unwashed odor. In an even voice, he asked us to call an ambulance, because, he explained coolly, he felt like harming himself. On one hand, I'd never take a chance with someone who says he's thinking about self-harm. (And we did call emergency services as he requested.) On the other, I'm a psychologist, and I wasn't seeing signs of mental distress. He had the energy and wherewithal to calmly approach a group of strangers, interrupt our conversation, and clearly express his requests. I fully suspect he needed some form of treatment but probably not emergency mental detention. Maybe he needed physical care or just a safe place to rest. (Many shelters bar men from their premises—even husbands.) Regardless of the reason, it's a commentary on our health-care system that some of the most at-risk Americans need to connive their way into receiving care. And it was a poignant epilogue to the Democratic Socialist health-care discussion.

After Morgantown, we wound through Charleston and Lexington, and then veered northward into Ohio. Road hypnosis started to take root. The cities seemed to blur together—Cincinnati, Columbus, Cleveland—like montaged frames from an art deco movie. *An art deco movie with no parking!* In Cincinnati, I drove in circles around the historic-turned-hipster downtown. Splashing through the puddles and dodging oncoming traffic as I tried to find harbor for my campaign land-yacht. Once we finally docked it, my mood lightened. The shiny waterfront didn't hurt, either, and while the Underground Railroad Center there couldn't be called mood lightening, it did refuel my sense of inspiration.

Later, as the sky continued to drizzle over my RV, I called Dr. Wallace J. Nichols, author of *Blue Mind*, for an interview.[2] He's a marine biologist interested in neuroscience, specifically the mental health benefits of water, which is what his book explores.

"As a kid, I was adopted, and I stuttered, so I didn't always feel like I belonged," he explained. Now in his middle years, J. (as he's known) bore no trace of either a speech impediment or his childhood self-doubt. "But in the water, I felt good; I felt whole. Water was my happy place. It led me to become a marine biologist, and I had a great career, but I always wondered: *What was it about water that healed me?* I wanted to study the neuropsychology of time spent near water."

"What did you find?"

"What happens when we engage with our water? First and foremost, it's about what we leave behind. We leave a lot of the noise. We leave the screens and to-do lists. If you're going to get wet, your laptop generally doesn't want to be in the water with you. We unplug and log out, and the auditory and visual environment is simplified. If we just stop there, that's pretty good; that's a rare commodity these days in our overstimulated lives."

I wondered, "When you talk about water, what do you mean, exactly?"

"It can be water metaphorically or literally. Some people have said, 'My water is music.' Some people have said, 'My water is Lake Michigan' or the Atlantic Ocean.' Some have said, 'It's my bathtub' or 'It's the food I eat.' Whether it's music, time with family, or time in nature—it's about making sure you have access to your reset button and that you know how important it is, because it affects everything you do: your ability to think clearly and make decisions."

"I come at it from the water perspective—our lakes, our rivers, our oceans," he continued. "Being near water helps us sleep, connect to ourselves, and connect to each other socially—even romantically. It boosts creativity and reduces stress hormones." J. ticked off more benefits. "Water is so valuable to our emotional health, to our creative health, to our spiritual health in ways that are underrecognized and underprescribed. But we're not taught about it. I was never taught in school, if you're having a really cruddy day, go to the lake."

"Could you imagine if we started telling children to go to the lake?" I interjected, and then I caught myself, "You know it's something they do in other nations. It's being explicitly taught in places like Finland."

"That's the educational side of this," he agreed, "to ensure every kid—and adult—understands this concept and knows about their own 'blue mind.' You could say it's a niche conversation, but when you begin pulling the strings, they're connected to public health, emotional and mental health, how we care for our first responders and veterans, and how we do end-of-life care. Imagine if hospice professionals had this in mind, if they asked their patients, 'Would you like to get in your water one more time?'"

J. gave me much to consider. Although, mental health, information overload, and the sinister effects of stress on decision making weren't new concepts, he had elegantly connected those ideas to something tangible and relatable. His *Blue Mind* work also underscores the intersection of our environment and our mental well-being—not only in a treatment or illness sort of way but as a continuous interplay affecting our daily lives.

The next day, I talked to Dr. Sheila Hoehn who continued many of the same themes. Sheila is a wunderkind with over a handful of advanced degrees. She's studied some of the most challenging mental health topics too, from the self-immolation of Afghan women to school shootings in America. During the interview, she stressed the difference between mental disorders and mental wellness.

"A lot of time you'll hear commentators say there's no link between serious mental illness and mass shootings. It's important to recognize when they say that, they're talking about mental *illness* not mental *health*."

Mental illness is a clinical diagnosis, like schizophrenia or a personality disorder, Sheila went on to explain. Mental health, on the other hand, is a universal concern; it's tied to our emotional and mental processes, coping skills, and interactions. Many of us go through difficult times in life where our coping skills fail us, and without intervention, the downward spiral of mental health can lead to grave outcomes.

"Mental health is a prevalent issue, specifically for school shooters. There's a strong link with poor mental health. A lot of these shooters had been depressed, had suicidal ideations for quite a while, and experienced multiple stressors, anxiety, and delusions. They also had problems coping and, specifically, problems dealing with conflict and developing resiliency. These are mental health problems; they're not mental illnesses."

She carried on, describing the typical characteristics of school shooters. "All of these shooters have difficulties processing grievances. They're injustice collectors. When something happens to them, they get very upset, and they don't know how to deal with it or those intense feelings. At first, they grow angry at the person or group who caused the injustice, but then it quickly spreads to a whole group of people. They're angry with everybody, and they want retribution. They also want to be famous and feel some sense of power. There is no one distinctive profile, but these are patterns they have in common."

"What can we do?" I prompted.

"Resiliency is developed if even one person of authority steps in and forms a relationship of trust, nurturing, and unconditional positive regard for that child," she explained, citing empirical research. "We have to create a narrative where it's OK to say something. We have to focus less on punishing that person, expelling that person, or sending them away—or even just stabilizing them in the midst of a crisis. If we can actually intervene and develop healthy relationships, they're less likely to commit these acts."

I pressed her, "But a lot of times people doubt what they're seeing or aren't sure where to turn if they have a concern. If someone is worried about another person's mental health, where do they go?"

"We have to have open discussions," she reiterated and then outlined many of the barriers in today's mental health system that hinder those discussions or otherwise obstruct access to assistance. "We need to work together as health-care professionals and primary doctors and address this from many different levels."

"I think this a place where the government could help," I added, "but we have to look at all the layers of this equation. I feel so much frustration when I hear health care oversimplified into 'let's have (or not have) Obamacare' or 'I'm for (or against) Medicare for All.' The real answer takes a more nuanced response."

After Ohio, we explored the upper Midwest for a few more days, visiting my son's high school alma mater in Michigan and a children's center in Indiana. I temporarily suspended my health-care research and took advantage of the opportunity to interview those experts about education reform, but within a week we zigzagged southward again, back into Kentucky, toward horse races, bourbon, and more health-care exploration.

July had just given way to a sweltering August as I pulled into Bowling Green, a city famous for its Corvettes and cave systems. It also has a large medical center and is home to a University of Kentucky medical campus. None of those were the reason for my visit, though. Hidden in a nondescript strip mall between a grocery store and a tax preparation office, I found the Bowling Green Veterans

Affairs Clinic. Inside the unassuming treatment center, I met with Penny Ritchie, the outpatient clinic's operations director, and Colonel Bill Lytle, its Community Blueprint coordinator. Among other things, we talked about the challenge of getting care to our veterans.

"I was thrown off by the numbers," I admitted. "We have close to twenty million vets, but only like nine million in the health-care program.[3] So many don't take advantage."

"One of the biggest problems we have right now is getting regular vets (if they're not already in the VA when they retire) to sign up," Penny agreed. "They don't really understand how the whole process works. We need more education."

"When it comes to our vets, there are other things they're facing too," I observed. For instance, there are over forty thousand homeless vets on any given day.[4] "What are some of the recurring reasons many remain homeless?"

"It depends on when they've been deployed, when they returned, and the nature of what they've done and what they've seen," Penny considered. "A lot are used to having structure, and then they return to this world where that structure's gone. How do you survive like that, and how do you get a job that will suffice without triggering you?"

"You know, we make sure our lobby is designed to accommodate people with PTSD," Penny continued, using the acronym for post-traumatic stress disorder. "That's not something you'll find in a regular hospital, and it can be a barrier to access. If someone doesn't feel safe coming in, they won't get treatment."

One of the solutions the Bowling Green clinic has embraced is telehealth,[5] using networked digital technologies to support medical care. It involves things like video teleconferences with doctors, remote monitoring of vital signs, and online self-management tools.

Penny described their system. "If a provider needs to change your medicines and follow up on your blood pressure, she can give you a home blood pressure cuff. You can record your blood pressure, then she can call you on the computer. You can talk face to face, 'How are you doing with that medication? How's your blood pressure? Go ahead and take your blood pressure now.' We can do all of that without the patient needing to come in. It's a phenomenal experience."

My visit to the tiny strip-mall VA left me buoyant. There are so many health-care gems hidden across our nation! It also made me wonder, *If a small-town clinic in the Midwest can have such success with telehealth, then why can't we all benefit from it? Who doesn't want to skip the doctor's waiting room, whether for health reasons or mere convenience?* The answer, of course, is we can.

Once I started to investigate, I quickly found telehealth across the nation. Already, more than three out of four hospitals offer it, but nagging bureaucratic barriers—like payment processes and practitioner awareness—senselessly curb its use.[6] Some places are breaking that logjam, though.

One example is the Mercy Health System and their "no-beds" hospital.[7] It's a virtual care center, which means routine monitoring and recovery happen at home. That can include care for things like chronic respiratory illnesses, diabetes, heart disease, and even post-op care. Virtual medicine has a lot going for it in terms of therapeutic outcomes, satisfaction, and patient follow through. Which means, up to a certain point, all sorts of high-quality care can be delivered at home, better and cheaper.

How much cheaper are we talking about? The Mercy Health System pilot program began a few years ago, and it showed millions in saving, especially for elderly people or people in rural areas—people who frequent the ER or who can't easily make it to a clinic. I don't know what the costs would look like at scale, but even if we shaved just one percent off of nationwide expenses, wouldn't that be something? Every year the US health-care system costs Americans more than $3.6 trillion (that's with a *t*).[8] So one percent would be around $36 billion. Significant indeed.

For weeks, I talked to health-care stakeholders from around the nation. I read research reports until my eyes crossed and, despite my best attempts, ended up devouring a pound of Twizzlers during several late-night cram sessions. So much for kicking my bad habit! After all that research, I found three themes repeated time and time again.

First, although politicians like to yell from the podium, "We need this" or "We need that," we're not actually lacking for programs. We already have so many puzzle pieces, but they're scattered, disconnected, and hidden at the local levels. During my travels, I found homegrown health-care apps at the VA, mature telehealth programs in Missouri, free medical education plans in Montana, and environmental wellness programs in Iowa. (Just to name a few.) Innovative, low-cost, and successful ideas already exist, but like Dr. Mannan complained of his medical research, no one is looking for the connections. No one's helping the local programs scale-up to serve more people or encouraging the complementary efforts find one another. Couldn't the government play a more active role in sharpening today's systems, shining a light and lending a hand to those already-working prototypes, rather than trying to reinvent the whole wheel at the federal level?

I'm reminded of my visit to Bowling Green when I spoke with Penny Ritchie. She'd explained how the clinic had improved its quality of care by moving all of the medical specialties into a single, shared facility. At first, the improvement was modest, but the administrators soon realized that despite working under a common roof, the providers were still separated by floors and wings. So, they'd rearranged the offices, putting different specialty areas (primary care, nursing, administration, and so on) into the same spaces. The results were immediate. Instead of working in silos, focused on their individual problem spaces, the teams began operating in a more integrated and patient-oriented way. When we'd spoken, I'd asked Penny if that had cost more money.

I can still recall her face. She'd scrunched her expression and looked at me as if I were a bit slow. "Of course not," she'd replied, "and it made a huge difference."

Health care is a complex puzzle. The solutions aren't all as simple as rearranging office chairs, but many of the most promising opportunities require neither more funds nor new legislation. They do, however, demand we think differently. That leads into the second theme I found.

Nearly every health-care expert I spoke with emphasized the distinction between treatment and wellness. Although both are part of the same continuum, too much of the health-care debate fixates on the treatment side and its delivery costs, insurance rates, and prescription plans. Meanwhile, arguably more important facets like prevention, wellness, and quality of life are practically ignored. We need to flip that script. That's easy enough to say, of course, but the implications are far-reaching.

Most obviously, transforming our reactive approaches into proactive ones would mean turning today's structure on its head. Maybe instead of paying for treatment, we could pay for good health? Imagine if hospitals received regular co-pays from customers to keep them healthy but were liable for patients who developed chronic illnesses. Maybe that's not the ultimate answer, but it's also not so far-fetched. Mercy Health System (who championed the "no beds" idea) has already piloted a value-based health-care program where providers are paid for helping patients improve their overall well-being rather than for each treatment procedure. It's a great example of the kind of lateral thinking we need to reframe the health-care system into a wellness enterprise.

Changing programs and policies, however, won't be nearly enough. To realize that wellness enterprise concept, we'll also need to influence society's outlook on health. Our stereotypical national identity paints Americans as independent, self-made men and women who fend for ourselves. As the cliché goes: *When the world throws adversity at us, Americans brave the trial and tough it out. We don't need help or downtime or counseling. Similarly, at work, we drive ourselves to achieve, sacrificing well-being and balance for more hours on the clock. We wear stress as a badge of commitment and burnout as a sign of productivity.* Even though those stereotypes are changing, national health trends still indicate more progress is needed. To embrace a wellness culture, our outdated mindsets will need to change.

We'll need to remove the stigmas around mental health too. As Sheila Hoehn said, that means making it safe to have open discussions—and not merely at the time of need. We need deep, enduring wellness systems. As J. Nichols also emphasized, those healthy outlooks and coping skills will need to be explicitly taught. It's not enough to "allow" someone to seek mental health treatment when they're starting to crack or, as a nutritional example, to merely have access to healthy food options. People need to learn about how their brains and bodies work, how to cope, and how to monitor their own well-being.

All of this opens the discussion wider, demanding coordination with education systems and, as J. indicated, even environmental ones. Our infrastructure matters too. Many health-care advances rely on connectivity, which means upgrading the nation's broadband and cellular systems in places like Lancaster, New Hampshire. Ultimately, it requires us to look at health care—and wellness—as an integrated ecosystem across culture, education, economy, environment, and infrastructure. A national wellness system will require top-notch Rubik's Cube decision making.

Given all of this, I had to wonder, *When it comes to health care, are we asking the right questions of politicians?* Today, it feels like political success hinges on brand-name programs: protecting the Affordable Care Act, passing Medicare for All, or repealing similar legislation. That's such narrow thinking; although, it is the kind of uninventiveness our political system encourages. Legislators are rewarded for passing bills and allocating money, not for tending to the garden of existing initiatives. Similarly, executive appointees and elected officials are mired in politics, competing with legislators for the next shiny object while simultaneously struggling against their own misplaced incentives. They act as if there are major puzzle pieces missing and loudly campaign for their pet program. More often, however, we already have many pieces of the solution, but they need coordination, communication with the public, or help to expand in size. I don't think that slogan wins as many votes, though. It's difficult to chant "incrementally improve routine administration and do a better job of cross-organizational orchestration!" at a rally (although, I'm willing to give it a try).

Could we change the way politicians are graded? Rather than earning points for drafting new plans or winning votes for their favorite bills, what if there was a different reward structure? What if politicians' health-care scorecards included things like the well-being of their constituents or efficiency of their communities' medical access? What if politicians were rewarded for searching out those local success stories or for advancing health outcomes without new legislation? Admittedly, that's all a pipe dream, but it's a worthy goal.

News anchor Walter Cronkite once famously quipped, "America's health-care system is neither healthy, caring, nor a system." Until we change government incentives, recast their top-down system as a wider interconnected ecosystem, and change its standards for success, Cronkite's observation will likely remain poignantly true. Reinventing our health-care system isn't easy—if it were, we'd have already done it—but I don't think it's as insurmountable as the tabloid news or conventional wisdom would lead us to believe. We do, however, need to reframe our thinking and conceptualize solutions in different ways. It's time to flip that script, adjust our mindsets, and force politicians to change theirs as well.

CHAPTER TWELVE

Who's Who in the Political Zoo?

What do you call a collection of politically minded types? A litany of legislators? An assembly of activists? A filibuster of politicos? Whatever their sardonic moniker, I've reliably found a certain pecking order among those who venture into the political realm. First, there's your "wannabe politician."

Wannabes are fueled by righteous indignation or some all-consuming passion that drives them to political office. What marks them as wannabes, though, is their utter inability to achieve any meaningful outcomes. They register to run, yell a lot about their passion project, and frequent political events. Beyond that, they wing it, seemingly without strategy and with no awareness of the implicit rules of politics.

You can spot wannabes by their intensity and, more often than not, by their attire. One wannabe I've seen around the Florida circuit wears a uniform of jeans and garish campaign T-shirts littered with slogans—even to ostensibly formal events. Bless his heart, he's a kind man who means well and is on a mission to make things better, but he's blind to his surroundings. Another fellow I've encountered litters his suit jacket with more than a dozen campaign pins, all loudly proclaiming his stances on various topics. He never misses a Florida Democratic event and is unafraid to talk with anyone at them. He loudly shares his message with anyone he can pin down. He's trying to do good work—he wants to change campaign finance laws to reduce corruption—but he's going about it the wrong way. It's not enough to proclaim a good idea loudly. In my mind, I imagine him as a traveling vacuum salesman, going from house to house to push his product. You don't want to be harsh because he's doing honest work, but you still don't want a vacuum. These two gentlemen are among the more savory wannabes I've encountered. Many slide even further down the social-awareness scale.

Another would-be politician around Florida, let's call him Eugene, personifies the dregs of the wannabes. Eugene cuts a portly silhouette, with pronounced rolls of fat straining against his perpetually too-small shirts and spilling over the waistband of his unwashed jeans. Eugene's raison d'être is the minimum wage. He spreads that message across the state at political conferences and partisan rallies, and he cornered me at one of those meetings.

"Don't you believe people should be able to take care of their families?" he grilled, spraying spittle as he talked and standing too close for comfort. I tried to back up, but he followed as he pressed another question.

"Don't you think people who work a full-time job are worthy of a living wage?"

Of course, no one could reasonably say no to his questions. He walks any listener down a path with no off-ramps. You can't have a discussion. You can only hang on for the ride as his argument hurtles toward the inevitable syllogism that, obviously, we must increase the minimum wage.

I wanted to ask, "Are you worried about people getting fired because businesses can't afford the added costs?" I wanted to have a discussion with him about small businesses and to ask if he's ever talked with corporate executives or company owners. He might still have come to the same conclusions, but I wanted to know, "Have you ever run a business? Have you ever walked in their shoes?" Eugene gave me no entry points for those thoughts, though. He had already made up his mind. He wasn't open to changing it or considering any nuances around the question. The discussion only had space for his black-and-white thinking—only room for him to aggressively state his good idea until listeners were convinced by his dogged persistence.

Talking with Eugene felt like being deposed by a lawyer. That's another characteristic of the wannabe: They're aggressive. Their aggressiveness is driven by heart and passion—they each want to right some wrong or champion some well-meaning idea. It's just that these individuals aren't going to succeed in politics. They're lacking some critical awareness that prevents them from putting all the pieces together and effectively influencing people to change.

After wannabe politicians, the second political character is the "devoted activist." Like wannabes, activists are driven by their passion for a particular issue, but beyond that similarity they're starkly different. Activists are good at bringing people together around a central message, and they're undeterred by adversity. In fact, I think rejection makes them fight harder. It almost seems to fuel them.

Activists also have an uncanny energy. I don't know if they sleep. I guess they must, but they clearly run on a different clock than the rest of us mere humans. Unlike the wannabe politicians who exude aggressiveness, the activists have the kind of hyperactivity usually only found in young children. It's the kind that makes everyone else feel tired just watching them.

One of my political friends, Lisa Santoni Cromar, is an issue activist fighting for an equitable Puerto Rico, and she the vice president of a corresponding advocacy group called the Diaspora En Resistencia. She's committed to galvanizing fellow Boricuas, specifically fellow Florida-based Puerto Ricans, to mobilize for the island's rights. We've met a few times over coffee, and each time it's the same scenario. She speaks just a touch faster than the rest of us and radiates that telltale activist intensity. She always seems to have a mental agenda, and, inevitably, the conversation meanders to her talking points—but not in a rude way. Rather, her focus and dedication come through in everything she does, even a social call.

Lisa spoke at my #Tour50 campaign kickoff event back in May at the American Legion. I thought she buzzed with energy over cappuccinos, but she practically exploded with zealous fervor on the rally stage. When she grabbed the microphone, it must have flipped a switch. Her normal language changed; she went from energetic spokesperson to professional evangelist. She chanted with exaggerated intonation and played call-and-response with the crowd, rallying them around her slogans and building their energy to an eager tumult.

That's another trait I've found in activists: They're good with a megaphone. They know how to get people excited about what they're doing. They're leaders of movements. They bring a voice to people who want to be energized by a given cause. Unlike political wannabes, though, activists aren't trying to write new legislation or change policy by themselves. Activists want to convince politicians to make different decisions. They wield the tools of political influence and civil persuasion. Wannabes, on the other hand, (unsuccessfully) try to wield the tools of elected office and formal authority. Wannabes seem to believe they can make decisions better than the rest of us (or, at least, better than the current politicians), and they're vying for that power. To be fair, I've occasionally seen some fed-up activists run for office—even successfully at times—but I've rarely seen wannabes at an activist's rally. Go figure.

For the third archetype, we've finally reached the "quintessential politician."

When my daughter Madison was a toddler, I took her to a parent-child meetup. Everyone sat in a circle while the organizers played music and ran activities for the kids. One little boy, who must have been around eighteen months old, started the event by walking around the circle, looking everyone in the eye, smiling and waving, and then walking on to the next. The kid had no sense of self-consciousness or bashfulness. With no prompting from his mother, he almost methodically acknowledged every adult, beaming with affable charm toward each of us. Impressed and astonished, I turned a questioning eye toward his mother.

"I know!" she replied with a slight laugh, "People call him the little politician."

I had to agree with the nickname. Less than two years old and that little boy had the political personality down to his core. It was fascinating to watch.

I had a somewhat similar revelation the first time I saw Andrew Gillum speak. He's a Florida Democrat and, by now, familiar to the political community, but when I first heard him, he was an unknown, just one of several potential candidates at the state convention. As soon as he spoke, though, I knew he'd win the crowd. He commanded an innate bearing of calm assurance. He moved with a smoothness, and when he spoke, it sounded like honey. The audience couldn't take their eyes off of him. It didn't matter what he said, it mattered how he said it and how he connected to people. He had personality and poise. I wonder if he had been like that boy at the meetup. I suspect young Andrew Gillum had many of those same inborn traits.

In addition to a silver tongue and mesmerizing charisma, quintessential politicians have tenacity. They're goal-focused and achievement-oriented. They have to be. Every day they face an onslaught of rejection, criticism, and second guessing. They have to gird themselves in emotional armor, shut out the negativity, and adopt a win-at-all-costs mindset. Along those same lines, quintessential politicians are dedicated—not necessarily to a cause or a platform but to holding their office. That takes substantial time. Consider the time they spend doing their actual jobs and then add all of those extra hours spent fundraising and political horse trading. In the end, they work incessantly. I knew of a former senatorial candidate who, while campaigning, only saw his wife twice in one year—and both times were at official events.

Quintessential politicians are willing to gamble everything, effectively leave their families for months or years at a time, and withstand a flurry of criticism, all the while constantly begging for money (not an ego-affirming activity) and getting doors slammed in their faces on a daily basis. They have to get up, even when they're exhausted, put on a polished mask, and find it within themselves to carry on. After dozens of rejections and scathing op-eds, the quintessential politician has to think, "That's OK. I can handle it. I'll take another step forward." Just to survive they have to be hyper-extraverts, able to thrive off of social energy while ignoring all of the negative cues that would make most people walk away. Do you ever wonder why the top politicians have a reputation for being headstrong or for not listening to others? If they listened, then they wouldn't survive the political gauntlet long enough to make it to the top.

The last archetype in politics is the "problem solver." These are the designers, thinkers, and strategists; they're the ones who develop the functional plans and draft legislation. They're the nerdiest of the bunch and often serve in the shadows. You might find them at a think tank, a lobbyist league, or in a few fortunate cases, on a politician's staff. Problem solvers have a unique affinity for complexity; they're not afraid to dive down the rabbit hole, pick apart a problem from a hundred angles, and then think through its intricate solutions. Problem solvers are blessed with penetrating insight and analytical creativity. On the other hand, they sometimes grow so enamored with a problem that they disconnect from normal life, and they're cursed with the inability to talk in sound-bites. They tend toward overwrought explanations and often express solutions with at least a dozen caveats. They also frequently insist on pursuing the right answer while stubbornly resisting any ancillary political dealings that might distract from those direct outcomes.

Personally, I consider myself a problem solver who's learning to play the role of a quintessential politician. I've occasionally met other problem solvers around the political arena. One was a former representative—a brilliant man. Nothing left his office without his direct stamp of approval, and often, he personally penned the plans (full of evidence-based assertions and hundreds of footnotes). He focused so intensely on defining the optimum courses of action, though, he often ignored office politics and let all of those subtle relationships flounder. He would step on toes in his pursuit of the perfect proposal, and, at least in one instance, I saw those petty politics defeat his picture-perfect policy work.

Wannabes, activists, quintessential politicians, and problem solvers: These are the four starring roles I've found in politics. Of course, there's an ensemble of supporting characters. There are the "smarmy kingmakers," like the Duke of South Florida, who peddle wealth and influence. There are the "professional volunteers" who doggedly attend community rallies and willingly loiter on street corners asking strangers to sign petitions. There are the "faithful citizens," who never miss a Women's League or City Council meeting and who you're likely to see staffing the polling stations on Election Day. These and others too make up a whole cast of (political) characters. Still, the starring four—well, except for the wannabes—are key.

We need the trifecta: the dedicated activists, quintessential politicians, and problem solvers. All three mutually reinforcing each other. Activists give a voice and mobilize constituents, the politicians know how to negotiate outcomes and reframe ideas into manageable sound-bites, and the problem solvers can architect true solutions.

Often the three categories are mutually exclusive too. Someone inclined to activism is often too rigid and righteous to perform well as a long-term politician. They're usually too fixated on their goal to manage all of the other relationships and extraneous tasks politicians need to navigate. Quintessential politicians don't necessarily have the experience or ability to strategize about long-term outcomes, construct complex solutions (with Rubik's Cube thinking), or orchestrate existing programs. They have to focus on their outward message and on navigating the viper's pit immediately before them. They're also incentivized to look for the "shiny new thing" to sell to the voters rather than "waste" their time improving existing programs or, heaven forbid, making programs in a different part of the government work better. And problem solvers tend to grow aloof. Unlike activists who dive into the heart of their causes, problem solvers see how the puzzle fits together because they stand apart from it, far enough away to consider all of the pieces. They don't necessarily have the magnetism needed to mobilize a crowd to action, and they struggle to reduce the complexity of their solutions into easily chanted mantras. Similarly, problem solvers rarely have the stomach to play the partisan games that fill politicians' worlds—the utilitarian trade-offs, bureaucratic fights, and self-promotional schemes.

In a perfect world, our political leaders would be problem solvers. They'd rely on trusted communication directors (quintessential politicians) to handle political dealings, and they'd work hand in hand with dedicated activists who help them liaise with the community. Of course, that's a fantasy. The entire system is set up against it. Still, as I told my son years before, we don't brook idle grumbling here. If you name a problem, you also need to recommend solutions. You can't bellyache about a broken system if you're unwilling to try to fix it. So, how do we address it?

Part of the underlying issue is that politics is short-handed in the problem-solver category. Across our nation, I've found thousands of viable problem solvers, people who've figured out (at least a part) of the governance puzzle, people with plans and strategies, and more often than not, data to back them up. But they don't want to come across as political, so rather than infusing these ideas into the system, they stand back. Maybe they post them online or implement a small-scale local program, but they keep well away from the dirty political machine. And in so doing, they cede that system to the wannabes, activists, and quintessential politicians.

More problem solvers need to contribute. It's not enough to simply vote, monitor the political news, or donate your ten dollars. It's not enough to lend your sweat equity, spending a day holding a candidate's sign or an afternoon collecting signatures. We need problem solvers to contribute their talent. That could mean jumping with both feet into the political fray, learning the ropes like I did at state events and local rallies. You could even try a harebrained fifty-state tour!

There are millions of entry points. The key is to enter somewhere—anywhere—and begin to learn those unwritten rules and inexplicable nuances of our political system. I think politicians, on both sides of the aisle, benefit from the perception that we're dependent on them and that the political system is too complex (or maybe too boring or too time-consuming or too fill-in-the-blank) for average citizens to meaningfully affect. After more than a year of living politically, I can tell you that's not the case. It's not only feasible to get engaged, no matter what archetype you favor, it's also critical. People across this nation are disgusted by politics—countless have told me that quite colorfully—but walking off the field won't change the nature of the game. The only way to change its rules is from the inside, which could mean running for office or simply becoming active in the larger political system. Either way, it means millions of people across the nation need to swallow their bile and get involved—if not with both feet then at least by sticking a toe into the water.

CHAPTER THIRTEEN

The Little Red Hen Strategy

I've spent years working with the military. I know its crazy acronyms and ridiculous sayings, like "that's a self-licking ice cream cone" (a pointless self-perpetuating system) or "do you have any alibis?" (a way of asking, "Does anyone have an unmade point before we end this discussion?"). I've thought seriously about the strategic level of defense too, and even before my presidential bid, I'd filled several mental notebooks with insights and gripes about how the Defense Department is run. All of that experience was a double-edged sword. It gave me a leg-up on writing my campaign strategy, but I also found it difficult to edit my thoughts. I kept wanting to dive down rabbit holes and overcomplicate my thinking.

To rein things in, I started at the top. The government publishes libraries of reports every year, and a lot are publicly available. The highest-level strategies include the *National Military Strategy*, the military's overall implementation plan written by the chairman of the Joint Chiefs of Staff, and its cousin, the *National Security Strategy*, which serves a similar purpose for the broader government. The top-dog strategy document, though, is the *National Defense Strategy*, authored by the secretary of defense. Then-Secretary James Mattis signed the most recent edition in 2018, and it outlines three directives for the department: rebuild military readiness while forming a more lethal force, strengthen alliances with international military partners, and make business processes more efficient.

I couldn't argue with the strategy's points; of course, that doesn't mean everything is perfect. Military spending is a hot-button issue. Similarly, there are valid questions around military missions and the overextension of our forces. And don't even get me started on the department's acquisition policies! So even though I felt no compunction to rewrite the military's strategy, I certainly had things to say about national security. The challenge was to hone my thinking, keep it focused on the presidential swim lane, and try to pinpoint what—if anything—was missing in our current system.

Officially, I kicked off my presidential focus on national security at the beginning of August, transitioning from health care to defense while visiting the Bowling Green Veterans Clinic. It seemed poetic, moving from medicine to military at a military medical facility. While I was at the VA clinic, Colonel Bill Lytle planted seeds that would catalyze my thinking. Although neither of us knew it at the time, his ideas around a "community blueprint" began to gradually shift my concept of national security. But all of that would come later, after I'd had time to wrestle my thoughts into a campaign-worthy strategy. First, I needed to continue my fifty-state tour.

After Bowling Green, I drove northwest into Illinois. I spent a handful of long days on the highway, passing through Carbondale and Champaign. Eventually, I arrived in Chicago. Robert's friends live there, and they kindly let me park at their house while I did some campaign work around the city. I stayed a few days, catching up on tasks and commitments and letting the road weariness seep from my soul. On the third day, hosts Mike and Laura Nadeau arranged a small get-together, a genial send-off before my departure the next morning.

In her work life, Laura oversees a private school, so she invited her team to dinner. Ostensibly, it gave them a chance to hear about my government experiences with education strategy, but it was also an excuse for all of us to geek-out about teaching and learning. Laura and her teachers had a lot to say. She explained, for example, that the philosophy of their school is unique. It takes a different tact than most conventional schools.

"We try to teach young people to recognize their roles in society," she shared with pride. "We want to help them learn to connect to others and become civically minded. We're trying to get them to think beyond 'What's happening on Planet Me.'"

"We have programs that tie it all together," one of her colleagues added. "We teach lessons that combine the traditional subjects, you know, like math and history, with those other themes: service, interconnectedness, and social respect."

The conversation continued for quite a while, but in a nutshell, it swirled around the unspoken question, "How should schools encourage kids to develop a civic mindset?" Laura's commitment to the interplay of education and society resonated with me, so I broached a budding idea that had been swirling around in my mind since Kentucky.

"What do you think about the idea of a national service strategy?"

It could resemble security-sector strategies, I explained to the group, but instead of defense objectives, it would have goals and pathways for citizen engagement. Bill Lytle had shown me his community blueprint in action. It coordinated the efforts of others who wanted to contribute to veterans, and as a result, it multiplied all of their outcomes. I kept circling back to the concept and thinking about it in a national context. That idea seemed to intersect with the educational approach Laura and her coworkers had highlighted. Imagine teaching civic mindedness and having a national plan that helps students to apply what they've learned in more coordinated ways. Unsurprisingly, these educators (who come from a school known for its social and societal curriculum) loved the idea. With their encouragement, the seeds Bill had planted began to flourish.

The next morning, I bid Mike and Laura farewell and then drove into Wisconsin, cutting across the state through Milwaukee, Madison, and Eau Claire. My eight-year-old daughter was still traveling with me at the time, so in the middle of the state, we paused for the obligatory photo next to the city sign that shares her name. Then we took a detour to the cheese chalet. It boasts one of the best selections of cheese curds and (bonus!) the largest roadside cow sculpture in the state. Sissy the Cow must stand four or five times the height of an average person. Inside the store, they have heaps of curd in every form and flavor. Of course, we diligently contributed to the local economy before continuing on to Minnesota.

I'd spent my preschool years in Minneapolis and still had fond, albeit fuzzy, memories of my childhood home. I wanted my daughter to see some of those personal landmarks and for her to experience Minnesotan culture. One of its pinnacles is Corn Days, a summer festival themed around (you guessed it!) corn. It features corn fritters, corn bread, buttered sweet corn, corn on the cob, and every other corn variation you can imagine. There's also a corn-themed parade with (real non-corn) candy. As a child, I'd bring a shoebox and fill it to the brim with sweets—a sort of corn-themed Halloween. My aunt and uncle, who still live nearby, met us at the festival, and even my husband flew in to join us for the starchy fun.

While in the area, we also had to visit the Mall of America, one of the nation's largest shopping centers. It's a gleaming marvel of glass and metal spanning nearly one-hundred acres. It's not just a temple of consumerism, though. The mall also stands as a sanctuary against the bleak Minnesotan winters, among the coldest in the nation. Living under those conditions must have been an ordeal for the early settlers, and while it's still not a picnic for modern residents, the local infrastructure has adapted. That's how you end up with a temperature-controlled megamall with over five-hundred stores and an indoor amusement park. It's a triumph against the elements.

My family moved to Florida during my grade-school years, and I remember how shocking the tropical climate initially seemed. I felt like a fish out of water, moving from snowdrifts to suntans. Similarly, people in Orlando didn't understand the cold; they couldn't even layer properly on the occasional Florida winter's day (what Minnesotans would call "late spring"). Florida has its own challenges, of course. Take hurricanes. Like northern snow days, Florida schedules a few hurricane days every year, anticipating those storms will interrupt normal activities. The state also builds seawalls, and in school, kids learn hurricane preparedness and evacuation procedures.

Every part of our nation has infrastructure, but the kinds of systems and services each needs vary widely—and I'm not sure DC pundits always appreciate those distinctions. We often hear political arguments about "this state" or "that region" getting its "fair share" of federal funding, comparing one place against the next in a tit-for-tat contest for infrastructure dollars. As I reflected on the Mall of America, it struck me just how different each area is. States shouldn't be vying for equal slices of the pie. It's not about the equality of spend; it's about the equality of outcome. I started to percolate on that concept's implications for national defense. Is every corner of our country getting its fair share of security?

After Minneapolis, Chris flew home to Florida with our little one in tow. Then I migrated to Fargo, stopping for a night at the 4e Winery. It sits on a wide grassy landscape, with the horizon broken only occasionally by a copse of distant trees or the peaks of red barns. Not only does the winery produce some interestingly beautiful North Dakota wines, but it also allows overnight camper parking—what's not to love?

That evening, I visited the tasting room, along with an assorted collection of fellow RV travelers and local wine connoisseurs. These included the winery owners, who also had day jobs as an economics professor and professional artist, a politically far-left factory line worker, and a far-right former Navy SEAL. It didn't take much time for the tasting room to transform into a group dinner party. Everyone had a story to tell.

Caleb, for instance, the former Sailor, told us about his unexpected life adventure. From the outside, he looks like a fit, unassuming middle-aged man. He wore a friendly expression and sported a salt-and-pepper beard. You probably wouldn't have guessed that behind his family-man exterior he's a highly trained warrior. Never mind that, though. As he soon explained to the group, he'd left that all behind to become a traveling organic farmer.

Caleb had retired from the Navy a couple years prior. After that, he and his wife sold their home, downsized nearly all of their possessions, and packed themselves and three small children into an RV. Then he took an entry-level internship with a training farm. (Yes, that's a thing; they teach would-be ag professionals the ropes.) He made such a radical lifestyle change, he explained, because he wanted to help build the nation's agricultural self-sufficiency.

"What kind of country am I leaving to my kids?" he ruminated. "Sure, we can put effects on target. We can go toe to toe with anyone in the world, but what does that matter if we're starving at home?"

While researching environmental policies I'd heard similar thoughts (although perhaps less militant). It's not so remarkable to find environmental activists who express concerns about seed diversity, agricultural sustainability, and water access. As I began easing into my defense research, though, I was surprised to hear similar warnings raised by national security professionals.

"A lot of people don't realize how bad it can get when you overuse resources," Caleb explained. "Nothing else really matters if we don't have an earth to live on, water to drink, and crops to eat. Ensuring those basic needs are met long-term ought to be a national priority."

If you'd asked me before the fifty-state tour, I'd have assumed only green-blooded activists would say things like that. I came to discover, though, there are different types of environmentalists. At one extreme, there are gung-ho tree-huggers who upcycle wine bottles into plant holders and only flush their toilets every third visit. On the other end of the scale, there are the business-minded pragmatists. They scoff at (what they see as) futile individual efforts and look for ways to make large-scale changes to systems and policies. Caleb definitely fell closer to the pragmatists' side of the spectrum. And he made good points. Protecting the homeland requires more than infantry brigades and aircraft carriers. Concepts like the security of natural resources and protection of our supply chains also play a role.

Caleb's points complemented the ideas already churning in my head from Bill Lytle and Laura Nadeau. Those thoughts were congealing around the idea of national service—something that connects education, environment, and civic engagement with defense concepts like stability, resilience, and readiness. In case you've misplaced your military jargon decoder ring, that means connecting citizen service to making our communities safe and functional (that's *stability*), and it means making sure we bounce back from emergencies, both the natural and man-made kinds (that's *resilience*). Finally, it means our nation is ready for whatever we might face. *Readiness* roughly means preparedness, sort of like an outfielder poised to catch a fly ball, but it's a more nuanced concept than that image implies. Fortunately, I had an opportunity to talk with one of the leading experts on readiness, and I picked his brain about it and the idea of a "ready nation."

Years ago, Lloyd Thrall had served in the Army's First Ranger Battalion. That's a special forces unit. Today, more than two decades later, he still shows the telltale mannerisms and physical fitness the rangers are known for. When I'd first met Lloyd, he was serving as one of the Pentagon's deputy assistant secretaries of defense. (That long-ass title is usually shortened to DASD and, in the tradition of all good military abbreviations, pronounced as a word—*daz-dee*.) DASDs are senior subject-matter experts who work just two- or three-steps down from the secretary of defense. Lloyd was the DASD for readiness, which meant he was responsible for monitoring whether the military was *ready* (in terms of supplies, equipment, manpower, personnel health, training, and so on) to conduct possible missions or face conceivable threats.

Having served his time in the Beltway, Lloyd now works as a scholar in residence at the University of Colorado Boulder. I sat down with him on an otherwise quiet Monday and grilled him on military—and societal—readiness concepts. I started our discussion with a hardball, and he rose to the challenge.

"Let me ask the direct question. You oversaw readiness. Are we ready?"

"I think, in a word," he paused and shifted, "no. And that's a pretty sobering thought, with some sad and troubling historical precedent. What I mean is, the United States has a history of being unready for war, and there are pathologies in peacetime that prevent us from lifting the fog of peace and thinking clearly about war. You can dance around it with euphemisms, but ultimately, that means we lose war fighters who would otherwise be at home with their spouses and children. So, this haunted me as the DASD for readiness—this question of 'Are we ready?'"

" . . . and it gets worse," he continued. "I'm of the opinion that we'll see an increasing frequency and severity of disruption, chiefly brought on by technology, that will challenge large bureaucracies to adapt in ways they're not traditionally or culturally incentivized to. I think that's the great challenge for our age. It's not cybersecurity or artificial intelligence; it's one level deeper. It's about how to make strategic decisions about things like cybersecurity, AI, and whatever's next. And we'll be competing in that space not only with China and Russia, but also with non-state actors—terrorists and insurgents—who are much like start-ups.

They'll take a commercial drone off the shelf and innovate in ways that large organizations, like the United States Navy, struggle to match."

"In working with our NATO allies," I put in, "I noticed many of the smaller nations were able to be more agile when it came to innovation."

Lloyd nodded but also parried, "What is America? We're the creators; we're the dynamic. We're the capital of innovation. So, I think the good news is, it's not a matter of actually building things we don't have. It's a matter of thinking differently about what we do have."

I gently pivoted the conversation, "You're trying to develop those innovative future leaders in your Designing for Defense program here in Boulder, but what if we thought more broadly? How do we scale-up that kind of education across the whole nation? What could you imagine?"

"I think about this a lot, actually. All right, maybe I have a dog in the fight," he admitted with half a smile before retreating to a more serious tone. "When most people think about innovation—we think about California, Boston, or New York. But this *nation* has a rich, innovative history, and here in Colorado we're in the middle of it. I think we've all heard the critique: America's not just a country of two coasts. We're a country of everyone, and yet we're not accessing the talent that lies out there. Or, I should say, the government isn't accessing it. People go out and have dynamic careers. They create value in the commercial sector (and we're all better for it), but government's not getting its share of talent. We have wonderful people in the military, and we recruit from well-stocked pools. But we need a broader swath of the American experience—in uniform and out of uniform, in government and out of government—in a permeable relationship with government where their expertise can be part of national service. It's time for fresh thinking in these models."

Finally, like a coda, he observed, "We live in a changing world, and the military and civilian spheres are converging at such a rate that traditional security thinking is not going to get us there."

In that moment, my mind was entirely made up. Even though the Defense Department dominates the federal government in terms of size and spend, it wasn't the right focus for my presidential examination. Like Lloyd had said, I needed to think differently. I needed to think more broadly about national stability, resilience, and readiness, and I needed to open my aperture beyond our men and women in uniform. I needed a nation-wide strategy that cuts across domains and has something for everyone.

★ ★ ★

A hundred points from my discussion with Lloyd stood out. One was his comment about technology and its disrupting influence on traditional security methods. The digital world is the next great battlefield, and no matter what kind of strategy I decided to write, my plan needed to account for its effects. I already had a healthy appreciation for advanced technology and the importance of cybersecurity, but I'm no technophile. I needed some coaching before I could work the technology thread into my campaign platform.

I called my colleague, Dean Pianta. Now middle-aged, with gray lining his temples and peppering his goatee, Dean is the director of cloud solutions at a large national security company. We'd met a few years earlier and, thanks to Dean's magnetic wit and keen intellect, soon became friends. That's how I knew that, in addition to having deep technical knowhow, he could explain those complex technology concepts to a mere human like myself.

"Hats off to our modern federal programs," Dean enthused as our interview began. "Civilian government programs, like FedRAMP, have done a good job at evolving with the times. Five years ago, every government agency had different ideas on how to secure their cloud systems. Everyone had their own, long, drawn out process to seek an 'authority to operate' for every application (you know, the certification that says a system is in a good state and can't be compromised). If ten agencies bought the same software, they didn't trust each other enough to re-use or help each other with securing it. Talk about inefficiencies and cost overruns. The most important point, though, is that not everyone did it right. So the weakest link made a doorway for the bad guys. It's getting better now, especially in the Federal Government. We're speaking the same language (NIST Security Controls), sharing best practices across offices, and beginning to embed security into how we develop and operate solutions."

"There are so many facets to this," I observed. "When people talk about 'defense,' we usually focus on our active duty and reserve personnel, and we talk about our vets, of course, but there's also a huge infrastructure beyond them. Particularly when it comes to cybersecurity; there's an expanding requirement to recognize how everyone's part of that greater puzzle."

"Everyone involved needs to stay abreast," Dean concurred and then shared an example. "Shame on us if Company A learns something about, let's say, a software patch or cyberattack, and then Company B fails because it didn't know about it. Those solutions could have been passed on, or people could have been trained to completely avoid the situation. With today's technology we can do these types of things, but at the end of the day, it comes down to people. Can we start to change our culture? Can we transform ourselves into a culture of feedback and really crowdsource information? It's about collaboration and knowledge transfer—how do we maximize that? This isn't done by one person. It's done through communities who then ripple up and share information across a common fabric."

I thought about all the systems that might touch a common digital fabric. The list is nearly endless: everything from Maddie's grade-school records to the MRI machine at our local hospital and, of course, our personal technologies. Our smartphones, digital footprints online, and the data exhaust from our smart cars are all avenues for cyberattack. It's pretty overwhelming.

"Most importantly," Dean continued, "Shame on me as a software company for thinking like I did twenty years ago—as if I could just develop software, put it out, and say, 'Oh yeah, the military will take care of it.' It's a shift we have to recognize."

After interviewing Dean, I turned my camper southward. About an hour in, as I drove beneath the unassuming overpass that divides North and South Dakota, it struck me that I'd just reached the halfway point of my fifty-state tour. South Dakota was my twenty-sixth state. As I reflected on that, a glimmer of emotion started to kindle in me, but before I could probe that more deeply, it was time to get off of the highway. I gently veered the RV down a nondescript exit and headed toward the Watertown Veterans Memorial. I'd found it online but didn't know what to expect. Following my navigation app, I pulled onto a wide empty road. Beyond its ample shoulders, green cropland stretched as far as the eye could see. Trees dotted the landscape, and as the road looped around a thicket of pines, the park came into view.

The memorial sits on the picturesque banks of Lake Kampeska. Similar to the Vietnam Veterans Memorial in Washington, its heart is a collection of black granite walls each lined with service members' names. Low benches and tall flagpoles bearing military banners line the walkway around it, with each aligned in perfect geometric harmony.

I was completely alone for the first time in ages. My husband and children had all returned home, and even my periodic traveling companions had all left for other commitments. Standing there, in the quiet shadow of the memorial, my eyes grew unfocused as I stared aimlessly across the lake. I let myself reflect, and that spark of emotion I'd felt earlier reignited.

Watertown's memorial lists thousands of names—just a fraction of the men and women who've fought for this nation. They risked life and limb and, often, mind to ensure our security. So many of them ran toward the sounds of danger so that the rest of us could live better lives. Once I began mentally prodding those feelings, the emotion spread across my other thoughts. I felt a penetrating sense of gratitude.

I'd crossed the halfway point of my national tour. I'd had the privilege of interviewing dozens of experts and making hundreds of videos. I'd visited monuments, museums, and universities—not to mention a giant roadside cow. I'd sampled strange local delicacies, reconnected with friends and family, and experienced the magnificence of the American countryside. I was living a lot of people's bucket lists and felt staggeringly grateful for it. I felt grateful to my family for supporting my unusual presidential gambit. I felt grateful to my Geek Team, who volunteered their time to spitball ideas and research campaign finance. I also felt a glow of appreciation for everyone I'd met along the journey.

Only halfway through and I'd already learned so much. Few Americans get to see all of the corners of our nation, let alone immerse themselves in its people and their cultures. Not only was I privileged to hear their stories and walk a few steps in a thousand different shoes, but the folks I'd met so far—from lauded professors to traveling retirees—were also giving me the gift of hope. I'd started this journey as an exploration of American politics. After what I'd heard from the campaign consultants and cable news pundits, I'd worried about what I might uncover. Although I certainly found vitriol and vice in places, more often I found an inspiring citizenry rich with insights, determination, and grassroots solutions. They had stories the nation needed to hear—an antidote to the partisan rhetoric and distorted news clips. What a blessing to play even a small part in sharing that message! I didn't serve in uniform, and I've never had to face the sacrifices some of our war fighters make. Still, this was something I could do to contribute to our country.

★ ★ ★

After visiting Watertown and Sioux Falls, my road trip continued south along the Iowa-Nebraska border. I passed endless acres of yellow-topped corn and, several monotonous hours later, finally saw Omaha's grain elevators crest the horizon. (I never expected to be so excited to see a storage silo!) I exited toward the university and then got ready for my upcoming interview with Dr. Jonathan Benjamin-Alvarado.

Jonathan works at the University of Nebraska Omaha where he wears several hats, including one as a political science professor with more than thirty years' experience. We met at one of the university's reading nooks, a lounge filled with dark wood paneling and chartreuse couches. Jonathan wore the favored uniform of university administrators: reading glasses, comfortable slacks, and a matching blazer hanging open over a black T-shirt. When I arrived, he greeted me warmly, his face easily folding into a dimpled smile. To kick things off, I asked about his background.

"I enlisted in the Navy after one year in college, and then after that stint, I realized I wanted to look into some of the things I'd experienced. We were still in the Cold War, at loggerheads with the Russians. That experience really opened my mind to exploring why we were doing the things we were doing."

Jonathan went on to explain how he'd come to work as a nuclear policy analyst and an international arms control consultant. "Then a number of years back," he continued, "I stumbled into the classroom, and it sent me in a whole different direction. Now, I've spent nearly twenty years teaching foreign policy, national security policy, and intelligence studies. I have the opportunity to parlay what I know to encourage students. For the last ten years, I've been helping to prepare young people to pursue careers in the intelligence community."

"Government service," Jonathan added, "It's the highest calling and something I'm very passionate about."

"Tell me about the American Security Project," I prompted. I'd already done my homework and knew Jonathan was involved with the nonpartisan group.

"The university is fortunate that one of its graduates is former-Senator and former-Secretary of Defense Chuck Hagel. He's always been an ardent advocate of public service. He's really enabled our institution to take great pride in it. He decided to partner with other former legislators and Department of Defense officials to create a think tank, so to speak, that would focus on the intersection of ideas that aren't strictly in the domain of defense policy but that have an influence on it. So, you know, American Security Project looks at issues of climate change, issues related to energy, or elements of our technology platforms and cybersecurity. Some of the best universities in the country today are working on those issues."

After the camera clicked off, Jonathan bantered a bit longer.

"You know, I think the defense and security folks like us better here in Nebraska than the guys and gals in California."

Clearly, he was baiting me, so with affected naivety I asked, "Why's that?"

"Here in the Midwest, we keep our feet on the ground and our heads on our shoulders—versus on the beach and in the clouds! The agencies do recruit heavily here, though," he added sincerely. "We have a good relationship with Strategic Command, which is just down the road, and special structures to work with the Department of Defense."

"It's about the diversity," I nodded. Then recalling back to a discussion we'd had earlier, I added, "It's like you said before: It's not enough to just train people to understand the technical side. We need managers and designers and even cheerleaders all contributing to the same team."

"And," he chimed in, "across the different disciplines: economics, policy, environment, global affairs, energy—"

"That's right," I interrupted slyly, "along with both pragmatists and daydreamers!"

I put pen to paper on my transformed defense platform—now a national service strategy—as my camper crawled through the Midwest. I cut east again, crossing through the heart of Iowa on Interstate 80 before looping south into Missouri. It was my first time in St. Louis, so I felt compelled to visit the Gateway Arch. We've all seen it in pictures, but in person, it has a magic that photographs can't capture. You feel small; it gives you perspective. I spent the next several days snaking westward, through Columbia and Kansas City (which, despite its name, is largely situated in Missouri), and then into Kansas, passing through Wichita, Salina, and Hays. Driving through the world's breadbasket made for a mind-numbing backdrop, the perfect white noise for pondering the concepts I'd uncovered.

Over the intervening weeks, I'd been able to interview a broad swath of experts. I'd talked to the chair of the Computing Security Department at the Rochester Institute of Technology, delving into the interplay of cybersecurity education and the workforce, and chatted with Jim Broome, the president of a security company, about protecting our energy grid. I'd found research and supply-chain experts, like Dr. Jen Murphy, who highlighted the critical role of military innovation, and Karen Fray, who talked about everyone's favorite topic: defense contracting. I found experts on peripheral issues too, people involved with things like veteran employment and military families. And I even called one of my daughter's childhood friends, now a petty officer in the Navy, to get a young enlisted's perspective.

After all of those interviews, my brain hit a saturation point. Plus, it felt like each one was treading around common themes: This is a multifaceted problem space. Technology is changing the character of national security. And an effective defense strategy involves a lot more than conventional warfare and the traditional warrior caste. As I considered that broadened perspective, I was reminded of a lacrosse game I once saw.

As mentioned before, my daughter Monica played competitive lacrosse in school. In case you're unfamiliar, lacrosse resembles hockey or soccer; teams score by getting their ball into the other guy's goal. During one game, Monica's coach benched their goalie, leaving their side undefended. Watching from the bleachers, the other parents and I had wondered aloud about the strange decision. Was there a problem? Was the goalie OK? Later, the coach explained to the team that he'd been trying to make a point: The goalie is your last line of defense. Don't saddle her with the full responsibility. Every person on the field needs to play a role in protecting the net.

I thought about that story as I contemplated national security. Too often, we treat the military like that lacrosse team treated its goalie. We focus on running after the ball (whether that be our careers, our hobbies, or other aspirations) and leave defense for "other people" to worry about. In today's environment, that's insufficient (if it were ever true). Every single player on Team America has a responsibility.

Not everyone can, or should, join the military or become a CIA agent. Playing a role in national security doesn't mean everyone becomes a goalie. A lot of other positions also need tending. The key is for everyone to be part of the team. That success begins with a common commitment to the outcome, a shared ownership of the game's final score. In this case, that means everyone contributing to our nation's stability, resilience, and readiness—but contributing in ways that go beyond our typical notions of volunteerism.

Usually, when we think about volunteering, it's as a contribution of unskilled labor, like driving meals to shut-ins or staffing the registration desk at a blood drive. Those kinds of contributions are laudable, but they're not the same as providing skilled talent. People can share their talents in a million ways, from volunteering with groups like Team Rubicon or the Red Cross to growing victory gardens or helping neighbors secure their Wi-Fi routers. As Laura Nadeau and her teachers highlighted, educators have a part to play, and as Bill Lytle showed me, there's also a critical role for connectors, for people who can transform others' individual contributions into a coordinated game plan. In other words, a national service strategy is about encouraging and empowering citizens to contribute, and importantly, it's also about combining the skilled capabilities, knowledge, and assets from across our nation into cohesive framework.

We have rich capabilities all over this country, but we've failed to harness the power of our people toward this end. We are squandering the treasures of our nation in the one place that they're most critical: in our safety and security and existential presence. As Lloyd Thrall, the former DASD, expressed: To become a ready nation we need the entire American experience—in uniform and out of uniform, in government and out of government—working hand-in-hand, bringing fresh thinking and multidimensional approaches to our nation's security and stability.

CHAPTER FOURTEEN

More than a Faster Horse

One of the most surreal experiences during my fifty-state tour happened in Hays, Kansas. I'd just passed the world's largest ball of twine and then pulled over for the night at an alpaca farm. (That's not the strange part yet.) Miles away from civilization, the farm offered free overnight parking along with a herd of fluffy companions to keep visitors company. Around 7:00 p.m., I heard a knock on my RV. Tentatively, I drew aside the curtain to investigate.

"Hi, I'm Terry," the stranger standing outside proclaimed affably. "I think we're related."

Curious, I grabbed my jacket and stepped outside. "What makes you think that?"

"I was driving by and saw your name on the camper," he explained. "You have the same last name as me—Walcutt."

Great, I thought, skeptical but still intrigued. *What are the odds?* Out loud I affected more patience, "What makes you think we're the same Walcutts? A lot of people have similar names."

"True," he agreed, "But most have surnames that are spelled correctly. Ours is misspelled."

In that moment, a nearly forgotten memory bubbled up. My husband, Chris, used to tell me a story about how his surname came from a Revolutionary War–era misspelling. For years, I harangued him about it. That fish story couldn't possibly be true.

"Back in the 1700s," Terry's wife, Deanna, was explaining, "one of our forefathers fought against the British in the War of Independence. He was honored for his service and received a handwritten commendation from George Washington himself—except Washington misspelled his name on it. So, rather than change the commendation letter, the family changed its name!"

Yep, that was Chris's story too. Unbelievable.

"We found most of this through one of those online sites," Deanna explained. "Here, I'll give you the information so you and your husband can look up the details."

There's so much knowledge at our fingertips today. In minutes, I can track down typos on three-hundred-year-old commendation letters or find the morning news from around the globe. And when my youngest daughter was born premature and critically ill, I was able to look up the latest medical findings on her unique condition (something I'm still convinced helped save her life). Information and communication technologies, not to mention all of the technical advancements in other sectors, have radically changed society.

Our lives today barely resemble those from a hundred years ago—let alone from the 1700s. Around the same time George Washington was misspelling letters, our modern concepts of education were being born in Prussia. Back then, the children would line up in desks, and a teacher would lecture or discipline them. The kids were largely expected to sit quietly, absorbing facts from their books and instructors—memorizing all the information they would need to become productive members of society. Fast-forward to today. In many ways, the modern classroom still resembles those Industrial Age schools. Modern students have left the one-room schoolhouse for different grade levels, and teachers use PowerPoint instead of chalkboards, but that classical design is still apparent.

If we envision a contemporary education system, free from the tyranny of its historical roots, what would it look like? That's a question I posed to my colleague Dr. Chris Dede, a seasoned education expert. Chris has a mop of white hair and wears thick-rimmed glasses. He looks characteristically professorial, which, of course, he is. He's an endowed professor at Harvard, where he focuses on learning technologies. I had a chance to talk with Chris earlier in my tour as I passed through Massachusetts. It didn't take much to convince him to agree to a video interview. He has a lot to say about modernizing learning.

"We're moving into an era where things are happening very fast, largely due to technology, globalization, social media, artificial intelligence, and the internet of things. So before we worry about changing the methods of education, we need to think about what we're educating for. I worry that in some ways we're preparing students to compete with artificial intelligence versus complement it. We're preparing John Henry to go up against the steam engine."

Chris and I had talked about all of this before; he was preaching to the converted, but for the sake of the interview's online viewers, he explained further.

"For example, students strive to do well on high-stakes tests like the SAT, the ACT, and the GRE. That's exactly the type of thing artificial intelligence does really well; it can score really high on standardized tests. What artificial intelligence doesn't do well, at least compared to people, is more on the creative side, the social and emotional side, the entrepreneurial side. So we need to think about a world where there's a kind of 'blended intelligence,' where artificial intelligence does the simpler things and that frees people to do the more complicated ones. People can only do those complicated things if they have the capacity, but our education system is still focused on teaching people to be really, really good at the simple things, which are not going to be part of the workplace."

I nodded my agreement. Chris has a way of explaining intricate ideas as if they were no more complex than his weekend plans.

To keep the conversation going, I asked, "What about the competency of thinking?"

"Yes, exactly! Even my graduate students at Harvard sometimes struggle with that. I have some students who are smart and dedicated (and I cherish them), but they've come straight through without any real-world experience, just moving up the academic food chain. They get into my class and are puzzled that I'm not doing what their other teachers have done. They come and talk to me about it. They're very polite, but basically what they're saying is, 'You're supposed to tell me the truth. I'm supposed to write it down and give it back to you, and then you're supposed to certify I'm a really smart person. That's what education is.'"

I laughed and nodded.

"Of course, the answer I give them is, 'Sure, I could do that, but what I'm doing is much more important. I'm teaching you how to figure out what's true versus simply accepting whatever someone tells you. I'm preparing you for life, which is based on figuring out uncertainty and complexity and coming up with new knowledge.'"

Chris's straightforward observation hid many implications below its surface. As he suggested, more than ever before, today's students need to think for themselves. Old Prussian-style information regurgitation won't cut it. In part, that's thanks to the increasing emphasis on knowledge work coupled with the fire-hose worth of new information the world produces every day. In part, it's also a reflection of our changing society. Everything around us, from the ways we order takeout to our core ideas about work, are shifting in response to our dynamic informational landscape.

Knowing Chris's work, I saw where this thread of discussion was going, so I prompted, "The country is changing dramatically, and in the future, people are going to have three to six careers—not just jobs but *careers*—across their lifetimes. That means we need to start looking at education not only as K-12, not only as the collegiate space or the trade space, but all the way through from early childhood to about the age of seventy-five." I drew my hand in an arc for emphasis.

Chris followed the thread of discussion I'd teed up for him. "So that leads me to the sixty-year curriculum concept," an idea the education faculty at Harvard have been refining for several years. "In mid-adolescence, we get serious about what our first job may be and really start to think about earning a living. This next generation is going to live into their nineties or beyond, so that means they'll need to work into their mid-seventies. That's six decades, and in those six decades they're not going to have just a single job or even a single career. And some of the careers don't exist yet, so you can't say, 'Why don't you prepare me in high school or college?'"

It's not just the next generation, I thought. In my own life, I'd been a therapist, an assistant professor, a stay-at-home mom, a military scientist, and a government program manager. Maybe I could add president to that list for my final hat trick?

Chris was still talking, "Education is set-up now so that we spend 95% percent of our time preparing people for their first job. Instead, we should be thinking about those six decades as a pipeline, and in school, we shouldn't just prepare people for their first job or their first career. Education should also make them flexible and entrepreneurial enough that they can handle the other careers that don't exist yet. That's a fundamental reconceptualization of what we've been doing in education so far."

If that's a reconceptualization, I thought, *then what's our current conceptualization?* I suppose that question is really asking, What's our philosophy of education as a nation? Do we have a collective notion about what education is meant to achieve? Has our concept of learning, let alone our nation's educational policies and practices, kept pace with the changing global landscape? Or, like a distracted driver, has the world shifted around us while our attention was pointed elsewhere?

I've asked a lot of people those kinds of questions. Some, like Chris Dede, have deep and thoughtful answers. Other times, though, it feels like the topic gets reduced to an oversimplified parody, focused on things like school lunches, classroom seating, and K-12 start times. Certainly, those are all necessary concerns, but I worry that federal-level educational leaders have become so fixated on those implementation details that they've forgotten to examine whether today's system is, fundamentally, still valid. In other words, we frequently ask if our education system is doing things right, but we rarely question whether it's still doing the right things.

That reminds me of a meeting I attended, hosted by the Florida Education Association, a massive labor union largely comprised of Florida's public-school teachers. They held it in one of those big conference hotels, and nearly a thousand people must have registered. I spotted some political folks, whom I'd seen around the state at other events, and there were business leaders, parents, and, of course, a lot of teachers. We all gathered in a transformed ballroom, sitting around circular tables and looking at a dais. The organizers did the usual welcome, and then the thematic sessions began.

One of those sessions involved a strategic thinking exercise—so fun! Each table had a slab of newsprint paper and a dozen pads of sticky notes. The organizers asked everyone to write down their ideas and then share them with their tablemates. Our group's question was, "How does education need to change for the twenty-first century?" I'd literally written the book on that question; it was the last thing I did before leaving my government job. So a lot of answers were already at the tip of my tongue—or, rather, at the tip of my pen as I jotted each idea onto a different Post-it.

When it came time to share, the others around my table talked about things like teachers' salaries, classroom supplies, and how state regulations constrain educators. Then they looked at my sticky notes, which said things like "implement lifelong education," "rethink assessment," and "incorporate social and emotional learning." The tone at our table shifted after that. We started to really talk about the future of learning, how our changing world needs different knowledge and skills, and how our comprehensive educational system—from preschool to professional development—ought to evolve.

The teachers sitting with me at that table easily joined the more strategic conversation that I'd prompted, but without my catalyzing comments, I think they would have stayed focused on those other, tactical-level issues. It's not like teachers' salaries or bussing schedules are unimportant. It's just that there are two levels to any problem. You need the tactical and strategic, and (as with health care or national security or any complex problem) it's important to start with the big-picture end in mind. And, at least for our educational system, that "end" probably looks a lot different from how most people envision it today.

One good thing about our education sector is it's filled with a lot of smart people and some of them have been working to define that vision of a modern learning enterprise. As part of my campaign research, I talked to several of these big brains, including Chris Dede and Aithan Shapira. There were a dozen others too, and every one of those interviews could have been its own feature-length documentary. To complement those experts, I took some scholarly field trips too.

In Michigan, for example, I visited The Henry Ford Museum of American Innovation. It sprawls across a manicured campus in Dearborn and includes a replica of Independence Hall. Ford founded it during his lifetime, with an eye toward fostering the next generation of American inventors and innovators. The museum still champions that mission, and as its chief of staff and chief learning officer explained to me, they've been expanding their efforts, looking toward entrepreneurialism and the larger talent pipeline. Of course, the educators at The Henry Ford aren't simply sitting on their laurels, waiting for interested future leaders to fall from the sky. They have dozens of programs across the state that reach out to kids and adults. They sponsor innovation challenges for high schoolers and bring experts together for whiteboarding events. The organization is eager to share its treasure trove of history and lessons in innovation.

The boarding school my son attended in Michigan is another great example. As part of my campaign research, I took the opportunity to visit his former high school and to interview one of his erstwhile teachers, Keith Aleo, head percussion instructor at the Interlochen Arts Academy. Truth be told, I stopped at Interlochen only partially for the sake of my political strategy; I also visited as a tribute to the academy. That school transformed my son. He not only learned to play music at a world-class level, but the education—like all good education—opened his mind. He lived and learned with kids from over fifty different countries and from nearly every US state. And I saw him blossom in that environment, growing confident and comfortable in his own skin.

The Henry Ford Museum and Interlochen Arts Academy are just two of the many bright spots of educational excellence scattered across our country. They're brilliant in their own backyards, but how do we connect all of those sparks of brilliance and expand them throughout our nation? How do we build these one-off programs into a more holistic shift across America's classrooms?

I posed that question to Dr. Jeff Borden, an education innovator with a resume spanning higher education and high school teaching along with learning-management companies and academic publishers. If anyone could talk about expanding educational innovation, it'd be him.

"I've worked in thirty-eight countries and in every state, except Alaska," Jeff began. "I've seen so many great ideas and so many ideas that could have worked—*if only*. If only *this* had happened or *that* had happened."

"What are some of the things you saw?"

"Avoid bureaucracy and politics!" he offered jokingly.

"Too late, there," I laughed.

He thought for a moment and continued, "At the national level, when we start looking at who controls the purse strings, where the money goes, and what people do with their money, there's not a lot of accountability across organizations. So you don't end up with a complete portfolio. Instead, you end up with a tremendous number of disparate solutions." He gestured with his hand for emphasis, bringing it up and down as he pointed toward imaginary programs and dubbed them, "disparate solution, disparate solution, disparate solution." Then he added, "And no one replicates them. Why?"

"How do we make that process shift?"

"I think when it comes to learning innovation there are a few things that need to start to take place. First of all, people need to start looking for the actual problem. Far too often, I think, we try to solve a symptom and not the root cause issue."

"That's logical," I agreed. "The first step is to figure out what works, and then the next is to figure out how those working solutions can multiply."

Jeff nodded. "We need somebody at the architect level looking across programs and saying, 'That's working,' or 'That's growing,' or 'Let's bring some of these projects together.'"

"The challenge," I posed, "is doing that at the national level with so many different states, accreditation bodies, and policies. So how do we bring it to scale?"

"I'm a big fan of the incubator concept. Put a little bit of money and resources toward them, and use the resources we have (the time, money, energy, and effort) to grow ideas within a particular group, like community colleges. Then start architecting how those subsystems connect to one another."

It all sounded painfully logical. Of course, from the fifty-thousand-foot level, it is. The problem, Jeff seemed to be saying, is that no one is looking at the educational system from that perspective. Instead, most of its actors are operating down in the weeds, necessarily tending to their own backyards but without the benefit of someone at a higher tier orchestrating across those segments.

Jeff continued, confirming my musings, "It's interesting because higher education really is open to share almost anything, with almost anybody, but they rarely have the right conversations. People rarely ask the right questions, and, again, you don't have an architect trying to bring these ideas together. Instead, we have a bunch of people sitting on the sidelines."

"So what's the solution for that?" I nudged.

"I think the punchline is: We need an architect."

The new school year began around the middle of my tour. My youngest was starting second grade, while my two older children were preparing for college. My son would be returning to his studies in New York, and my daughter was planning to attend the Rochester Institute of Technology. This marked Mitchell's junior year at the Manhattan School of Music, and he didn't need—or want—his mother trailing him to it. Monica, on the other hand, was beginning her freshman year, so I flew to meet her in Rochester as she settled into the freshman dorm. While in town, I also took the opportunity to interview the school's president, Dr. David C. Munson Jr.

The day we met, David sported the university-chic look: reading glasses, a button-up shirt, and an open blazer sans tie. During our chat, he alternated between steepling his long fingers and gesturing gently for emphasis. During the interview, I'd expected David would highlight the school's technology programs in areas like physics, computer science, and engineering. (*Technology* is part of the school's name, after all.) Instead, as the camera clicked on, he turned the conversation in another direction.

He started with his childhood. "As a youngster, I did two things: music and math. A lot of brains work that way. When I got into college, I didn't know what I wanted to study, but I eventually chose electrical engineering and ended up pursuing a PhD at Princeton. After that, I taught at the University of Illinois—minding my own business as a regular professor for twenty-four years. Eventually, I moved to the University of Michigan where I chaired the Electrical Engineering and

Computer Science Department for three years and was the dean of engineering for ten. Then I decided to move to the Rochester Institute of Technology. It really combines my passions for technology and the arts—that combination drew me."

He explained a bit more, "Arts are more than just something to look at or listen to or a hobby to do on a Saturday afternoon. For a lot of people, they're fully integrated throughout our lives, and within a university, they ought to be integrated into the research, mission, and education. The arts shouldn't be just standalone conservatories."

I thought about my own grown children: one focused on musical studies and the other engrossed in cybersecurity computing. Two fields that seem radically dissimilar. Yet around the dinner table, my kids often have these deep technical discussions, even though they're at either ends of the supposed art-and-technology divide.

David shared an anecdote, one of his own personal epiphanies on the matter. "I had an experience some years ago, when I was active in musical theater. I was at the dress rehearsal for a show, which is usually a bit of a disaster. Somehow it has to pull together for the very next night, and the person critical to this is the stage manager. The stage manager knows every aspect of that production, from the mics and audio to the lighting, blocking, sets, and everything else. Stage managers make the magic happen because they understand the whole system. When I saw what that person did, all I could think of was a systems engineer. Suppose you're working for an engineering company, and they're designing a new satellite communication system. You've got to worry about the design of the satellite, the launch, and its functions later on. It's so complicated, and the person who coordinates all those components is the systems engineer. A systems engineer and a stage manager have the same job—but they don't know it! A lot of the arts and the technologies overlay one another like that."

David's point, as our conversation continued, wasn't merely to highlight the similarities between artistic and technical fields. Rather, he emphasized their synergistic connections, how one bolsters and deepens the other.

"We haven't traditionally looked at arts education as a required space," I observed. "We've worried about our reading and our math and our writing—"

"Yes, it's been a 'nice to have,'" David interjected.

"But the way you're describing it, it sounds like a necessity."

"Well, I think it is," he agreed.

"In government," I posed, "we talk a lot about automation and how it will affect the future of work. Creativity, meta-skills, and all of those human pieces are going to be even more important. So beyond the benefits we get from the arts today, we'll need them tied into business and technology even more in the future. And education will have to evolve accordingly. What are the steps to get there, if you had to narrow them down to one or two?"

"As a first step . . . " he considered, "Would it be too obvious if I were to say, sitting here at a school oriented toward science and technology, that I think we need some base level of literacy among the general population in science and technology? That doesn't mean everybody needs to be a computer scientist or an engineer or whatever. That's not the point. The point is to be aware and have some understanding. A second thing I would probably mention is that we're tremendously undervaluing the humanities and the social sciences."

He paused for a moment. "Let me ask you this, if you think about who you'd want to help you predict the future, who would you consult? Who would you ask to help you understand the implications of a new technology? Sure, you'd have some technologists in the room, but I think you'd also have some psychologists and political scientists and historians. So I think the social sciences and humanities are incredibly important for our future for that reason as well as for their other contributions around our lives."

Yesterday's schools aren't as relevant nowadays. To be ready for the future (hell, even to be ready for the present day), young people need a broader and richer set of competencies. No one cares whether today's high-school graduate has encyclopedic factual knowledge when even the dullest among us has Wikipedia. Access to online encyclopedias is just the start, of course; technology has propelled countless changes to our society. We live in a faster, noisier world than ever before, filled with deepfakes and robots and AI, oh my! I'm pretty sure Prussia's educators never imagined any of that.

While I still worked for the government, I published a scholarly book about modernizing our nation's education system, not simply for children or for our workforce, but across the board as a big integrated enterprise.[1] Around ninety subject-matter experts helped to create that strategy, bringing together perspectives from industry, government, K-12 schools, colleges, and universities. The resulting four-hundred-page book outlined the reconceptualization of education that Chris Dede had mentioned. It talked about things like lifelong learning and twenty-first-century competencies, and it dealt with specialized topics such as artificial intelligence in education and contemporary theories of instructional design. (I promise not to delve into those details here!) But for all of its length and analysis, the book didn't venture into politics or the design of particular federal programs.

So while I already had solid notions about educational reform, as I considered it from a presidential perspective, new questions arose. First among them was: Why are most educational programs still stuck in an outdated model? Places like The Henry Ford or Interlochen Arts Academy are breaking that antiquated mold, and thousands of people have already reimagined the nature of learning and development. Clearly, it can be done. And across scattered silos of excellence, it is being done. Yet walk into an elementary classroom or college seminar, and more often than not, you'll still find teachers and students emulating Industrial Age schools. What gives?

I knew the issue wasn't technical, because in addition to those exemplars of excellence and thoughtful strategic plans, we also have tons of scholarly research on educational reform. Our own Department of Education has supported a good chunk of it, including two seminal works named *How People Learn I* and *II*.[2] The government has already done its homework. Unfortunately, at a federal level, those papers often just sit untouched on the shelf—at least untouched by US government executives.

As my tour passed through Tennessee, I'd had an opportunity to interview Dr. Xiangen Hu, a professor at the University of Memphis. We discussed his work in learning science and educational technologies, but we also talked about the differences between American and Chinese educational systems. Xiangen emigrated from China more than thirty years ago, but he still serves as a mentor for learning science students and junior faculty members at a Chinese University. So he has a unique perspective.

Xiangen told me about a Chinese experimental program to build the high-tech classroom of the future, and we discussed learning technologies. I was surprised to later discover how much Chinese programs are leveraging US government investments in that sector. China is voraciously pursuing educational innovation. It reportedly spends more than 4.6 trillion yuan (or around $685 billion in US dollars) every year on education,[3] and that doesn't count the extra money Chinese parents pour into their kids' extracurricular studies, an average of more than $17,000 a year per family.[4] Compare those numbers to how much China spends annually on national defense, around $240 billion,[5] and you get a sense of its strategic priorities.

China is just one example. Plenty of other nations also invest more in the modernization of their educational systems than we seemingly do, and those investments are often built upon the foundations we've sponsored. While other nations are seizing the opportunity to update their educational infrastructures, we can't find traction for those same ideas in our own federal government—who funded a lot of the research. We're paying the price to mine those valuable gems of innovation but failing to capitalize on our own intellectual wealth. As a result, we not only risk falling out of step with modern educational needs, but we also risk being left behind globally.

As I worked on my campaign's platform, one question came up time and again, posed by a lot of the folks I talked with on the street. "Why in the hell do we have a federal education program?" they'd more or less ask. "We've got the state. We've got the community. What are those swamp things in Washington adding?" (OK, I may have invented the "swamp thing" pejorative, but I think it was implied.) Anyhow, there's a good reason for the federal government to care about education. It comes back to that strategic versus tactical model.

State and local organizations need to focus on tactical issues: Are we doing things right? The federal level ought to have its eye on the other question: Are we doing the right things? The Department of Education shouldn't be telling teachers how to do their jobs or micromanaging pay for public schools. Alternatively, individual programs, and even individual states, aren't likely to design (or fund) the big-picture strategy. Or, if they do, without a unifying center of gravity, we risk replicating those efforts fifty times or more.

So the federal government has a vital part to play, and the Department of Education already works with some pretty smart strategists. I found faculty, teachers unions, military programs, Chamber of Commerce businesses, vocational trainers, and many others who want reform, but politicians are slow to support it. I don't think they're unwilling to change, but they've lost sight of that bigger picture. They're trying instead to patch the tactical-level gaps in our stagnant system, and they're wielding the one tool politicians love best: allocating money. Take ideas like free college for all, for example. Putting aside whether or not that would work from a policy perspective, I wonder if any politicians have asked whether a traditional two- or four-year degree is even the right model for national education? Have they thought about microcredentials, intelligent tutoring systems, or vocational apprenticeships? Perhaps they have. Then again, maybe they're unintentionally reinforcing a model of education from George Washington's lifetime.

As Henry Ford purportedly quipped about the automobile, "If I had asked people what they wanted, they would have said faster horses."[6] We don't need to invest in our old educational horse; we need a new way of conceptualizing the system. The vision of reform is already inked, and sparks of brilliance have already incubated around the country (and the world). We're simply waiting for that educational architect who can implement the blueprint that pulls it all together.

CHAPTER FIFTEEN

ʻOhana

Labor Day marked the third full month of my #Tour50 adventure, so I stashed my wheels in long-term parking and flew home for a few days to recharge over the holiday weekend. Before that mini-vacation I'd been on edge, quick to emotion and bone-weary. One of the many things this campaign has taught me is that I'm not a quintessential politician. They feed on extraverted energy. Me, on the other hand, I need to recharge after being social—and the campaign forced me to be social all the damn time. I wasn't just collecting interviews and asking people voter-on-the-street questions. I also had to tend my social media and be "on" pretty much constantly. Even when I was just pumping gas or connecting my RV's power lines, someone was always there to talk with me. (That speaks wonders for civil engagement, but it didn't charge my social batteries.) Running on empty, my solution was to visit home and spend some lazy days wearing yoga pants and snuggling with my family on the couch.

Later that week, I emerged refreshed and ready to restart my cross-country expedition. By now, I'd made it to my thirty-first state: Wyoming. I drove for ages in the Cowboy State, rolling along a nearly deserted highway that stretched across a barren grassland. It sometimes felt like I was the last person on Earth. I passed through Lusk, a town that couldn't have had more than one stoplight, and then pressed on to Laramie. My cousins live nearby, so I made a small detour to visit.

On a rainy afternoon, I pulled my campaign-mobile up to their one-story house. They live at the end of a cul-de-sac in a neighborhood where all of the pitched-roof houses press tightly against one another and the streets are more dirt than asphalt. As I splooshed down from the camper into their soggy lawn, my relatives greeted me.

The parents, Cathy and Jim, are both cresting senior-citizen status, and their daughter Libby, who's about my age, lives with them. Libby pilots a wheelchair and competes in the Special Olympics, and except for her wheels, she resembles her mom, both sturdy women with pale blond hair and thick glasses. Before he retired, Jim was a farmer, and when we met that September day, he sported denim overalls that wouldn't have looked out of place working the land.

I'd planned the day as a family visit, a social call where we'd swap cheerful stories about our mutual relations, but once I arrived, everyone seemed eager to talk politics. I was happy to oblige but hadn't expected it. Not only is there a strong vein of straight-ticket red in my family, but my family is also unaccustomed to active political involvement. Nonetheless, despite the novelty of being connected to a politician, they've all been supportive in their own ways. Cathy, in particular, engaged early, reliably following my campaign videos, liking my Facebook posts, and reading my monthly strategies.

So in the spirit of unconventional family gatherings, we leapt into the classically taboo subjects of politics and partisanship. We talked about how popular culture affects people's perspectives and about how difficult it is to have differing opinions within a family. Like so many folks I've met across the fifty states, my relatives felt frustrated by the political climate. They worried about biased news outlets and unconstrained social media concocting different bubbles of "truth," and they fretted about how politics has become a wedge, dividing brothers and sisters and, in some cases, overpowering those longstanding bonds of friendship and blood. Sadly, I had no answers to soothe their fears. Instead, I shared stories collected from my travels, like the man whose own mother hung up on him when she discovered he's a registered Democrat or the woman who wouldn't share a holiday meal with her family because she disagreed so fundamentally with their political beliefs. In every state, I heard accounts like that, a growing litany of examples exposing our political-familial divide.

After Wyoming, I dipped into Colorado where I'd reserved a couple days to spend writing and strategizing with colleagues. We pulled out the whiteboards and brainstormed about my campaign. I was in geek heaven. Like family, the best kinds of friends and coworkers help lift and energize you. In this case, my colleagues gave me the mental pick-me-up I needed, filling my nerd energy bar in a way that complemented the relief my family had provided.

Next, the campaign trail took me into Utah. I stayed a night in Price before driving on to Provo and Salt Lake City. There, I spent a day taking in the state capital. Like so many before me, I felt the magnetic draw of Temple Square, the heart of the city and the Church of Jesus Christ of Latter-day Saints. It looks like something from a fantasy movie, with its gleaming white-and-gold buildings and picture-perfect landscaping.

I'd been reading the Book of Mormon, and at home, several of my neighbors follow the LDS Church teachings. I was respectfully curious and intellectually inquisitive. While the public isn't permitted into events at the Temple, I was able to observe a service at the adjacent Meetinghouse, essentially a community chapel. I went inside to watch quietly from the wings.

I eased into one of the annex's wooden pews then turned my attention toward the service. The atmosphere felt more relaxed than the Methodist or Lutheran churches I'd experienced. The families were demonstratively affectionate, sitting closely with their spouses, with arms around shoulders or hands in hands. The children played quietly throughout the congregation; some sat in groups on the pews, and a cluster sprawled on the floor, apparently coloring in books. A few moms sat on the floor too, doting warmly on their little ones. In a word, it seemed comfortable.

The Mormon culture and doctrine teach traditional family values. They emphasize conjugal marriage, meaning a union between a man and a woman with a strong emphasis on raising children. The church also encourages traditional gender roles: women should nurture their children, support their husbands, and, ideally, stay at home to tend to their domestic duties.[1] I've met plenty of people quick to disparage those values, but sitting there, in the glow of the Salt Lake Temple, watching cozy families take part in their faith, I had to wonder, *Isn't it possible some people, both women and men, enjoy the comfort of their culture and traditional roles?* If it works for them, who am I (or anyone) to judge? Certainly, those boundaries become a cage if someone's unable to choose freely, whether pressured directly or by other means, but setting aside those cases, when someone has the option and chooses a particular way of life, even one so different from my own, I'm all for it. The trick, for any of us, is knowing what to choose.

When my first child was born, I tried the stay-at-home mom gig. I married at the age of twenty-one, just after graduating from college, and was pregnant soon after. I'd always wanted to become a mom and, growing up, had pictured myself staying at home, raising a family, and minding the house. After Mitchell was born, though, I soon discovered that being a stay-at-home mom (eventually of two) is one of the hardest jobs in the world—at least for me. I'm a terrible cook, and while I despise clutter, I hate cleaning even more. (This is likely thanks to years spent cleaning commercial toilets alongside my dad on weekends, a tactic that successfully discouraged any aspirations I might have had of becoming a janitor!) As a new mom, I adored my spirited toddlers, but I found the daily monotony at home mind-numbing. I crave challenge and achievement, and little did I know at that age, I love complex problem solving, which, it turns out, wasn't something my mommy groups were particularly interested in hearing about. To assuage my mental energy, I'd decided to enroll in graduate courses at the local university. They satiated my need for nerdy conversation and mental puzzle solving. As strange as it may sound, classes like parametric statistics and mental health counseling offered the release valve I needed from my meandering mommy life. So I kept taking courses, and then I started doing research studies, and eventually I ended up with a PhD (something my younger self had never intended to pursue).

Throughout my life, I've experienced a lot of roles: stay-at-home mom, single mother, and full-time working parent. At one time or another, I've pretty much tried every mommy archetype in the book. Thanks to that, I've gained some appreciation of the different options, and I feel particularly protective of our stay-at-home parents. I've talked to hundreds of people who see it as the pinnacle of their lives, people who swell with the love and fulfillment it brings. What a beautiful way to live, if it works for you.

Professionals in clinical psychology have a saying, "Don't 'should' all over yourself." In other words, don't get lost in what someone says you *should* do, following some custom or outside expectation. A lot of women, especially in my generation, are torn between the traditions of our mothers and the iconoclasm of our daughters. Should moms strive to be someone like June Cleaver? Should we try to "lean in" to professional ambition? Or should we try to play all the roles, adjusting our outward demeanors to whatever the situation demands? At some point in my life, I've tried all of those personas, and despite that wealth of experience, I still don't know what a woman or mom *should* be. I'm still figuring it out myself.

After my visit to Utah, I traveled to Idaho, stopping for the night in Pocatello, a mountain town seemingly ripped from the 1920s. It's not what you'd call a tourist destination. Still, its scenery is tourism worthy. Around the city, the countryside looks like one of Van Gogh's landscapes, with colorful rolling hills and perfectly dappled trees. Mountains frame the area, and with the sky filled by fluffy white clouds, the town feels cocooned against the world, as if it were its own private snow globe. Inside that bubble, Pocatello's residents seem to have adopted a slower lifestyle.

I hadn't scheduled any interviews or fact-finding field trips for the day;

instead, I spent the morning at a local coffee shop, just soaking in the unhurried pace and taking time to contemplate my strategies. Later, I politely asked one of the locals, a clerk of some kind at the nearby supermarket, how I should spend my time if I wanted to get a feel for the town. She pointed me toward a dry-cleaning business where the town's celebrity, a former state beauty queen, works. ("Former," in this case, means she won her crown over three decades ago.) My impromptu tour guide also recommended I visit the Museum of Clean, which boasts a collection of more than five hundred vacuum cleaners and a range of exhibits with names like "toilet collection" and "garden of clean." A part of me felt like I was paying homage to my dad and all those childhood weekends spent "bonding" over our janitorial conquests.

After a rejuvenating and hygienic day in Idaho, I drove northward, taking the opportunity to visit Yellowstone for the first time. If nothing else, this fifty-state tour has cemented my appreciation of our national parks. Yellowstone is as breathtaking as the hype implies; burbling streams run along the path, and wildlife bustles all around. I saw herds of grazing bison, which I've been instructed ought to be pronounced as "bi-zon" (with a *zee* sound) and shouldn't be confused with buffalo (an entirely different species). I stayed overnight near the park, and even though it was only mid-September, by the next morning a thin sheet of frost covered the landscape. Between the remoteness and cold, the world seemed locked in quiet.

Breaking the silence, I restarted my RV and ventured farther north into Bozeman, a sleepy but seemingly affluent town in southwestern Montana. It has a remarkable mix of homespun charm and contemporary engineering. A lot of the buildings have this particular aesthetic called mountain modern. It's black steel beams and gaping picture windows mashed up with rough-hewn stone and rustic flair. I think it's my favorite architectural style in the country.

Much of my extended family lives nearby, which gave my mom and youngest daughter a good excuse to fly in and for my aunt and her grown daughter to meet us in town. As a family-fun activity, we spent the day shopping. Every girl loves shopping, right? Sadly, as a failed feminine stereotype, it's not for me, but everyone else enjoyed it, especially Maddie, my little fashionista in the making.

After a few days in Bozeman and Missoula, my mom, Maddie, and I took

Interstate 90 into Washington State. We stopped in Spokane, where my mom had studied as a young woman. She reminisced about her younger days as we strolled along the riverside, Maddie walking hand-in-hand between us. During the walk, we visited some of Spokane's more peculiar destinations.

By this point in my campaign, I'd begun to see certain patterns across communities. One of the strangest trends has got to be the sheer volume of curious street-side statues. Are all the small towns secretly competing for the weirdest roadside sculpture? Spokane's entries into that competition included an enormous Radio Flyer wagon (only a two out of ten on the weird scale) and a metal goat statue that "eats" garbage thanks to vacuum suction (definitely a contender for the weird award). Naturally, we visited these distinguished attractions, and I added them to my mental tally of artwork oddities.

The next day, my mom and Maddie flew back to Florida while I drove to Seattle by way of Mount Saint Helens. Once in the Emerald City, I visited my extended in-laws, Alex and Lillian Adacutt. Alex is my nephew by marriage. He used to be a Walcutt, but he and Lillian merged their last names when they married. The couple is close to my son's age, and when we met, they were wearing what I mentally picture to be the requisite attire of the Pacific Northwest. Alex sported a blue hoodie, a shade darker than his cerulean-colored hair. Lillian wore a brown flannel shirt that happened to match her own shoulder-length fringe, and although it wasn't obvious at that time, Lillian was pregnant with the couple's first child. As we chatted, the conversation naturally turned toward the forthcoming baby and their plans to raise the newborn gender neutral.

"What made you decide to do that?" I asked.

"I don't think we had a culminating point where we decided to do the gender-neutral thing," Lillian reflected. "I think we've always just been on that page. We have a lot of friends who are trans or who question their gender identity, and we know people who say they're nonbinary. I think you see a lot of that in Seattle. More than that, it just makes sense. You know, calling a kid a 'pretty, pretty princess' or saying, 'Oh look, this little guy is so strong and tough,' it just seems pointless. At the same time, I know people will still buy clothes of all different varieties, and I plan to throw this kid in whatever people hand me!" she added with a playful laugh.

I smiled too and then fabricated a mask of seriousness. "One more question, and it's really important," I cautioned. Lillian and Alex waited attentively.

"Chris and I have decided that since we're the new baby's great-aunt and great-uncle, we think we should be called 'grantie' and 'grumpy.' Chris totally loses on that one!" Everyone dutifully snickered at my dad joke (or grantie joke).

"But then I realized," I continued lightheartedly, "if you're raising the baby gender neutral, what name do we use? Great-niece and great-nephew are both gendered, so I need a term!"

Lillian parried, "I've heard my sister say, 'I can't wait to meet my nibling—you know, like *sibling* but with a *n*.'"

The skepticism must have shown on my face.

"I don't know how sold I am on that," Lillian deflected, "but it's a starting point."

Amazingly, that linguistic puzzle seems to be the biggest barrier in my relatives' unique childrearing plans. It's a testament to the modern world that that's their only major stumbling block.

After I bid farewell to Alex and Lillian, I reflected on the day and then the last couple of weeks. What a dramatic contrast to go from the orthodox lifestyle of Temple Square to the unconventional humanism of northern Washington. Those two microcosms are so dissimilar, yet, I reflected, they seem to share a similar core. In Salt Lake City, I saw families focused on warmth and who built a bedrock of tradition meant to safeguard and strengthen their households. In Seattle, I saw the same sentiments but expressed as a boundless love, dedication to ideological freedom, and protection of the child's future choices. In some ways, the two are poles apart, yet they can still both exist in our nation and still both be right for different families. Interestingly, those two paths sort of reflect the mantras of our major political parties—stability and tradition versus freedom and choice. Perhaps, like our motley family values, we can find a way to harmonize and acknowledge all of those ideals.

Early the next morning, I left my RV and boarded a flight bound for the Last Frontier. It touched down mid-morning at the Anchorage airport. Robert had been scouring the interweb for possible campaign activities in Alaska, and he'd stumbled onto a listing for a federal funding workshop sponsored by the Administration for Native Americans. Governmental processes *and* local culture—sign me up! But there was a snag: That event wasn't open to the public. Only tribal representatives could attend. Fortunately, Robert had reached out to the organizers, and they'd graciously agreed to let me sit-in as an observer. So after the plane landed, I changed clothes in the airport restroom and then rushed off to the event.

The organizers had rented a meeting room at a local hotel, one of those midgrade chains that all feel the same. When I arrived, I found a handful of attendees mingling around the seminar tables and the workshop's facilitators prepping near the front. Throughout the space, they'd hung sheets of blank paper, and the tables were covered with notebooks, Post-its, and colorful pens. By the time the meeting began, about fifteen people had checked in, a smattering of both men and women. They ranged from fresh-faced twentysomethings to senior citizens, and their clothes were an assortment, spanning a generous definition of business casual. Despite that variety, everyone seemed to share a common lineage, each with similarly tawny skin and coal-black hair.

Predictably, I was the novelty in the room, an East Coast politician visiting their community event. During the breaks, the workshop attendees curiously approached me, asking questions about my time in DC or telling me about issues their tribes are facing. During one of these chance encounters, an older gentleman invited me to an event that night.

"You should come," he urged. "It's traditional tribal drumming. We do it every week at the medical center, and it really lifts people up. We bring our families and our drummers, of course, and it's an energizing experience for them and the patients."

How could I refuse? So later that evening, I found myself at the Alaska Native Medical Center. Even from the parking lot, I could hear the percussion. It sounded like a steady four-beat pattern, built upon the sharp thwack of a wide handheld drum and intermixed with chanting in a language I didn't recognize. Inside, I found a room filled to nearly bursting. Whatever furniture had been there before had been moved aside and, in its place, were people of all ages and sizes, from sprightly toddlers to wheelchair-bound octogenarians. Around the room, I saw families, partners, pregnant women, and breastfeeding moms. A handful of drummers sat in a semicircle near the room's center, and around them people danced or, in some cases, simply swayed, to the enthusiastic cadence. I spotted one little girl, who couldn't have been more than three years old, eagerly mimicking the choreographed movements, and less than an arm's length away, a burly man crouched on his knees, expertly moving his arms to the beat.

Standing closer to the periphery, I carefully approached some of the people nearby. Many were delighted to talk.

"I love this," one man in a button-up shirt and eyeglasses shared. "I love the fact that everybody's sitting here in a caring and curing environment, passing on culture, and . . . " He paused and looked back over the thrumming crowd, "And having a beautiful time."

"Where else you gonna find this?" he asked with a shrug and shake of his head. "Not in Oklahoma. Not in Chicago. Not New York. Come to A-K, baby!"

Then he encouraged me to get into the heart of the throng. The dance moves weren't too difficult to follow; the repetitive moves reminded me a little of country line dancing. So I gave it a shot. Smiling the entire time, I stretched my arms this way and that, following the lead of the crowd around me. I could feel the vitality in a personal, pit-of-my-gut sort of way. Even as a stranger, I felt that flicker of connection to the community and this tribal family. Seeing all of those happy faces and feeling the affection so palpable in the room, I couldn't help but think of my own family, now thousands of miles away. I missed them, and a sizable part of me wished they could have been there with me, laughing and dancing at that Alaskan jubilee.

What does it mean to have family values, community, or kith and kin? If you'd asked me before my nationwide tour, I'd have had a ready response. Now I'm surer of my feelings but less certain of how to answer—because there is no answer. At least, not one that works for everyone. The closest, most universal idea I've found comes from the Hawaiian culture's concept of *'ohana*. It means "family" in the broadest sense—relatives, friends, and neighbors—and I saw it in action when I visited Oʻahu the week after my time in Alaska. I'd scheduled an interview with a couple who own a software consultancy. The discussion was supposed to inform my economics strategy (and it did), but more than that, it shone a light on Hawaiian family values. Right from the start, Chuck and Anne-Marie Lerch focused on *'ohana,* emphasizing how committed they felt to structuring their business around it, which meant making room for everyone's family priorities as well as fostering a sense of connectedness in their workplace. Within my own life—and campaign—I've tried to adopt something similar.

When I first told my parents about my political plans, they weren't all that surprised. (I've been oddly precocious since my rug-rat days.) Of course, both of them offered to help. Mom lent a hand with Maddie, and Dad joined my Geek

Team. He came to all of our meetings and provided, in his own words, the "old-man Republican" perspective. It always added color to things. As it came time to kick off my campaign, my dad and I decided to take our polarizing discussions to social media. Just about every week during the tour, we made a video blog related to my monthly strategy focus. We looked, in particular, for topics likely to have different generational or partisan perspectives, things like women in the military and health care rights.

Before each vlog, my dad would poll his buddies at the lodge or the veterans club then bring their ideas into our conversation. After each video, he'd go back and talk to his friends. In my mind, I would imagine them standing around the canteen, beers in hand, bent over my dad's phone scrutinizing the video playback like a curious old-man book club. How ever it actually happened, I know they watched and discussed, because the next week I'd get follow-up questions, and in a few cases, some of his friends even donated. Each time, whoever was sending the money would invariably point out that he'd never before contributed to a Democrat.

My dad and I definitely uncovered some philosophical rifts. For instance, I remember when we were talking about people's distrust of police and at one point he observed, "I don't see what the problem is. I always feel safe." Naturally, my dad saw the issue through his own experiences, through the lens of his sleepy Florida coast retirement community. But what about someone from a different walk of life? When I nudged him to consider alternative perspectives, my dad was quick to revise his statement and acknowledge others' experiences. For my own part, one of the nuggets I took away from our conversations is that there's an undercurrent of anxiety among many in the older generations. My dad and his friends worried about what progressive ideas might mean for the nation, things like: Will those policies threaten their health, wealth, and lifestyles? Will new laws unmake what their parents and grandparents had built? Are their retirements safe?

My dad and I were able to talk through all of that unspoken baggage, almost like a joint therapy session. Change is hard, and for those benefiting from the status quo, it's even harder. But that doesn't mean we should allow ourselves to stagnate. So we examined policy and government through each other's eyes. In that light, we achieved a kind of both-ness: We weren't trying to win an argument or change one another's perspective. We were just trying to consider solutions from a two-way street. Ultimately, it worked because we realized that neither of us were advocating to take away someone's nest egg or destroy people's lives. We both just wanted to find solutions, and we approached them from a foundation of trust and mutual respect.

Those bipartisan conversations stand in stark contrast to the politics as usual stereotype, with its snappy sound bites and winner-takes-all precepts. Once you take the partisanship out of the political solutions, though, there's actually a lot of common ground. Healthy families might squabble, and most surely, they disagree, but hopefully, those differences don't undercut their affection for one another. That trust and attachment forms the bedrock for solutions. Ultimately, we're all part of a national family. When we allow party affiliation to take precedence over our shared national identity, it's counterproductive, at best. Instead, if we each embrace a little *'ohana,* if we each take a step toward that mutual understanding, we can begin to design the pathway forward.

CHAPTER SIXTEEN

A Dummy's Guide to Fundraising (Badly)

I'd just settled in at an RV park, a quiet campground nestled against a lazy river, and had struck up a conversation with my neighbor. He was a retired Soldier, and we bonded over our shared military connections. After a few minutes, as always happens, he asked about the curious signage on the side of my RV, and our conversation turned to my campaign.

"I'm trying to fundraise," I eventually shared with a grumble, "and I'm not excited about it."

"Yeah," he agreed, "I hate politicians! All they ever want is your money."

"You're not wrong," I soothed, "but what do you think we should do about it?"

By now, this was a conversation I'd had a thousand times. Invariably, it goes something like this: The exasperated person complains about all of the political panhandling, and then I explain the participation rules involving minimum donation amounts and how hard it is to get onto a ballot without sufficient funds. I ask them to think through all of the valid campaign expenses like renting spaces for town halls or traveling to events. Then I usually ask, "So should we only leave politics to the independently wealthy or the partisan drones?"

"Well, no," they always respond. "But we need people who don't care about money." Sometimes they're even kind enough to flatter, "We need someone like you: a regular person, not a career politician."

"You're right," I usually say, "someone has to step up and fix the system." To which, they can't help but agree. "Of course," I continue, "to be in that position you have to get into the system first, and at least for now, there's only one way. So if you're not donating to that 'regular person' or to some other candidate who's better than the least-worse option, then you're letting other people decide for you. By the time you get to the ballot box, money has already determined your set of choices. Until we change those rules, we've got to play by them, at least minimally."

"You're right," people usually concede, but that doesn't seem to matter. Their logical minds may be swayed but their pocketbooks remain securely fastened.

I hate fundraising. Any normal human finds it anxiety provoking. As soon as you ask people for money, they inherently distrust you. Even your friends start to wonder if you're only after their piggybanks. But I'd already turned my back on the traditional approach, working with the partisan machine and kowtowing to its kingmakers, so I needed to figure out how to raise funds by myself. It's an essential part of today's political game.

Before my campaign, I'd studied other candidates' shticks. I saw plenty of fundraising events, some good and some "other." I started at the local level, and more often than not those candidates were terrible fundraisers. From what I could tell, they poured more personal funds into their campaigns than they ended up recouping. One example that sticks out involved a gentleman running for the state's House of Representatives. He'd organized a happy hour at a local bar and brought in a beautiful spread of heavy hors d'oeuvres. Between the bar and buffet table, someone had set up two speakers and a microphone, and about halfway through the gathering, the candidate used them for a short speech. Not a terrible plan on paper, but (I found out later) the venue had charged him a $1,500 bar minimum. Worse still, only two dozen people showed, and most of them seemed related to the budding politician. He must have shelled out hundreds of dollars, and I doubt he gained any new followers.

Of course, plenty of politicians have figured out the art of fundraising. Two good examples come to mind. First, I attended an event hosted by a woman running for the local school board. That's a nonpartisan position, which likely helped. She also wisely held the event at a community pizzeria and asked every attendee to pay a small cover (around fifteen dollars), which also came with a slice of cheese and a glass of wine. The pizza joint only served what was ordered, so she probably pocketed a few hundred dollars from the forty or so people who showed up.

The second exemplar comes from a long-time senator. His son hosted a meet-and-greet. Ostensibly, it was open to the public, but to attend you needed to RSVP with a donation, ideally meeting one of the recommended benchmarks like a hundred dollars for students or three-hundred and fifty for early-career professionals. After that, would-be attendees received an e-mail with the fundraiser's location. When they arrived, visitors were greeted by a campaign volunteer sitting at a small table and wielding a cash register. He verified their contributions and recorded each attendee's contact details (to be sure the campaign could follow up with more donation requests in the future). Inside, the senator's fundraiser was packed; over a hundred people had squeezed into his son's row house. Like the state representative's fundraiser that I'd attended at the bar, this one offered hors d'oeuvres and drinks. The senator's snacks were more modest, though, and instead of a fully staffed bar, he served six-dollar bottles of Kirkland-brand wine. The senator's campaign clearly knew how to organize these things. I heard they made more than fifty-thousand dollars that night. Of course, he was a career politician and an incumbent. People inherently want to hobnob with those already in power. That was just one of the many advantages he held as compared to your average political hopeful. So while his event had been useful to see, it wasn't necessarily something I could replicate. The senator held a lot of cards that I just couldn't play.

In the years leading up to my presidential run, I saw a lot of campaign events, from black-tie galas and cozy dinner parties to bizarre open houses and partisan after-parties. After I'd plunged the depths of that market research, the next step was to become legal. Before I could start begging for money for my own campaign, I needed to learn the official rules.

I studied everything I could find about campaign finance and fundraising regulations. It wasn't easy, but I'll spare you all of the false starts and confusing rabbit holes. The first step begins with the Federal Election Commission. Federal candidates have to register with the FEC. Then they need to incorporate a campaign committee, a special nonprofit organization that can accept and manage campaign donations. Mine was called Team JJ USA. (Oh so creative, right?)

Next, your campaign needs a bank account—but not just any account. The bank has to meet particular oversight standards, and (although not an issue in my case) it needs sufficiently deep pockets to handle the high-dollar deposits and outlays that (most) federal campaigns experience.

Then you need an expert to oversee those accounts; specifically, you need a campaign finance accountant. Mainly, this elusive species is native to the DC Beltway, so with my Florida-based campaign, I had slim pickings nearby. Nationwide, I found around thirty options that fit my bill. I contacted them, and a handful even called me back before they declined. Campaign accountants, I discovered, aren't particularly interested in low-budget, no-name candidates from Central Florida. Thankfully, through my Florida Democratic connections, I eventually found one willing to give me a shot. (It made me wonder what unaffiliated candidates must have to do.)

My accountant helped me file the last few forms with the FEC. She also set up electronic filing so we could report our quarterly proceeds, and she registered all of the campaign officials who'd have access to the money (myself, herself, my campaign custodian of record, and so on). Everything has to be documented just-so with the FEC.

Last but not least, I studied the rules about accepting money. They're not intuitive. For instance, campaigns can accept up to fifty dollars in cash anonymously or up to a hundred bucks from a named source, but after that donors need to use a different process. You'd think the easiest way would be to use a payment app, like PayPal, or an online platform, like Kickstarter—except you're not allowed to. You have to use specialty apps, like ActBlue or WinRed, that account for state and federal rules. They charge candidates a pretty penny for every transaction, but they keep you out of jail with the FEC (so there's that feature).

Finally, after jumping through all of those hoops, you're cleared to begin collecting money. Of course, that's easier said than done. At first, I tried to hire a fundraising team, but I soon discovered: There aren't many unaffiliated fundraising experts in the political world. I did find someone who offered to give it a try, but he couldn't cobble together a competent team. All the big-name races had cornered the market on that talent. After a few fruitless weeks, he returned my retainer fee and left me only with a piece of advice: Go through your Rolodex and ask every single person you know for money. Ugh.

As a side note, you might be thinking: Well, if only she'd gotten more political experience first at the state or local levels, then this wouldn't have been so arduous. There's obviously some truth to that statement, but also consider that those rules differ entirely from the federal ones. So even if someone knows how to file with the state commission or throw an expert fundraiser at the neighborhood pizzeria, that person won't necessarily know the national-level equivalents. Also, while existing politicians undoubtedly have the upper hand in all of this, I was trying to see whether someone outside of the usual partisan system could get into the game based on competence rather than political connections.

My first fundraising idea was to sell T-shirts. I've seen the swag most campaigns peddle and thought I could do better. Instead of making basic shirts adorned with my name and the election year, I designed pithy sayings and cool gear (that I hoped) people would want regardless of political affiliation. For example, I made one that read, "Politicians are temporary; nerds are forever" (with the semicolon too). My Geek Team and I reasoned buyers would invest in a piquant idea or funny phrase more than a candidate they've never heard of.

Unfortunately, despite their obvious inherent appeal, the shirts barely sold. I quickly realized my oversight. Without an advertising budget, would-be buyers couldn't find the shirts. It was ironic. I needed funds (in this case for marketing) to raise funds. That proved to be a common theme: You need seed money to fundraise successfully. You can't start with empty pockets like I was trying to do.

My next clever idea was to raise funds by hosting virtual 5K races. I didn't invent this idea; they're already popular around the country. People sign up online and pay a small fee, then they complete the 5K and earn some token for their efforts. My campaign 5Ks would work similarly. Participants would learn about the events through social media, and then they'd sign up through my website—with their thirty-five-dollar participation fees going toward my campaign. They'd join me virtually at a particular time, and we'd run together. During the event I'd talk with my fellow joggers through a teleconference. We'd all be active and at least marginally productive, and meanwhile I'd have a paying audience for my stump speeches. Afterward, everyone would receive campaign-themed medals and one of my clever T-shirts as souvenirs.

We organized the first fundraising 5K for a Sunday in June. I was scheduled to be at the Nickerson Park Campground in Connecticut, and my children (the eldest two are genuine marathoners) planned to run with me. Let's just say things didn't go as intended. The night before, we arrived hours late, and by then it was too dark to map the route. We didn't have good cellular coverage and only just managed to get the 5K T-shirts shipped in time. Ultimately, the mayhem was inconsequential because no one (save for my parents and a couple exuberant friends) joined the thirty-minute call. Nonetheless, we all finished the route, which for me involved a scintillating twenty-lap circumvention of the RV parking lot. As I power-walked in circles, I discussed my environmental strategy and had flashbacks to traipsing around the neighborhood while training as an American Warrior Nerd Princess.

Despite the utter fundraising flop, the day wasn't a total wash. The walk-and-talk 5K forced me to distill my thinking around the environment into more palatable sound bites, even if no one came to hear them. Exercising with my family wasn't terrible, either, and of course, I also learned many valuable lessons on how *not* to fundraise.

Ostensibly wiser the second time, we tried again in Interlochen, Michigan. This time, we made it easier for donors. Instead of only hosting the race synchronously, people could sign up to run with me on Sunday morning or complete it on their own anytime that weekend. And instead of writing a half-hour speech, I filmed a casual five-minute summary, talking about my latest travels and the findings of my health-care research. This time, we got more traction, at least six or seven people signed up.

We held two more. The third one was over Labor Day weekend in Orlando, and I ran in the balmy heat of Florida's waning summer. Then in a dramatic contrast, I held the last one about a month later in Fairbanks, Alaska. Wrapped in a parka and shivering in the predawn darkness, I tried to lure donors into a talk about national education. Despite my valiant attempts, the races were largely a bust. It was like the T-shirt sales: I needed more than word of mouth. I needed to invest in advertising or find some other way to get the message out if I wanted people to get involved. So, I reasoned, perhaps I needed to try something more traditional.

What about rallies like my #Tour50 kickoff back in May? That had worked well as an event, but from a fundraising perspective, it had a fatal flaw. I'd held it at the American Legion, which is a nonpartisan venue; that means no direct solicitations. Where else could I campaign? I tried to find community centers and other civic groups, but they usually had similar apolitical rules. And the partisan places only welcomed their own preordained options. So that left public spaces. Parks and libraries worked, but those don't have a steady flow of interested donors. Just imagine how eager you'd be to donate to that hungry politician stalking the book return.

I tried speaking at universities. Weren't they supposed to be hotbeds of political activism? That didn't turn out either. I had scheduled talks—not even fundraising rallies but nonpartisan discussions about the political process—at universities in Massachusetts, Colorado, and Arizona, but the schools all canceled at the last minute. Supposedly, each university claimed its administration had decided it wanted to remain apolitical, which, I was told, meant a would-be politician couldn't talk—not on any topic, even if it was nonpartisan and preapproved. That was a particularly tough pill for me to swallow. I'd spent my career among academic-types and had even worked for a time as an assistant professor. I know the ropes. I wasn't just a wannabe politician off the street. I was one of their own. But I'd committed the apparently mortal sin of studying politics. *So much for open minds!*

Eventually, I accepted the truth: If I wanted to hold a public rally, I'd need to rent a space. That meant dolling out hundreds or thousands of dollars a pop—with no guaranteed return. So, like my T-shirts and virtual races, I ended up at the same chicken-and-egg conundrum: In order to raise funds, I needed to first have funds.

Maybe, I thought, *rather than the shotgun approach, I should try a more focused method*. What if I found a few significant donors to get my fundraising snowball going, two or three people with enough disposable wealth and political interest to help seed my campaign? But why would they do that, I fretted. What am I selling? What would make someone agree to invest triple digits in me?

I decided to write an investor's package, like the kind small businesses make for corporate sponsors. It forced me to think about the real-world value my unconventional presidential campaign offered. It proved a great exercise. It made me articulate all of those intuitive ideas that drove me to run in the first place, and it made me sharpen my thinking around why we should challenge the status quo. The package talked about systemic issues across government and the need for a problem solver–type in the White House. It talked about my tangible plans for how I'd use campaign funds, with earmarks for things like public speaking and voter infographics. Overall, its message was, "Invest in me because I'm going to do good work for the country." I don't have to win the election to accomplish that outcome, the package explained; my nationwide tour, the political conversations I planned to have, and the other artifacts, such as interview videos and strategy reports, would have an impact regardless of who wins the race. Then the package ended with a call to action, encouraging readers to look differently at the political process—to invest in political innovation. If you want a different climate in politics, it urged, then you need to try a different approach. You'll get nowhere running the same marathon every four years and expecting a different outcome.

I circulated the investor's package and got some good feedback. Several people even said, "I like your ideas. How do we get you into office?" When it came to forking over real greenbacks, though, they demurred. The most common response went something like this, "I'd be happy to give you money, if you can get X amount from another source." Even these handpicked patrons weren't willing to invest solely in the quality of my governance ideas. They needed another metric—a certain minimum dollar threshold—before they were willing to climb on board.

★ ★ ★

My political friends and reluctant patrons didn't leave me completely in the cold. A few threw fundraisers for me. Since I was an unknown quantity, I couldn't pull off a masterful moneymaker like the senator I'd mentioned earlier; instead, these ended up being more like meet-and-greets.

I held my first town hall in Traverse City, Michigan. Thys DeBruyn arranged it. I'd met him serendipitously when I had first passed through the area in August. Thys has a no-nonsense national security background, and he's also a staunch Republican. Like so many voters, though, he's more interested in performance than party labels, and he resonated with my campaign ideas and governance strategies. I gratefully accepted his offer to organize the gathering.

It's nearly impossible to fully prepare for an event like this. I didn't know the audience, and I wasn't sure of their expectations. I had to be ready for town hall–style questions, but I couldn't monitor current events 24/7 and didn't have a team of analysts whispering in my ear. What if the crowd asks me something I don't know about? What if I make a gaff or laugh at the wrong time or have the wrong body language?

By this point, the second Democratic presidential debate had aired, and I figured it was a good place to look for inspiration. I downloaded it along with another copy of the first debate and studied them on the flight to Michigan. I boarded the plane, said a few pleasantries to my seatmate, then popped in my headphones and got to work. I scrutinized the video, looking especially for those more implicit cues like tone of voice. I watched their facial expressions too, both when they spoke and while others were speaking. It was interesting to consider which candidates seemed nervous and which were calm, which ones would roll their eyes at another's reply or interrupt a speaker. I also dissected their responses. Did someone answer with depth or try to deflect? Did they use facts or platitudes, directives or narratives?

I noticed a divide between the candidates with prior executive experience versus those with legislative chops. The legislators did what legislators do: They promoted legislative policies—things outside the purview of the presidency. Maybe I'm projecting, but the candidates with executive experience seemed frustrated. I kept wishing one of them would call out the offenders. Just picture one of them interrupting to say, "You can't do any of those things! That's not how the executive branch works. If you want to be a legislator, then run for Congress!"

When the flight attendant brought our pretzels and soda, I took a break. My neighbor, making small talk, asked what I was doing. I sketched out the high points, filling her in about the town hall and my presidential cramming.

"Well, I'm not so interested in watching those debates," she shared gently. "But I'm entertained watching you watch them. Between the forehead slapping and exasperated sighing, it's like you're giving running commentary!" We both had a warm-hearted chuckled.

I arrived the next day at the fundraising site, a classy bar near downtown. People started to trickle in, and I mingled. Most of the two dozen or so attendees had backgrounds in national security, government, or education, which made it easy for me to strike up conversations. It also turned out that about half of the guests were registered Republicans. The others were Democrats. I felt elated—people had come together across party lines! It reminded me of good parents after a divorce. Despite diminished affection for one another, they're willing to set aside their squabbles when it comes to the well-being of their kids. In this case, the metaphorical child in question is our nation, and I thought, if the partisan groups are willing to compromise for her long-term well-being, that's a good sign.

Then it was time for me to speak. I'd prepared something ahead of time, but after circulating through the crowd, I realized it needed to change. These weren't curious spectators, merely looking for a primer on politics and a free beer; they had wisdom and intensity. These were people who cared—really cared—about our government. So I threw out my script and just spoke from the heart. I talked about why I'd decided to run and shared stories about the things I'd seen in government that motivated me to try an alternative campaign.

Afterward, they peppered me with questions, although not the ones I had expected. Before the event, I'd studied the typical political issues, like health-care policy and tax law. No one quizzed me, though; instead, they asked about things like problem-solving approaches and strategic decision making. Their questions sent me into problem-solver mode. My politician's persona cracked a little, and some of my authentic nerdy core peeked through. Fortunately, these were my kind of people; they ate it up.

I felt buoyed by that town hall. Thys's dedication to organizing it and the attendees' unprompted encouragement brought literal tears to my eyes. I felt like I'd achieved another level-up on my political journey. Unfortunately, my pocketbook remained on level one. Despite the outpouring of compliments and reassurances, they weren't ready to back their words with their wallets.

I held a few other similar events in cities like Boston and Colorado Springs. Each time, the fundraiser differed significantly. In Massachusetts, for instance, I had an elegant dinner with an intimate crowd, primarily comprised of business investors. In Colorado, we had something closer to a political house party with beer and wine, tons of finger food, and social mingling. The differences ran well below the surface, though. Whether because of the region or the organizers' contact lists, the guests at each fundraiser were distinct. They asked different questions, wanted different types of answers, and reacted differently to the same tone or body language. In Michigan, for instance, they asked me about process and resonated with my nerdy way of thinking, but in Colorado, I found a closed and skeptical crowd. They were a sociable group, but instead of vigorous nodding and attentive discussion, they wore forced smiles and asked perfunctory questions.

It's not like I received zero donations. They just tended to come in smaller amounts and usually through word of mouth or social media. Overall, these provided meager sustenance. I'm immensely grateful for the bread and water my campaign received, but it was still starving. I tried to feed it from my own bank account, but that wasn't enough.

In the midst of that famine, I had a few questionable offers of support. For example, there was a guy online, someone I didn't know from my regular life, who quickly became my number-one fan. He liked and commented religiously on my posts—on the surface a good thing, but he seemed to take it too far. He had, somehow, too much enthusiasm. My psychologist Spidey-senses tingled. He didn't show the typical boundaries or go through the usual getting-to-know-you rituals. Why was this stranger so obsessed? Then he wanted to donate. *Hooray!* I thought at first. But something felt wrong, so I looked him up online. Sure enough, he was listed on the sexual offender registry. Someone could argue that he still deserves a chance, that his life isn't defined by the worst thing he ever did. At the same time, there's a big difference between forgiveness in your personal life and condonation as a professional politician. Just look at the fall-out over the donations from sex-trafficker Jeffrey Epstein.

When politicians and university presidents accepted Epstein's contributions, there's a good chance they didn't know about his criminal activities, but their ignorance didn't protect them from getting embroiled in the scandal. What's worse, maybe some of them sensed something was off with Epstein—like I had with my own online admirer. It's easy to overlook behaviors you don't want to see or to justify the forbidden fruit by your noble uses of it. I can imagine how people talk themselves into accepting contributions that they probably shouldn't.

I felt the pull too. You have to feel desperate for money to really understand the lure of that slippery slope. It's easy to judge politicians' fundraising choices from afar, but when you're the one starving, you can convince yourself that even moldy bread is appetizing. I had to draw a hard line for myself—under no circumstances would I even consider crossing my ethical boundaries. Of course, I'd been a professional politician for less than a year and was only getting a small glimpse at that hunger. I can only imagine how struggling career politicians must feel. It was a potent lesson to see those cash cravings from a different perspective.

After a year of fundraising badly, I learned a few things. First, fundraising belongs in one of Dante's circles of hell. Quintessential politicians may be immune to its effects, but for me, every time I asked someone for money, it felt like a paper cut on my soul. It was one of the most draining things I experienced during the campaign.

Second, politicians should never fundraise. If I had a magic wand, this is the first thing I'd change. I'd wish fundraising was impenetrably firewalled from elected office. Imagine if our top surgeons or chief engineers had to fundraise to buy their jobs. There's a reason we don't do that. It's somewhere between ludicrous and an abomination of the natural order. It's particularly harmful for presidential candidates and federal legislators. The sums and scale on which they fundraise naturally pique voters' cynicism. Inherently, politicians become distrusted agents, potentially paid for by the highest bidder. That suspicion follows every politician, even those with the highest ethical standards. Justified or not, it provides fuel for ad hominem attacks and distracts from more substantive debates. The emphasis on fundraising also means politics rewards and attracts good fundraisers while discounting those who are less skilled in the monetary arts, even if they'd make outstanding lawmakers. And of course, there is the opportunity-cost issue: Every minute someone spends begging for dollars is a minute not spent listening to constituents or designing solutions.

Imagine if we picked our presidential hopefuls differently. What if we used an entry model like the New York City Marathon? Some candidates could still buy tickets to run. Other hopefuls would be selected from a random lottery. Some people could earn their way in by demonstrating tenacity. For the NYC Marathon that means running nine other races and volunteering at, at least, one. Still others would be selected through merit. For the marathon, that means meeting some pretty demanding time standards. For politics, of course, we would probably want a different yardstick than candidates' overland speed records (although someone could argue even that would be better than the status quo).

What if the merit path used a corporate model with resumes and expert headhunting teams to find the best—truly, the most qualified—candidates in the nation? Imagine if the political parties played along, mentoring their top talent over years for a shot at the meritocracy nomination. Picture young high-potentials getting trained in history and governance, taking field trips to real-world America, and gaining experience through outcome-focused apprenticeships.

Of course, we don't live in that fantasy world. If you've only skimmed a portion of this book, you already know: The only coin of the political realm is gold. The political machine guzzles money like a race car devours gasoline. Campaigns start and end with their bankrolls, and political careers rarely survive without gorging on funds. I hate it. But I felt compelled to ride the politics train, so I needed to get a ticket.

Before my campaign, I'd never been an advocate of those legislative proposals that use tax money to fund federal campaigns. Publicly funded elections always felt like politicians trying to line their own pockets. Now that I've caught a glimpse inside the system, I'm converted. Plans like Voting with Dollars or Clean Elections might not eliminate financial influence, but they're a start.[1]

I've come to view public campaign funds a lot like financial-aid scholarships: They open a door to the opportunity. As a young adult, I couldn't afford college, and without a scholarship, I either wouldn't have gone or would've been crippled by debt. A scholarship got me into Colgate, and after that, it was up to me. I still had to work hard and prove myself each semester. I still waited tables and saved every penny, but the scholarship gave me the initial leg up.

Federal elections have no equivalent. They're truly a members-only money-driven system. As a consequence, we've weeded out people who would be good at the job by making the campaign portion so expensive. We haven't just made it improbable for others to participate; we've made it impossible.

CHAPTER SEVENTEEN

How Are We Still Talking about Money?!

Here's a quiz. Don't read ahead or peek at the answer! OK, ready? What's the yardstick for the American economy? I'll give you a moment to consider. Did you say GDP or the stock market? How about the unemployment rate and jobs growth? Or, if you're really clever, maybe you said the Consumer Price Index or the Federal Reserve's money supply. All of those indices work, and I bet (now that the mental monetary juices are flowing) you can think of a dozen more, even if you can't precisely define what they all measure.

As I studied other presidential candidates and federal politicians, I noticed they'd often quote these sorts of indicators. "The Dow's hit a new record," they'd crow, or "The national debt is a ticking time bomb," they'd warn.

I started to wonder, why do we quote these things? I'm a fan of evidence-based policy, but a lot of the time, at least to me, these quantitative figures don't seem to reflect the qualitative reality of Americans' lives. Or, I should say, different figures reflect different realities, depending on your preselected viewpoint. The full picture is more complex than a single digit. Why, then, do our political pundits love this kind of economic play-by-play? Are federal policymakers genuinely using financial statistics to drive their policies, or as I've started to believe, do politicians more often use them as hand-waving shortcuts for their established platform positions?

Of course, that's an easy trap to find. Even everyday Americans tend to fall back on numerical surrogates, especially for the more partisan issues. Take, for example, one woman at the RV lot. Unasked, she volunteered her financial wisdom, explaining, "The stock marking is soaring. I don't care what anybody says. The economy's the best it's ever been, and that's all we care about!"

Or consider her counterpoint, a bright-eyed socialist I met at a coffee shop, who dejectedly shared that one in five American children are going hungry, and with that math as a given, the only possible answer was universal basic income. Of course, it's fine to argue the underlying position in either case, but problematically, we're overblowing the reality of these benchmarks and, in general, using those indices poorly.

Part of the issue, I think, is looking at our lived economic experiences in a superficially academic way. On paper, the stock market might have the velocity of a rocket ship, but if you've lost your job or can't pay your bills, then who cares? As a nation, if our health index is sinking and our suicide rates are climbing, then is it still fair to say our national resources are in the black?

Don't get me wrong, I love numbers. I'm an advocate for data-driven decisions, but the information used needs to be meaningful. As Mark Twain famously wrote, "There are three kinds of lies: lies, damned lies, and statistics."[1] How many economics discussions on Capitol Hill are above board, and how many of them fall into one of Twain's buckets? I needed to see for myself. So that's how I started my monthlong deep dive into the politics of national economics, by first attempting to uncover if we're even asking the right questions.

I began in Alaska. As I mentioned a few chapters ago, I eased into my economics research at a seminar on contracts and grants in Anchorage. A couple days later, I flew to Fairbanks. That city could've been just about anywhere in small-town America, which surprised me. The houses and stores didn't seem rugged enough for the harsh Alaskan winters. Most business buildings were one-story boxes that showcased a distinctive 1980s strip-mall aesthetic. The houses, scattered across rambling neighborhoods, often gapped with sagging siding or bowed behind boarded windows. Pockets of greater affluence exist, of course, but as I drove around the potholed streets, a sense of poverty seemed more common.

I'd scheduled an interview for the afternoon I arrived in Fairbanks. It was with a manager from the International Brotherhood of Electrical Workers, one of the largest labor unions operating in America. Given the amount of political airtime dedicated to both celebrating and denigrating unions, I'd wanted to learn more about them for myself.

Doug Tansy and I met in his office on a crisp, sunny day. He wore a light-blue button-up over his burly frame, and as we talked, he leaned comfortably in his chair, approaching every topic in an open, down-to-earth way. As soon as we began, Doug proudly shared his Native Alaskan heritage—half Tlingit (which he pronounced like "klink-kit") and half Athabaskan. Then he summarized his resume. That includes being the assistant business manager for the local electrical union and serving as president of the Fairbanks Central Labor Council, part of the American Federation of Labor and Congress of Industrial Organizations (or, more commonly, AFL–CIO).

"Doug, I often hear people wonder: Times have evolved, and our country has changed, so do we still need labor unions? What are their benefits and drawbacks in the modern era?"

"Well, I can share my personal story, as far as what the value has been," he offered. "I got an education that I didn't have to pay for. I did a nearly ten-thousand-hour apprenticeship (something we all do), and I came out with zero debt. I was provided health-care coverage as well as a starting retirement. I immediately came out of school and was able to be a contributor to my community. I can volunteer to coach wrestling—I have time to do that because I have a good income. I'm able to contribute by purchasing a home in my community as well as shopping at the local grocery store, the local vendors, the local coffee stand, and buying bicycles for my kids locally. And being part of the labor union has given me a voice in my contracts. It's given me a chance to have a secure income and make a secure lifestyle for my family, and it's given me a chance to enjoy the things I value: the time for stuff like hunting and traveling and spending every night with my kids doing homework."

"It's allowed you to live," I observed.

"Yes! It's not survival. It's allowed me to live my life." Doug nodded and raised his eyebrows, which given his otherwise stoic demeanor, I took as an enthusiastic response.

"I've been so fortunate," Doug reflected. "I've seen the stuff some people experience when they don't have a voice or don't have benefits or just don't make a livable wage. I hear a lot of stories where people are trudging through their lives, tiptoeing to the grave because they don't have much else. At the core, there's not much optimism or hope. They're going to work until they're shoved out. And then," he continued, "I have friends who are struggling to pay for their parents, and that's set their own retirements back. It's set their own finances back, and it's going to set their own children's finances back. It's going be a generational problem."

"So the union gives you peace of mind, knowing you won't become a burden to your children or your children's children," I observed. "But something you didn't say: That also means you're not a burden to society, to the government, or other people. You're self-sufficient, which is fantastic for you personally, and at the national level, it's fantastic for everybody."

My mind wandered to my recent health-care exploration and to the notions of wellness and mental well-being. *Workplace self-concepts*, I recalled from psychological practice, *often plays a big role in our mental health*. So bonus on top of bonus.

And Doug still wasn't done answering, "There are a lot of things we're doing that benefit the lives of folks who work on these contracts and their families, their spouses, their parents, and children. In the end, we look to elevate the fabric of our community, and by doing that, whether my friends and neighbors are represented through the labor union or not, their lives are improved."

"There's a ripple effect of benefit," I noted, "and I don't think that story is being told."

After the interview, I considered what Doug had said. I'd expected him to talk a lot more about wages or employment packages. Instead, he focused on living life, with financial compensation only a small part of that picture. Looking at unions from a different perspective—as a tool to help families and uphold the community—really humanized them to me. Doug's points also lined up nicely with my Rubik's Cube way of thinking, emphasizing the interconnections of work, health, freedom, support, retirement, and security. Finally, perhaps because it was top of mind, Doug also reinforced my doubt in the usual economic metrics. Rather than focus solely on income, he seemed to be using a different and more robust yardstick to measures success.

After five captivating days in Alaska, I flew back to Seattle where I rejoined my RV and restarted my cross-country commute, driving from Washington down to Oregon. As my campaign-mobile lumbered toward Portland a few things surprised me. First, the whole area is larger than I'd expected. It's sprawling, and downtown Portland is packed with high-rise buildings. There are also all of these stacked highways, crisscrossing like concrete spaghetti. Looking down from those skyways, I found another surprise: You can see the tops of buildings, and a lot are covered in greenery. Who knew Portland was the unofficial capital of rooftop lawns?

I had a couple interviews planned, so as soon as I found a spot for my RV, I got to work. Afterward, I didn't have much time to explore the city; although, I did find a brewery that, in my humble opinion, must have the world's best nachos.

It definitely earned Portland an A-plus in my culinary diary.

The next morning I traveled to Eugene, and later that day I attended a community meeting about microdwelling held at a local beer hall. It promised economic dialogues along with tasty pints—my kind of party! Even niftier, the bar was formerly a church, and its architectural roots couldn't have been more apparent. The building sported a peaked wooden ceiling and colorful stained-glass windows, and its tables and chairs had a pew-like aesthetic. A small group congregated in the center of the onetime chapel. Most of them looked to be in their retirement years (as civic events are wont to attract). I sat and listened.

Everyone was campaigning for more microdwelling options. Some wanted an alternative for the area's lower-income or homeless residents. Others sought less costly options for themselves, to relieve the anxiety of their fixed-income lifestyles or, in the case of one professional editor, to live free from the shackles of a high-paying but loveless corporate job. After the meeting, I approached that editor. She seemed a few years younger than the others and was compellingly articulate. After a little small talk, she agreed to sit down for an interview.

The next day, I met up with Sherri Schultz at her microdwelling.

"I generally define microhousing as anything under four hundred square feet," she clarified, even though her own private space is smaller yet. Still, her overall apartment complex felt spacious. She lives in a community of microdwellers, each with tiny rooms situated within a shared, dormitory-like facility.

"This style of living is much more common in Europe, but it's getting started here," Sherri explained in her animated style, hands moving to emphasize each point she made. "There's the tiny-house concept, which I think a lot of people have heard of, and also a parallel movement called co-living. That's where you have a small individual private space and then shared communal spaces, because, you know, we don't all need to buy a washer and dryer or big containers of cleaning supplies. About forty-five or fifty people live here, for example, and it's just a tremendous savings of time and energy."

It certainly seemed like a smart plan to me. Everything Sherri or her neighbors could want is included: a dedicated community chef, shared laundry, Wi-Fi and utilities, and a stockroom filled with groceries and supplies. Not only is it convenient; it's also practical.

"I actually was a homeowner in Seattle," Sherri continued, "and that city became very expensive. So I specifically moved back to Eugene, to a place that would allow me to live and do what I want to do, and not just spend a lot of time making money to pay the rent or the mortgage."

Sherri's words led me to reflect on my son, Mitchell. He's a musician in New York City. He'll probably never live in a staffed luxury condo, and he may never have a nuclear family of his own. I can imagine him happily doing the bachelor thing for, perhaps, his whole life. But he was also born with a congenital heart condition, which adds an element of risk to solo living. What if he has a medical emergency? What if he needs to spend time recuperating at home?

Once upon a time, people had to rely on their families, or maybe a small-town community, in their times of need, but in a co-living situation like Sherri's, the neighborly support network comes as part of the package. If she were to need, say, meals delivered when she was sick, she said one of the community assistants would probably bring them up, or she could ask a neighbor. There are also different types of microdwelling communities, including some organized around groups like artists or indie performers. Yet despite their many varieties, each emphasizes a common theme: the autonomy to live life on your own terms.

"Everyone is so different," I observed. "So maybe someone wants a standard home, or maybe someone really just wants the freedom of a place like this."

Sherri nodded. "I'm not saying everyone should live this way. I'm saying that everyone should know that this is a way you can live—and live well."

After our interview, Sherri gave me the grand tour of her room and apartment building. I have to admit, I felt a bit jealous. Back at home, Chris and I have a large traditional house with a grassy backyard and in-ground pool. As beautiful as it all seems, too often those amenities feel like paperweights on my life. As Sherri and I walked around her space, I daydreamed about downsizing, selling off my upkeep commitments, and moving into a co-living space similar to what I envisioned for my son. (But don't worry, Mitchell, I promise to find a different complex to live in!)

The next morning, I packed up my little house on wheels and drove south to Medford. The city sits in a lush plain, surrounded by agriculture and wineries and a dramatic ring of mountains that stretch across the horizon. As I approached, I couldn't help but gape at Mount McLoughlin, a cone-shaped volcano that eclipses the nearby foothills. But I hadn't come to Medford for sightseeing, so I turned my eyes away from the landscape and headed to the city center, a sprawling downtown filled with yawning parking lots and squat business buildings. I'd scheduled an interview with Reverend Murray Richmond, the pastor of the First Presbyterian Church and an advocate in the fight against homelessness.

I found a spot for my unwieldy motor home (without much hassle for once) and then quickly changed into a dress, grabbed my video gear, and set out for the church. As I approached, a mannerly gentleman greeted me, handing over a crisp paper bag he'd been carrying. I looked at him quizzically, not quite comprehending what had just happened.

"I'm sorry," I stammered, "I don't think I'm the person you were looking for."

"It's OK," he smiled kindly. "It's a free lunch. They're for anyone and everyone, no questions asked."

"Oh! Thank you," I replied in realization, while handing back the brown bag, "but I'm not here for the food bank. I have an appointment with the reverend."

"Oh, sure, no problem. Let me help you to his office."

I looked down at my attire: high heels, lace dress, and well-combed hair. It seemed professional enough to me. I was surprise to have been mistaken for someone in need of a handout, but I quickly put the question out of mind as I shook hands with Reverend Murray, a fatherly man in his fifties or sixties with wispy gray hair and a white goatee. The reverend had moved here about six years prior from Fairbanks, where he'd spent eighteen years as a pastor and ten years as a hospital chaplain in a behavioral health ward.

"When I came to Medford, I'd known this was a downtown church," he shared, "and I knew we'd have some of the problems of a downtown church. What I didn't expect was a congregation that took those issues so seriously. For instance, we do a food bank every week. When I first came here in 2013, we were running an average of twenty families a week. Now, a small week for us is sixty families, and we've had weeks with almost a hundred."

"Is that because you're servicing more people, or is it because the problem has increased?"

"The problem has grown," he clarified. "Food insecurity is a major problem. We see all these statistics about the economy doing better, but that doesn't necessarily mean the mass of people are doing better. A lot of people are barely eking it out on minimum wage, and if one thing goes wrong—if you have a car repair you can't afford, then you can't get to work, and then you lose your job, and if you lose your job, then you lose your house. It just throws everything out of whack."

I shuddered trying to picture such an anxious and tenuous situation. "I'm exhausted just hearing that story. I'm trying to imagine how hard it must be just to survive."

He nodded sagely. "People who live in, what I call, a 'culture of poverty' . . . It's hard to understand what that's like. Everything is really hard—and I do mean *everything*—and if one thing falls out of place, it all falls apart." The reverend's brows furrowed with compassion. "A large portion of the people we serve are the working poor."

"What's the difference in demographic between those who are homeless and those who are the working poor?" I asked and then quickly added, " . . . besides the obvious factor."

"Two big reasons for being homeless are drug addiction and alcoholism or mental health, and often they all come in the same person. But it's a chicken-or-egg thing. Frankly, if I had to sleep out on the streets every night, I don't know if I'd want to go to bed sober."

"Yeah," I considered aloud, "if your life is miserable, and you have the opportunity to do something for yourself . . . Like last night, it happened to me. Everything in my RV went wrong—my heat, my generator, and my power all went out, so you bet I had a glass of wine and some popcorn. Of course, I shouldn't have been eating them, but it was a terrible day."

"And that terrible day for you was just a blip," Reverend Murray noted.

"That's right, it was," I agreed, "and yet I went to the coping mechanisms. Would we have allowed those same affordances to somebody who every single day is facing these challenges and is exhausted?"

Rather than answering directly, the reverend shared a personal example, "I heard a woman outside wailing, and when I went to check on her, I realized she had covered herself in her own feces. (I assume it was her own feces. I don't know.) She was wailing at the top of her voice and clearly schizophrenic. So we cleaned her up and took her to the crisis intervention center. When we got there, this guy comes over and looks at the woman, who's there on the floor. We're still wiping crap off of her (literally), and the first question out of his mouth is, 'What kind of insurance do you have?' She looks up and says, 'F— off!' It's the most coherent thing she'd said all day," he shared with a bit of dark humor.

"You know," he confided more somberly, "the mental health system we've designed in this country assumes that the people who use it are not mentally ill. In order to take advantage of the system, you have to be pretty smart, you have to be a good planner, and you really have to have your stuff together. But we're dealing with people who, from day to day, sometimes don't know who they are. Anyone who's out on the street can't manage appointments. If they'd had watches, they've been stolen, so they don't know what day or time it is. They tell time through the chimes from our church." Then offhandedly he added, "That's why we schedule our food bank around the chimes."

"I was walking in today to the chimes," I recounted, "and someone handed me a bagged lunch."

"We give a bag lunch to whoever comes to the church," the reverend nodded. "There used to be a guy who came every day for I don't know how long. Our policy is, if you come to the door, you get a lunch. But he came every day in a suit. People were beginning to grumble a little bit, and then he disappeared. A few weeks later, he comes back and says, 'I just want you to know I lost my job, and every day I set myself a goal to get three or four interviews. So I wore my suit every day for those interviews, and your lunches were all I had during those three weeks. But I got a job! And here I am, coming back to thank you.'"

Reverend Murray clarified the moral of his story, "We often think of a poor person as someone who doesn't have anything, but often, they simply don't have what they need. So, you know, you might have a car but have lost your house. Sure, you can drive, but you still have nowhere to stay and maybe no food to eat."

Reverend Murray and I chatted a bit longer, talking around the themes of homelessness, mental health, housing, and pragmatic charity. Throughout, he kept highlighting two underlying ideas: First, that people need different types of interventions; being poor isn't simply a lack of money. And, second, housing is the cornerstone. Once someone has housing, then they can muster the energy to stabilize in other ways, build social support, get treatment (if needed), and begin the journey back to our collective society.

After the reverend and I parted ways, I climbed back into my camper, feeling grateful to have it (despite the broken onboard heating). Then I drove to my campsite. Once parked for the night, I continued my string of interviews on housing and homelessness. This time, I had a video-chat with Terry McDonald, the executive director of his local St. Vincent de Paul Society, an international charity organization. An older man with a lined face and thick glasses, Terry wore a powder-blue shirt and a puffy orange vest for our call. To kick things off, I encouraged him to talk about the creative strategies he uses to secure housing for people.

"We have a ladder of housing. It starts actually with free housing. We do 'car camping' for homeless individuals. For homeless families, we have a shelter program. We have an interesting and strange tent village, called Dusk to Dawn, where we house two-hundred homeless per night in old military tents that are heated and air conditioned. Then we have the warming centers that we run during the winter when it gets to thirty degrees. Those serve about five-hundred to six-hundred people. And we have some other temporary housing, some transitional housing, a veterans housing program, and supportive services for veterans' families. We purchase and repair derelict mobile homes, and we have about eight of those parks. We have Section 42 housing, which is a program of affordable housing for families and singles, and then we have home ownership projects for people who get to 100 percent of median income."

"Wow," I responded, a bit taken aback, "that's a lot to digest! What sticks out to me is the progressive scaling you do. I've heard other people mention this, so can you talk a little more about the beginning of that scale or 'pre-housing?'"

In his calm, matter-of-fact way, Terry walked me through the answer. "For better or worse, there are more individuals and families than we can house. So we work with people who are still homeless and say, 'Can we find a more stable place for you until you have the resources or the ability to be in housing?' Then we move them into the tents, which are these big MASH tents. They're huge. It's congregate housing in those units, and we provide the bedding and everything else. Then we start working with them on a plan. Like if someone is on a fixed or very low income and can't afford the price of rent, we find a way to link that person up with someone in a similar situation. We see if they're compatible, and then see if we can repair their rental histories and credit scores. So that's what we mean by pre-housing. It's meeting people where they're at, before they have the resources, and getting them some stability."

"Love it!" I exclaimed, "And how many communities around the country are doing this, in the manner you're doing it or to the extent that you're doing it?"

"None."

"None?" I sputtered. "Why do you think that is?"

"Well, it's because the organization isn't relying primarily on largesse or on government grants. We bring our own resources to bear on this very difficult problem. You know, I'd like to say the federal government funds 100 percent of our activities, but they don't. Instead, we have a large retail footprint and a large recycling footprint. Both of those businesses have been profitable, and those profits can be used for the human services around us."

"How does that work? Are the businesses run by the people living in these housing options?"

"Um, some are, but most of the time it's people just coming out of difficult life situations, like ex-offenders getting out of incarceration or people with multiple barriers to employment. Those are the folks who run the various businesses for us. We have fifteen retail thrift stores, a car lot, and the largest mattress recycler in the United States. We're also one of the largest freon gas recyclers in the region. We own an interstate trucking business with four-hundred trailers to move product around, and we pillage a lot of stuff from transfer sites and dumps. So it's a multidimensional response to business, working with the resources available in the waste stream and with people who have multiple skills but are not typically employable."

"Did you see the business growing to where it is today back when you started it in the 1980s?"

"Well, back then, I did see the potential. And I see the potential everywhere in the United States. You can do this to scale almost anywhere."

"So if we wanted to bring this to every major city in the country, what would be the first three steps?"

Without missing a beat, Terry replied with cool confidence, "First, identify a nonprofit organization that has the same type of mission that we do and is interested in taking risk, stepping out of their comfort zone, and being entrepreneurial. The next thing is to look in that community for the waste stream or the place in the system that fits best for that group, like book recycling or mattress recycling or appliance recycling or maybe automobiles or retail thrift. The last thing is to go out to the public sector and the philanthropic sector and say, 'I see you have contracts to do this. We could do the same thing they're doing but for less.'"

"What are the hiccups?"

"Risk. Most nonprofits are risk-averse, and anything that you're going to do in the business world requires risk. You have to be interested in maintaining a business that's viable in the private marketplace, and that's tough."

"Yeah," I agreed. "It's the same in government. We're fear-driven instead of mission-driven, and I've seen so many problems because of it. Wait!" I interrupted myself. "Let me ask you this: Do you serve on any boards for HUD?" which is the federal office of Housing and Urban Development.

"Nope."

"Has anyone ever approached you to do that?"

"Nope."

"Do you even know about those boards?"

"Nope."

"You're a nugget that our country needs, and nobody's reaching out to you," I pointed out with a twinge of annoyance at our system. "OK, if you had a recommendation for the people in Washington, what would it be?"

"When you're talking about landfills and transfer sites, stop thinking of it as waste. You have to think about it as opportunity or as 'resource recovery.' We have so many resources available through the waste stream, and we have an unlimited opportunity to move that product around and make money, and also to decrease our carbon footprint dramatically. So you can tie all these pieces together around a theory: We need to treat our so-called waste—both material and human—as assets instead of liabilities."

The next morning, I stashed my camper at the airport and flew to meet Chris and Madison in Hawaiʻi. They'd decided my campaign stop in the Aloha State was perfect timing for their visit. (I can't imagine why!) Chris used traveler points to book a beautiful hotel, complete with a spectacular view of Waikiki Beach. I'd blocked off a few days for rest and family, and we spent our first night together just reconnecting and admiring the tranquil vista from our balcony.

The next day, I took my morning walk and then joined Chris and Maddie at the pool deck. They'd already settled into some chairs by the time I arrived, so I ran back to our room to change into my swimsuit. Before I could return, my gregarious husband had struck up a conversation with our lounge-chair neighbors.

"You're not going to believe this," he exclaimed as I reappeared in my suit.

"What?" I asked with a flicker of anxiety. That excited tone didn't bode well for my plans of daydreaming and mai tais.

Chris gestured to the adjacent couple, who gave a friendly wave.

"They just told me that there's a protest this afternoon. They're going to be marching down that street right there, the one next to the beach."

Well, *shenanigans!* I couldn't miss the opportunity to see democracy in action. So, reluctantly, I returned to our room, changed back into my street clothes, and headed out to Ala Moana Boulevard. It didn't take much time to find the protesters. They made a dramatic scene; although, it looked more like a celebration than any demonstration I've seen. Some people wore traditional robes and jewelry; others wore only a loin cloth. A lot of the protesters had shown up in bright red or yellow shirts, which had clearly been made for the event. As I watched the main parade route, some women trotted by on horseback, swathed in regal robes and wreathed in flowers. Groups of men danced the haka. People sang or drummed or chanted in unison, and everywhere I looked, I saw protesters carrying Hawaiian flags: big ones, tiny ones. It was a sea of striped red, white, and blue.

I soon discovered the crowd was marching in opposition to a new telescope being built by the National Academy of Sciences, called the Thirty Meter Telescope or TMT. It's being built on the now-dormant Mauna Kea volcano, a place many Hawaiians view as sacred ground. With camera in hand, I approached people in the crowd and asked for their perspectives.

A massive man in a red protest shirt and sunglasses explained, "I'm here to support my Hawaiian people, my culture, my blood, my island. I think, all in all, we're just tired of it. We're done, not only with TMT but with everything that's going on, on the island—the rail, the taxis, everything. And, this isn't only about Hawaiian issues"—he gestured with a thick, tattooed arm—"it's about all of us here."

Down the street, a grandmotherly woman wearing a matching red T-shirt further explained. "Our Unity March is based on *Kapu Aloha*," a sort of non-violent political and philosophical code, "and our love for our land. When the *Hōkūleʻa*," which are the traditional double-hulled sailing canoes, I later learned thanks to Wikipedia, "went around the world, it was to save the earth not just to help Hawaiʻi. We are the protectors, not only of Mauna Kea but of the earth, and we need to save it for our generation and for the generations to come."

Everyone I spoke with seemed to have a similar story: This is our land, and people continue to come from the outside, acting as if they own it, only to corrupt it. How can someone halfway around the world in DC just decide to build on our mountain? There's a perception in Hawaiʻi that "other" people are running the islands' affairs and exploiting the local resources. The high-priced Honolulu Rail Transit is just one example. Opponents argue that the less-privileged communities, where many indigenous people live, will pay its price without reaping its benefits—that it wasn't made with those Hawaiians' interests at heart.

Similarly, some locals lament their lost land on Oʻahu. They feel like the island is being gobbled up by wealthy foreigners, shell companies, and commercial holdings.[2] Meanwhile, native Hawaiians are often left working for those businesses, which are now growing wealthy on the land that once belonged to the Hawaiian people. Fair or not, I heard that sentiment frequently, throughout the

demonstration

"Who do you think those hotels are built for?" One man draped in a yellow protest banner asked as he gestured toward the high-rises on the beach. "We can't afford to live there."

While I could appreciate everyone's sentiments, I also wondered what actions, beyond protests, people were doing in response. I began to ask, and in particular, I found surprising results with the question: "Of your family and friends, how many people do you know in government?" Emphatically, across the board, everyone replied with, "I don't know anyone."

One woman grew visibly angry at the question. "It doesn't matter if I'm in the government or not. They should come talk to us."

It breaks my heart; these protesters' courage and message have been largely unheard, and now that construction has been underway for years, things are unlikely to change. They're being overlooked, I suspect, because of the unwritten rules of government and politics, like knowing where to apply pressure or how to get a seat at the decision table. I've seen a similar pattern in a lot of places: Administrative roadblocks, intentionally complex paperwork, and inexplicable regulations create hidden barriers to representation. Laws and policies aren't always meant to protect the masses. Rather, in some cases, they're meant to protect those already in control. In a way, knowing the unwritten rules and secret handshakes is a sort of second economy, one that trades on the currency of connections and power.

After a couple more days on Oʻahu, and a few more campaign engagements, I found myself back in the Continental US and ready to explore California. The Pacific coast is breathtaking. California, in particular, boasts spectacular views, but as I entered the state, those weren't the first things I noticed. Rolling along the highway in a gas-hungry camper, the price of petrol caught my eye. From Oregon to Cali, the price jumped by more than a dollar. Another thing impossible to miss was the smoke. The air quality resembled a 1970s pool hall. Everything reeked, and warnings signs flashed all around. To make matters worse, the electrical grids were shutting down too, and in the hardest hit areas, people were leaving their homes or, in some cases, hunkering down for an indefinite, apocalyptic wait. I found the situation disconcerting and worried how our largest state (at least in terms of budget) could end up in this *Mad Max*–like situation.

Turning my sights back to my economics research, I stopped a night near Redwood City and took an interview with Prasad Ram, or "Pram" as his friends know him. A slight man, in his mid-fifties, Pram is a former Google executive who founded a nonprofit focused on delivering free, technology-based education to K-12 students and the workforce. We met at his office near Silicon Valley, and I asked him about the skills workers will need in the future. Rather than answer directly, he asked his own question, broadening the discussion toward a more holistic theme.

"What does it mean to prepare for a job, right?" he replied, a slight accent tinting his words. "You have a particular set of skills, and this job requires a certain other set of skills, and there are clear gaps." His tone and gesture seemed to satirically imply that training for a job is easy and obvious. Of course, it's not so simple.

"But technology," Pram continued, changing his tone for effect, "Technology can help. We can use artificial intelligence to understand your competencies, and we can determine which competencies you need to gain and help you work toward them. And when you get to the full set, we can use technology to show employers what you have mastery in."

"So I feel like people believe they have that right now," I pointed out. "Companies have a list of requirements ('this is what you need to apply for the job') and then you make a resume that says, 'I have those competencies.' I feel like some of the major issues we have, both from an equity perspective and from a jobs perspective, are the unwritten rules, or what I like to call them, the game rules."

Pram nodded, a knowing smile on his face. I took that as a positive sign and continued. "I often tell the story about when I went to college. I thought my job was to go to class and do well in school. After I graduated, it was a big lesson for me when everybody else called their parents—not because their parents would give them a job but because their parents got them interviews, and those interviews helped them get their first jobs. My parents didn't have those connections, and I ended up working the register at a pharmacy because I needed health insurance and enough money to eat. I hadn't prepared—I didn't even know to prepare—for these other pieces of job development. I think a lot of people in this country feel frustrated, and it seems like doors are closed because those game rules aren't evident to everyone."

"What we do now," Pram responded, "is ask for a one-page resume and, generously, maybe three or five questions during an interview, and that will determine whether you get the job or not. There's no objectivity to the entire process, right? In terms of networking, in terms of building connections, all of that is required simply because we have a big mess in the rest of the system. And, you know, employers want to hire the best fit, because they're looking for profitability. But they don't have a way to find those people today because, again, there's no objectivity."

"So," I asked, counting off points on my fingers, "if we can personalize the education system with educational technologies, have verified evidence of someone's competence, start to credit people for their personal skill sets, and then match them to jobs in a better way—how does that impact our country?"

Pram paused for a beat, as his thoughts focused inward. "I think this could be transformative," he answered evenly. "There are a lot of studies that show if we can close the income inequality gap then all of the social indicators improve, right? All of the social indicators—whether it's poverty or health care or child mortality or whatever—all of these will transform. So, now, the question is, how do we close the inequality gap? I'm sure you've heard, very often, there are so many jobs that go unfilled and so many people who are unemployed or underemployed."

I nodded.

"The question," Pram continued, "is what do those jobs need, and what are the competencies of people who are underemployed, and is that distance bridgeable?"

Enthusiastically, I picked up his line of thought, "I often look at this and say, 'When we don't match our people to the jobs we need, we don't just have unemployment. We actually lower our nation's overall capacity for success.'"

"Exactly," Pram smiled.

Unemployment and underemployment impact everyone. They have a ripple effect, similar to how Doug Tansy framed the impact of unions—but in the opposite direction. And like the pictures Doug, Reverend Murray, and Terry McDonald all painted, workforce development is a more complex issue than initially meets the eye. It needs a multilayered solution, a slice of which includes getting rid of those hidden rules. Or maybe, at least, training the AI to help everyone else learn how to get our foot in the door.

After chatting with Pram, I pressed on to Santa Barbara and Los Angeles. Outside of LA, I camped for the night at an RV park perched atop a hillside. Looking down, I could see the glow of city lights and a halo of smoke around the city. In the distance, I thought I could see the glow of flames against the predawn sky. During the days, I tried to push the wildfires out of my mind. I worked on my strategies and interviewed people around town. I explored the sprawling metropolis, but the scratchy air kept reminding me of the threatening flames, and I found myself futilely hoping the firefighters would triumph quickly.

My next official stop was Las Vegas, but before I reached Nevada, I passed through hours of California countryside, including one of the strangest places in our nation: magical Nipton. I'm surprised Quentin Tarantino hasn't filmed something here. It's a surreal one-street town, adorned with painted classic cars and perplexing roadside art. It claims a population of fifteen people and is situated in an isolated stretch of desert. Despite this, there are dozens of highway signs advertising the place, and it has a hotel and café. But Nipton's winning feature, in my book, is its massive rainbow squid, built from sparkling glass and hypnotic shimmering lights. After a brief pit stop at the Nipton saloon, and some decidedly eerie conversations with the locals, I got back on the road the next morning.

Once I made it to Sin City, I met up with Sean Wagner, an entrepreneur and digital marketing expert. What a contrast to go from the bemusing stillness of Nipton to the pulsing intensity of Las Vegas! And Sean reflected the city. He's one of those people who can't sit still; he's so full of exuberance and drive. When we met, he wore a "No Excuses" T-shirt that hugged his tattooed biceps, and during our interview, he kept up a rapid pace, often gesturing with his arms to drive home his message.

"So I took business as my major, specifically international marketing." He reported, "But I'll say this, I don't believe college is worth a lot for that kind of thing. If you're getting a doctorate of mathematics or science, then I think college is critical, but for business . . . " he made a grimace. "Business is so much about who you know and how you put deals together on the golf course. It's the game rules. You know, it's about going to work and being able to hustle."

"OK, so how did you find your path?" I asked.

In response, Sean explained how he'd gotten involved in internet marketing in the mid-1990s, on the ground floor of the world wide web, so to speak. He'd translated that experience into sales, lead generation, and eventually to his own apparel business. Throughout his account, he kept emphasizing the importance of tenacity and hard work—or, as he called them, "the hustle."

"So," I observed after Sean shared his story, "I think the number-one thing people can learn from you is the entrepreneurial mindset. I mean, the future of work is not going to be nine-to-five jobs. People will be changing jobs, getting nontraditional gigs, and more people will need that hustle."

Sean nodded, with his eyebrows raised in animated agreement. "It's about productivity, you know? You can burn hours all day long without achieving much. Early on, as an entrepreneur, I'd spend sixteen hours a day doing things—a lot of that was just to feel like I was working, but it wasn't achieving much. You know, you can pull a nine-hour day at a warehouse, just sitting on your ass. Sure, you were at work for nine hours—but did you *work* for nine hours? That's a big difference"

"It sounds like we need to work smarter not harder."

"Totally," he agreed, "but that's not a new concept, right? I feel like, today, people aren't risk-takers. There's more complacency. To be an entrepreneur, you need to be a risk-taker. You're going to have to work longer hours. You've gotta put in the elbow grease, and you've gotta be hungry."

After a monthlong exploration of the politics of our economy, I returned to my original rumination: Are politicians asking the right questions? *No,* I decided, *I don't think they are.* Economic indices serve an important role, particularly in monetary research, but in the public sector, those data points are too often distorted, taken out of context, or cherry-picked to suit a particular stance. What's more, I'm not sure the statistics economists use ought to be so readily or, at least, so singularly embraced by elected officials—even if they use the numbers sincerely. Policymakers need a different, larger scope.

It's like Doug Tansy's underlying message: Real-world economics is about more than income. Ideally, our personal and collective economic environments provide a bedrock for our own multifaceted lifestyle goals. And as the Hawaiian protesters highlighted, the economy involves more than money. Power and knowledge are also forms of currency, as are other seemingly intangible assets like influence and access. Even mental health could be considered a kind of resource, as Reverend Murray's stories showed. When you open the aperture, the economy has onion-like layers, and if we're only looking through the lens of a dollar sign, then we're missing a lot of important parts.

To be fair, politicians and others involved in governance discussions do talk about practical economic effects. Some circles engage in those discussions almost daily. Still, in practice, there's a tendency to fall back into the rut of "what gets measured gets managed"³ and, as a result, concentrate efforts on policies aimed at the pick-your-favorite monetary metric, whether the S&P 500, national debt, joblessness figures, minimum wage base, or any of a hundred others.

Maybe we need new metrics? How about the "I'm having a swell life" index or the "history will judge us favorably" scale? Or, at a minimum, perhaps it's enough to more widely emphasize these broader derivative goals in policy discussions. If we start with the downstream outcomes in mind, we may even discover that the monetary targets we hype so much today were never on the critical pathway to begin with. Or maybe not. But one thing is clear: At the end of the day, the human side of the economy is much larger than our typical political discussions of it. So, perhaps, it's not all about the money, after all.

CHAPTER EIGHTEEN

Black Swans and Little Green Men

"There's a valley of death: We take research to *this* point. Industry's over *there*, and no one's building the footbridges in between." That was Clarke Lethin, a retired Marine Corps colonel who served in both Afghanistan and Iraq. After his time in uniform, Clarke moved into military research, first working with the Office of Naval Research and now with the Institute for Creative Technologies, a university affiliated research center. He still looks more Marine than academician, though, with his close-cropped gray hair and chiseled features, even in his late fifties.

"What's the pipeline," I prompted. "How do new ideas move through the process?"

"It's taken me a while to really learn the equation," Clarke admitted. "So there's basic research, which creates knowledge, and from that knowledge, you may be able to create an application—a piece of the puzzle. Then, eventually, you can take the pieces of the puzzle and make a picture. That becomes the prototype."

"Why don't we just turn that process over to industry?"

"Think about what industry has done," he replied. "The products that industry has created are based on the foundation of government-invested basic research dollars. So if we want to be looking two-to-three ridgelines out into the future, if we don't continue this basic research, well, then no one's going to create that knowledge. Industry has a very short timeline. They have quarterly timelines and profit margins. They do have some internally invested research, and I'm not taking that away from them, but they're not going to make the discoveries."

Clarke made a knife-hand gesture, bringing the edge of one flattened hand against the palm of the other. "Case in point, I visited a government-funded research lab back when I was with the Office of Naval Research, and I'm listening to them talk about all this research they do. The one thing that really hit home was their work on SAPI plates—the body armor, you know. They did the basic research necessary to improve the manufacturing process that's allowed industry to mass-produce viable and effective SAPI plates. At the same time, I'm listening to industry tell me how they have this unique process for creating a SAPI plate, and each business says they're the only ones in the world that can do it. I hear that from a few vendors, and then I get it. I see the equation. Government is really creating the knowhow, and industry is taking advantage of that and pulling it through."

A smile spread across my face, and I couldn't help myself. "I mean, exactly right!" I exclaimed with wonky exuberance. "While I was working for the government, I did a study on innovation in the executive branch. One of the things I found was that 60 percent of all economic growth in the country is due to government innovation and research investments that go largely unseen."[1] Nerdiness shared, I turned the conversation back to Clarke, "So what do you think would happen if we reduced that amount? What's the ripple effect of that?"

"We will be surprised," he answered calmly and quickly. "I mean, 9/11 was a surprise, and if you look back on our history as a country, we've been surprised a number of different times. That could be in warfare or in business—or anywhere else. If we aren't constantly investing in the future, then we will be surprised by it, and that could be detrimental in a number of different ways."

Over a year before, when my Geek Team and I were making our hierarchy of national needs, we'd brainstormed about political approaches. Across scattered whiteboards, we'd scrawled our personal principles for effective governance, things like "use what you have," "be more efficient," "connect the dots," "creativity not money," and "think about the big picture." It wasn't until after the exercise that the common theme had become apparent. That's how innovation landed the top spot in my political playbook. It's the pinnacle of the pyramid because it defines the overall solution style: the lens through which we view the other domains and the strategic approach that guides interventions. In other words, it's the how versus the what. And that's why, for the last month of my fifty-state experiment, my presidential focus shifted—away from identifying the individual components of our nation and toward the conceptual methodology used to achieve those solutions.

When last we left the tale of my intrepid road trip, I was in Las Vegas, a city no doubt brimming with innovation (even if it's not to your personal liking).

While in town, I sat down with Al Light, head coach of one of the most brazenly innovative organizations, Cirque du Soleil. We talked about some of the parallels between the circus and the government, things like the shared need for clear policies and common desire to write regulations that motivate positive action rather than stymie or frustrate. Of course, we couldn't settle for a normal conversation. So after my cirque-theme government crash course, Al insisted I complete our discussion on the trapeze. How's that for campaign innovation!

After Nevada, I drove to Arizona. The scenery felt like the backdrop to a spaghetti western, with miles of empty sand and bone-dry scrub. As I drove, it lulled me into contemplative frame of mind. I was transitioning into the last month of my scheduled tour and beginning to consider my life after. Ironically, as my campaign was nearing its swan song, the news media had finally started to pay attention. In just one week, I gave an on-air interview in Phoenix and two more back on the East Coast.

That media attention felt like a small triumph. Even though most voters hadn't learned my name, I could still check a TV interview, YouTube newscast, and DC news column off my list. On top of that, by this point in my tour, I'd held several town halls and fundraisers. So even if I was playing in the junior varsity presidential league, I'd still made it onto the field. I wasn't just a hanger-on or a wannabe. I'd gotten past the first miles of the presidential marathon—and using my nontraditional approach (my innovative flying machine) rather than the conventional footpath.

After my weeklong media blitz, I returned to where I'd left my RV in Tucson. Then I ventured on to New Mexico, passing through a small town called Truth or Consequences (no kidding) and eventually reaching Roswell. Like a lot of people, I was fascinated by aliens as a girl (and, truth be told, as a grown woman too). My obsession really peaked in college, and although I've never owned a tinfoil hat, I still couldn't pass up the opportunity to visit some extraterrestrial landmarks.

Roswell is a smallish city. It could be any nondescript little town with wide streets and low-slung buildings. That is, of course, if it weren't for its special attractions, like the quaint Main Street museum dedicated to the famous 1947 alien encounter. The place claims to be a UFO research center, and it exhibits (alleged) eyewitness testimony and visual recreations from the legendary crash site. As I walked through the gallery, which seemed more like a B-grade art installation than anything else, I mused about the potency of ideas.

Decades ago, a handful of people started talking about an alien crash landing, and with little to no evidence, they created a worldwide movement. Today, Roswell has become one of bees in the bonnet of ufologists (as they like to be called). That idea spread with plague-like efficiency, as have many others: take the antivaccine movement or Flat Earth Society. Of course, the power of thought isn't reserved solely for conspiracy theories. Good things can also benefit from this idea-contagion phenomenon, like the rapid normalization of LGBTQ+ lifestyles in America over the last twenty years or, historically, the lightning uptake of medical anesthesia across the world.

In all of the cases, a small seed of thought sprouted into a giant beanstalk. Whether we're talking aliens or ether, they're all examples of concepts spreading like wildfire, and they're great exemplars of the classic axiom: The pen of ideas really can triumph over the sword of force or ambivalence of idle minds.

After facing our (wax recreation) alien overlords in Roswell and conducting a couple of decidedly terrestrial interviews in New Mexico, I continued my tour across the white-noise landscape into Texas. As I crept east, grass and trees began to replace rocks and tumbleweed. Houses started to dot the horizon—as did flags. The sheer number of flags Texans fly is strangely remarkable, and there were at least as many bearing state emblems as there were with Stars and Stripes. So one stereotype, at least, seems valid: There's a lot of pride in Texas.

My first campaign stop in the state was scheduled for San Antonio. Along with a couple hundred local professionals, I attended a VelocityTX event focused on business innovation. After I checked in, I wandered into the meeting space, which was situated in a museum ballroom that had been transformed with tables and a presentation stage. Displays bordered the room, with different companies selling their wares or ideas at each. It was an eclectic scene. For instance, a portly scientist stood behind one display, talking about a battlefield wound-care tool he'd developed for the military. Next to him, two animated women hovered over their exhibit of boob-themed cupcakes. (Later, during the on-stage presentations, the two ladies talked about the importance of nipple reconstruction for women who'd undergone mastectomies—hence, their memorable little tata cakes.)

Throughout the afternoon, I learned an impressive amount about San Antonio's business innovation ecosystem, and I talked to scores of people. One of those bystanders directed me to a nearby business incubator. So later that day, I found myself at Geekdom, a program for aspiring technology entrepreneurs.

Adrian Machen, a buoyant business development manager showed me around, and as we toured the office space, he explained the incubator's origins. "One of the founders of Geekdom, Graham Weston, got an infamous letter from one of his business partners. Graham had expected the guy to move to San Antonio, but the e-mail said, 'San Antonio doesn't have a scene for developers, and it's not a place where entrepreneurship thrives. I'm not moving there.' Graham forwarded the e-mail to the mayor at the time and said, 'This is the city we must build.' Graham took that e-mail as a challenge. So, along with Nick Longo, he founded Geekdom."

Adrian then proudly motioned to an oversized city map covering one entire wall. Fist-size boxes, like oversized pushpins, were spread across it, each highlighting one of the many businesses Geekdom has helped to develop or attract to San Antonio.

". . . and that's what separates us from a typical co-working space," he continued. "We're here to actively develop the city of San Antonio."

Business incubators are nothing new, but what sets Geekdom apart is its holistic approach. It wasn't designed merely to give start-ups a boost. Its mission is to transform San Antonio into an epicenter of technological innovation. The incubator space is just one part of that. The relationships built around it, the coaching and transition assistance it offers, the venture capital matchmaking, and community outreach—it's a comprehensive program. They even have mentorship agendas designed to teach budding entrepreneurs those tricky unwritten rules. It's an innovation pipeline designed from tip to tail, from idea to success.

Man, I thought, *I'd love to be twenty-five again and starting my career in a place like this, a whole system that uses good ideas and creativity for its currency.*

It took me a week to drive across Texas, passing through Austin, Houston, Dallas, Fort Worth, and a dozen small towns. Along the way, I interviewed more innovators, including Patricia Rodriguez Christian who talked about entrepreneurship and diversity, Bonnie Hagemann who discussed innovation in leadership, and a handful of folks attempting to overcome that research-practice gap Clarke Lethin had bemoaned. One interview that stands out actually happened a few weeks prior.

I'd met Dr. Brie Linkenhoker and Nancy Murphy on my way through the Bay Area. The two run Worldview Studio, a company focused on connecting science to society. In other words, these two highly educated women and their creative team work to overcome that chasm between research and practice.

"As a nation, we're not doing a very good job of connecting what we're learning in academia to people in the real world," Brie shared, when I asked why she'd founded the company. "We have so much knowledge across so many different areas—like criminal justice, education, health, and governance—but we have these barriers between the knowledge generators and the people who really understand the problems"—she clapped her hands in front of her, like a miniature wall—"barriers between those potential solutions and the people who could put that knowledge to work."

"It's important to think big and to think broadly," Nancy added with lively enthusiasm. She wore a colorful scarf and matching jewelry on her wrists and ears that bounced as she gestured. "When we do that, it gives us so many more opportunities to find the solutions. They're out there, all around us."

"And this is true in so many different domains," Brie chimed in, matching her colleague's effervescence. "We actually do have solutions, and data that show they work. But part of the challenge is getting that information out to a broader audience. It's about helping people figure out how to take a program, let's say, that was done in rural South Dakota, and make it work in, say, an urban area in Pennsylvania. Sure, some design work needs to be done, but the fundamental takeaway is that there's already a treasure box of knowledge and information and solutions. We're just not fully opening it."

The two ladies' zeal was contagious. I jumped in eagerly, my own animated gestures rising to their energy levels. "I had a hypothesis when I started this journey," I explained. "We probably have way more solutions at our fingertips than we realize. In government, we always refer to it as 'low-hanging fruit.' What's already working that we can start with, and then how do we refine it to make it more useful? But one of the challenges is finding that information."

Brie and Nancy nodded as I continued, "For instance, we have all of these think tanks in government, and they produce white papers that are a mile long. I had an experience once while I was still in government: I was working on a research project and had to read this report that was six hundred pages long. I'm pretty sure I was the only one to read it. That's a problem."

"Yeah, we're antiwhite-paper," Brie agreed dryly. "People just don't read a hundred pages—or six hundred pages or even fifty—so why do we keep making these formats? I mean, it would be like releasing all of your knowledge on, like, a Beta videotape—"

"I'm pretty sure most people don't even know what that is," I interjected lightly.

"Right, it's something people don't even have a player for anymore," Brie amended with a smile. "The point is, if you aren't putting your best ideas into a media format that's accessible, shareable, and engaging, then you're not doing the work necessary to get the full value from them. So, here at Worldview, we try to work with people who have those terrific solutions. We come to them and say, 'Fantastic that you put out that forty-page journal article, now let us help you do a video version or an infographic. Let us help you make those great insights more usable.'"

Nancy picked up the thread of discussion, the two practically finishing one another's thoughts, "And it's more important than ever because the biggest constraint that people have is time. And more than that, there's a clear difference in how generations prefer to take in knowledge. Either we wake up to those realities and start sharing ideas in new ways—and in ways that invite people to respond and contribute—or else we lose huge opportunities to tap into the collective brilliance of the people on this planet."

"Why don't people already do that?" I asked.

Brie considered, "One of the problems is that academia is still structured around guilds—a medieval approach to managing people and knowledge and skills." And Brie would know, given her academic experience, first earning a doctorate in neurosciences at Stanford and then serving as a senior research scholar there.

"If you're a psychologist, let's say, then you work with the guild of psychologists, and you frame everything you do to impress other psychologists. That's who matter. They're the ones who determine whether you get tenure. So everything you do ends up getting directed to this very small group of people, and nothing about your advancement in academia has anything to do with how well you engage the public."

She made a sarcastic face, "And if you engage the public really well, people probably think you're a bit of a lightweight because you're spending your time with the public instead of those people who 'really matter' in your guild." More seriously, although no less dynamically, she continued, "Part of the solution is changing the incentive structure within academia. For instance, the National

Science Foundation has a requirement that all grantees talk about how they're going to achieve broader impacts with their research. I think that's fantastic. The next step would be to have the NIH and other funding agencies, like DARPA, do the same. And then we need those agencies to say, 'We're going to help you by connecting you with people who do it well.' Another thing is that knowledge producers really need to learn from social media. Those influencers have figured out how to create engaging media. There are lessons we can learn from them on how to make useful knowledge for the social and natural and behavioral sciences available to broader audiences."

"You know, it's also broader than academia," Nancy supplemented. "It's about having empathy for everyone: How can we help each other learn? How can we help each other do things better? You know, just because you're a brilliant academic that has a PhD doesn't mean you have all the answers. It's about connecting the dots across all kinds of boundaries—whether they're geographic or disciplinary, state or local or national. It's about fostering those kinds of conversations. It's about listening, asking better questions, inviting in diverse perspectives, not judging those ideas too soon, and really creating the conditions for learning and curiosity. And I think if we connect the dots—and there are a lot of dots out there to connect—that we'll be a lot further along."

Mentally, I cheered. Nancy and Brie had just echoed and validated what I'd seen across our nation. The emperor really had no clothes! Too many of our so-called problems stem from communication and orchestration challenges rather than gaps in knowledge or lack of resources. Bridging the research-practice gap is no trivial matter, but it's a fundamentally different kind of predicament—and one, I think, our nation can readily overcome if we set our minds to it.

After the Lone Star State, the campaign trail took me into Oklahoma. I stopped for a night in the capital and chatted with Matt Stafford on digital innovation. He works with companies to help bridge the gap between people and technology. His company even coined a term for it: *humalogy*. We talked about getting the right blend of humans and automation, and Matt emphasized that more automation—more technological innovation—isn't always better. Instead, it's about the mix, the confluence of insights across domains. Although Matt was referring to a relatively narrow slice of business fields, my mind saw patterns in the conversation.

Across domains and subjects and capabilities, it's all about the connections. There's a growing sense, or in some cases (like with Brie and Nancy) a well-researched fact, that so many pieces of the solution already exist. But we're not always looking in the right places for them.

Beyond the local interviews and campaign events, the downtown memorial in Oklahoma City really stands out in my mind. Built over the remnants of the 1995 federal building bombing, the site radiates an aura of quiet reflection like sacred ground. In its center, a long shallow pool reflects the sky, and next to it stand 168 empty chairs, representing those who lost their lives in the attack. Nearby, the National Memorial Museum has exhibits about the victims, the first responders, and the city's outlook on the assault and its aftermath.

One display that caught my attention described the city's revitalization efforts undertaken after the tragedy. From the damage and heartache, the community came together to rebuild and press forward. Oklahoma City experienced a renaissance after the bombing, the display explained. Congress provided more than $50 million for reconstruction, and local businesses and private investors added millions more. Since that fateful day, the city has transformed its old warehouse district into a modern entertainment area, attracted a professional NBA team, started an annual marathon, and constructed a new music hall. And today, the memorial contributes almost $50 million a year to the region.[2] In the exhibit, a lesson plan made for students asks, "Can good come out of a bad situation?" For OKC, at least, the community has clearly rallied with resilience in face of tragedy. Sometimes something negative—even something evil—can be a catalyst that inspires good.

I'd never been to Arkansas before, and it was fall by the time I crossed the border. All around me the trees were turning into brilliant shades of canary and crimson. I was surprised to find so many Arkansas cities have a New England–sort of feeling. I'd had no idea there were so many hills and foliage throughout Little Rock, and Fayetteville seemed like the architectural kin of Providence. I'd also underestimated how small its streets would be. Once again, I found myself in camper purgatory, trying to navigate all of the diminutive boulevards with my unwieldy land-yacht.

In Fayetteville, I did some presidential exploration at the Clinton House Museum, a remarkably unremarkable little bungalow where Bill and Hillary lived in their younger days. Today, it houses Clinton-themed memorabilia, including a flying pig sculpture in front of the house. (OK, it's supposed to be a Razorback mascot from the University of Arkansas but let me live in my funnier fantasy world!) Inside the house, the predictable political keepsakes were on display, like photos and old campaign swag. I was surprised to also see less flattering artifacts, including souvenirs of defeats and some hilariously sarcastic merch. One card in the gift shop featured a caricature of Hillary Clinton with a line that read, "I meant to send you a birthday e-mail but it disappeared!"

After a few days in Arkansas, I pressed south to Louisiana. As I neared the border, I noticed one of those shifts in the local atmosphere. Expressways lined with colorful trees gave way to narrow roads framed by churches. One village I drove through was so small that it didn't even have a fast food restaurant or grocery store, but it somehow supported three churches. (That's a lot of worship!) In every direction I looked, I also saw boatloads of American flags, often accompanied by biblical signs. The whole region, particularly in the smaller towns and countryside, felt sharply Christian and hyper-American.

My route took me through Natchez and Alexandria and, eventually, to Baton Rouge. Before exploring the capital, I first visited the nearby Bluebonnet Swamp Nature Center, an educational conservation area. After a few hours spent exploring the park's boardwalks, I was famished. So I followed some online reviews to a local Creole joint. Being a Monday night, the place was pretty quiet. There was just the one bartender and another fellow nursing a beer at the bar. Climbing onto a nearby stool, I took a proffered menu.

"Anything look interestin'?" the bartender asked, a Louisiana accent blurring his words.

"I don't know," I admitted, "What do you recommend? I'm looking for local flare." That piqued his interest, so I added, "I'd also love to hear about the bar too, you know, some local stories."

"Well, I'd say you'd do all right with some étouffée and," he added with a grin, "a *proper* hurricane."

I nodded my agreement, and he set about mixing liquors for my drink. As he worked, I asked what made this hurricane different from its presumed impostors. That was the right button to press because it launched him into a well-rehearsed diatribe on why his concoction was objectively superior to the tourist swill in New Orleans. The other guy at the bar couldn't resist chiming in, and by the time my dinner arrived, we were all having a lively conversation.

I told the two about my presidential aspirations and nationwide road trip. They told me about the region, the local bog (that's their own phrasing), and some of their respective family histories. We talked for a time, although never really about politics. Instead, my unofficial cultural guides shared stories that brought the region to life, and like my time in Alaska and Hawai'i, I felt a dawning sense of all the many customs and traditions I'd never experienced before. Take the Cajun and Creole cultures. Despite their exceptional roots and vivid pasts, we rarely learn about them in school, and beyond a handful of (typically lousy) portrayals on TV, those cultures get short shrift in all kinds of media. I was reminded again of our great American salad bowl, and I thought, *If we did a better job integrating all of these extraordinary perspectives—now that would spur innovation.*

The next morning, I woke before sunrise and was in New Orleans by midmorning. That Creole bartender got one thing right: New Orleans is so different from the rest of the state. Although last night he'd meant that comment as a good-natured taunt, it still rang true in the light of day. New Orleans has strong French foundations mixed with Spanish, African, Haitian, and many other cultural influences—all blended together in the pressure cooker of the city's volatile history. Grown from those varied and sometimes embattled beginnings, New Orleans today has become a magical melting pot, a peerless place unlike anywhere else in America and, probably, the world.

Like every tourist before me, I went to Café Du Monde, the historic coffee-and-beignet spot dating back to the 1700s, and then walked through the French Quarter. The area's best known for its raucous parties, but the classic architecture is also a subtle reminder of the city's ignoble history as the onetime hub of the southern slave trade.[3] On top of that, the scars of Hurricane Katrina still blemish the urban landscape, whether as old watermarks on buildings or as shining new edifices out of step with their neighbors.

Well over a thousand people died from Hurricane Katrina, and nearly half of them were killed after the storm, when the levees broke.[4] Residents who'd survived the hurricane and thought they were out of the woods suddenly found themselves in the worst kind of trouble. Many of those who had stayed simply hadn't had the means to leave, perhaps because they were homeless, bedridden, or lacked access to transportation. For whatever reason, thousands were stuck. It was a gut-wrenching tragedy—not merely an act of god or assault of nature but the result of our own fallibility, shortsightedness, and after-the-fact thinking. Sadly, the busted levees and abysmal evacuation were predicted in advance. Some experts, like Ivor van Heerden from Louisiana State University, proverbially waived their arms and screamed their warnings, but they went unheard. It's like what Brie and Nancy from Worldview Studios lamented: Too much knowledge and too many good solutions are trapped on the far side of that research-practice gap, and in this case, that treasure trove of research knowledge was only truly explored with the benefit of hindsight.[5]

As I walked down Bourbon Street, my mind naturally circled back to my campaign strategies, my time in Oklahoma City, and my political philosophies. In the midst of those roiling thoughts, I wondered, *What lessons can we learn from this tragedy as a nation? What good can come from this bad?* The most obvious answer, I thought, was a question to ourselves: *How do we want our society to run? Do we want to be proactive or reactive? Do we want innovation or afterthought? Will we continue to build fences between or begin building footbridges across the research and practice divide?*

The next day I drove to Mississippi. Months earlier, I'd met one of the state's residents on a flight. Characteristically, I'd been carting around a heap of policy documents, which led to a rousing political chat on the plane, and by the time we landed, Bethany Culley and I had exchanged e-mail addresses. That's how I ended up in Jackson at the Broad Street Baking Company and Café on a gray and clammy afternoon. On certain days, like that one, the café doles out free cups of joe to people who drop in for community conversations. So, along with Bethany, an ideologically diverse group joined our conversation including a community pastor, a city planner, and a former educator.

Bethany is a fantastically energetic redhead who loves Jackson, the South, and real estate. She's also one of those community pillars who knows everyone's name, their children, pets, and lives. While planning my visit, Bethany and I had originally agreed to talk about innovation in real estate (her business area), but what started as a simple discussion about housing and districts quickly turned into a community seminar on life in the region.

From my coffee-klatch tutors, I learned about some of the issues affecting Jackson. They chided local leaders for living outside of the area (despite their ostensible in-city addresses), and they observed that many government officials seem more focused on personal power than on helping residents. A culture of poverty and disempowerment also pervades the area, they explained. But that's not where their stories ended. Bethany shared her experiences with local investors groups who've banded together to assist neighborhoods, and her friends chimed in with their own anecdotes about civic organizations that are making a difference, even with limited political support and meager resources. In the end, the conversation embodied more hope and progress than finger-pointing and dejection.

Although initially surprised by the discussion's direction, I wasn't shocked by where it ended. When I'd first met Bethany, her vibrancy had immediately impressed me, and after our coffeehouse conversation those sentiments redoubled. It's not just her energy and openness that stand out; it's also her willingness to question the status quo and to act as an agent of change. If you'd asked Bethany before whether she saw those characteristics or their application in the local community as innovative, she likely would have demurred. To me, however, she's a touchstone of innovativeness. Scientific geniuses and eccentric inventors don't have a monopoly on that concept. True innovation has many forms; although, they share some core characteristics. Innovation is about pushing yourself to look at everyday situations differently, approach problems resourcefully, and move forward continuously. That's just as true for solving big issues, like the global environment or national health care, as for local ones.

After Jackson, I spent a day in Oxford and then crossed the border into Tennessee, stopping for the night in Memphis. It's home to the FedEx headquarters, University of Memphis (where I snagged a couple of expert interviews), and the Memphis Pyramid, a gleaming skyscraper that houses a Bass Pro Shops megastore. But perhaps the city's most notable attraction is Elvis Presley's Graceland. As luck would have it, the RV park where I stayed connects to the estate, and although I barely had an hour to spare, I couldn't pass up the opportunity to see Elvis's iconic pad.

Later that night, one of my campground neighbors admonished me for the meager time I'd dedicated to The King's abode.

"You need at least three or four hours," she explained as we chitchatted between our mobile homes. "This is my seventeenth time visiting. You know, Elvis has always been a part of my life. When I think back to when I was a little girl, well, those memories are chock-full of his music and movies. And so I keep coming back—and dragging my family with me!" She raised her voice with that last line, playfully teasing her husband who stood nearby.

Returning to a normal pitch, the woman continued our small talk, "I've brought all my children and grandchildren here over the years. It's turned into a family ritual, our little pilgrimages."

Elvis was never a big part of my life, but I can relate to her ideas. For me, this whole year has been a kind of pilgrimage, and although I didn't know it, like the literary pilgrim's journey, I was about to face an unexpected ordeal. It started innocently. Someone at the university had tipped me off about a one-of-a-kind little bakery. So the next morning, I decided to stop by for some sugary confections on my way out of town. As warned, the bakery didn't have parking for my campaign-mobile. Instead, I wedged my camper into the tiny lot of a nearby boutique. It was Sunday, so the boutique's lot was empty, leaving me plenty of dockage.

After loading my camper with maple bacon and vanilla sprinkle goodness, I set out for Nashville. Throwing my RV into drive, I pressed the accelerator, turned the wheel toward the exit—and then heard this sickening, screeching metal-on-metal sound. Horror-struck, I stepped outside and took in the scene. I'd violated the first principle of motor homes: Don't run into the overpass. I'd run into the underside of a concrete arch. Ostensibly, my RV should have fit under it, but the AC unit on top had caught on the girders. I tried to reverse out, but somehow the metal beams and AC unit intertwined themselves. As I gingerly worked to untangle them, the drywall inside my house started to tear. Every movement threatened to open my camper like a can of sardines.

I sat down on the curb, head in my hands, and felt defeated. For a time, I let myself wallow in alternating waves of anger and self-pity, as I stress-ate my doughnuts. Then, with no other options, I quit my pity party, picked myself back up, and called roadside assistance. About an hour later, an oddly matched pair of men arrived. One was older, with crooked teeth and rural overalls, and the other was a younger, beanpole of a man in trendy streetwear. As soon as they saw the scene, they both laughed uproariously.

"You win!" The older one exclaimed between guffaws. "This is the worst we've ever seen."

They spent the better part of the afternoon working to free me, eventually using a Sawzall to cut through my AC. That ended in a dramatic scene where the younger fellow, who'd precariously wedged himself between the RV and the concrete awning with only his shoes showing, shoved the damaged air conditioner off the camper. It shattered theatrically onto the asphalt. After that, the pair were able to shimmy the camper forward without inflicting any more damage. That freed me, but my ride was in sorry shape. Technically, most of its roof was still there, aside from an AC-sized hole in the center, but if I hoped to make it back to Florida, emergency surgery was needed. So after thanking my rescuers, I beelined it to the nearest home improvement store.

The sun was starting to set, so before I lost the last vestiges of daylight, I stormed into the store and raced to buy tarps, insulation, and of course, some miraculous duct tape. With my makeshift repair kit, I patched things up the best I could and then slowly crept back to the highway. I still needed to get to a campground for the night. By this point, frazzled and exhausted and comically still losing pieces of my RV as I drove, I decided to skip Nashville altogether and head straight to a closer port.

I limped into Birmingham, Alabama, stopping en route at a nearby soul food place to drown my woes. I ordered practically everything on the menu: mac and cheese, collard greens, pulled pork, and fried corn. Oh, and they had two different kinds of desserts that night. You know I got them both. Amazingly, it worked. That comfort food really did salve my soul.

In retrospect, I can look back at that terrible experience and appreciate it. I can even chuckle a little at how ridiculous it must have looked, and I can see the beautiful irony in my hands-on learning opportunity. Sometimes, innovation means figuring out how to use what you have, overcoming problems with improvisation and tenacity—and maybe a serving (or two) of cobbler.

I spent a little time in Birmingham licking my wounds and reinforcing my crumbling camper. The following afternoon, I made it (more or less intact) to Montgomery, my last campaign stop—the final city in the fiftieth state of my national tour. I interviewed two military educators. Initially, we talked about innovation in learning, but the discussion soon meandered to my RV incident and then to the distinctive places I'd visited over the preceding six months. Brandon and Julie were eager to highlight Montgomery's own exceptional heritage, and with well-deserved pride they talked about the city's history and extraordinary role in the civil rights movement. That afternoon I visited some of those celebrated landmarks we'd discussed including the Civil Rights Memorial, National Memorial for Peace and Justice, and Rosa Parks Museum.

In my last #Tour50 video, I reflected on the civil rights movement and, in particular, on the museum dedicated to the mother of that movement. Parks, and her friends and neighbors, took a stand and found creative ways to activate. Through courageous local action, they helped spark a movement and have become shining examples to us all. While it's easy to tell ourselves that individual efforts and singular voices don't really matter, in reality, a single grain of sand can set off the torrent—whether that's on a national stage, within our own local communities, or on a downtown bus in Montgomery, Alabama.

After Montgomery my next destination was home. Feeling desperate to get there, I forced myself to a grueling pace. I drove until I couldn't see straight, and then snagged two hours of dreamless sleep before pressing on. With my camper still rattling dangerously, I pulled into my Orlando driveway a few hours after sunrise on a Thursday in late November, exactly one week before Thanksgiving. I breathed a heavy sigh of relief and then fell into a daylong hibernation—the first time in six months I didn't set a wake-up alarm. Over the next several days, I disconnected from campaigns and politics, focusing instead on family and recuperation.

Just before the holiday, I met my two eldest children in Pennsylvania and cheered from the sidelines as they ran the Philadelphia Marathon. (The irony of watching a literal marathon in our nation's onetime capital was not lost on me.) After that weekend, we all returned to Florida and spent a quiet Thanksgiving, each sharing our most recent adventures. Monica, Mitchell, and I talked a lot about marathons—both the literal kind and figurative political ones. I cheered a little, congratulating myself on crossing that fifty-state finish line, but my kids weren't so willing to concede victory.

"Mom, weren't you running a presidential race?" Mitchell teased rhetorically.

"Yeah, I don't think anyone's giving out participation medals," Monica piled on.

"Fair enough," I agreed, "but we always knew 'the impossible' wasn't likely—shoot, that's why we kept calling it *the impossible*."

Mitchell shrugged noncommittally while Monica reminded me, "You always said it wasn't necessarily about winning the election but more about understanding all of the hidden systems. So do you think that happened?"

"Well," I responded with a slow wry smile, "I still haven't seen a caucus, yet . . . "

★ ★ ★

Admittedly, innovation is an overused and under-clarified term. In this book alone, it's been referred to as creativity, a willingness to change, and the imaginative use of existing resources. Ultimately, I think each of those concepts is right, or more accurately, all together they paint the right picture when also combined with one other aspect: pragmatic effect. Innovation, in my mind, is no navel-gazing exercise. Only ideas and actions that withstand the trials of real-world application can truly be called innovative. (Good-idea fairies can take their stargazing elsewhere.)

Sadly, as I traveled the country, I found too many good ideas trapped on the far side of the research-practice gap. Like Brie and Nancy explained, spanning that divide takes user-friendly communication and a willingness to reach out beyond one's own guild. Still, even those efforts can fall short. Because, like so many things in life and politics, there are also hidden game rules, which can sabotage a guileless player.

As Jeff Leitner, founder of Unwritten Labs, explained during one of my campaign interviews, hidden rules are a fact of life. As social creatures, humans naturally develop collective customs and sanctioned norms. Those unwritten rules help organizations and communities maintain stability, but there's a dark side to them. By design, these invisible social systems prevent change, and the rules themselves resist alteration. There are plenty of valid and evolutionary reasons for these social constructs to exist, but in the civil space, they can stifle innovation and bar access to already disenfranchised groups. Uncovering the invisible rulebook is the first step to either using those implicit conventions or, potentially, circumventing them. Either way, understanding the hidden pitfalls is a necessary part of successful innovation.

Naming those unwritten rules and bridging the research-practice divide, however, are no small feats. Still, they're worth the effort. As a nation, innovation helps us avoid surprise, as Clarke Lethin mentioned. It helps us compete in a global market and withstand black swan events,[6] those unlikely and unforeseen catastrophes, like 9/11 or the 2008 financial crisis, that send agonizing ripples around the world. When applied to governmental programs, innovation also encourages efficiency and better outcomes. Look at the environmental and health-care sectors. Already, countless programs are spending trillions of dollars to stockpile solutions for those domains. But when progress fails to materialize, policymakers (and many others) are quick to call for new projects or additional funds. It's often the case, however, that workable ideas already exist. They're merely trapped—thwarted by a resistance to change, hampered by miscommunication, or tangled up in the invisible spiderweb of unwritten rules.

CHAPTER NINETEEN

The Last Mile

A year ago, I launched my journey into fact-finding research, experimental politics, and an unconventional candidacy. Over my year of living politically, I learned to navigate (at least some parts of) the dark maze of politics. I researched and wrote six strategy reports, engaged thousands of people in civil discourse, and spent time in all fifty states. I even garnered a modicum of media attention and kindled a modest social media following. Although, not the dark-horse Cinderella story-ending I'd been hoping for, surely, by November, I'd reached my own personal finish line. Or had I?

I thought about our conversation on marathons over Thanksgiving dinner. Athletes will tell you: The halfway point of a marathon is the twentieth mile—at least, that feels like the midpoint when you're running the race. The dreaded wall lurks at mile twenty, along with its crippling fatigue, nausea, and self-doubt. It made me wonder, *In my own political marathon, had I truly reached the finish line or was I really hitting that twenty-mile wall? Was I measuring my success by the calendar or by the effects of my actions?* Ultimately, I decided there were a few more miles to go. I couldn't call myself a true presidential contender if I didn't contend in the Iowa caucuses.

Of course, I had no hope of competing with the big-name frontrunners. Not only was I still largely unknown, but my personal gas tank was depleted, my RV was out of commission, and both my pocketbook and campaign coffers were in the red. I couldn't hope to win the state, or even a major precinct, but maybe I could make enough noise to be heard. So the question became: How can I elevate my message to a mainstream media level?

I thought about how the news channels cover Iowa. Candidates who earn at least one percent of the delegates become part of the national discussion, so reaching that mark became my goal. Unfortunately, I knew relatively little about Iowa politics, and until this point, I'd never campaigned for presidential primary votes. I had so many questions about where to start, and despite my yearlong exploration on running the government, I still had few answers on running a campaign. Naturally, I fell back on my nerdy roots: I planned a scouting mission to learn about the lay of the land, the local people, and some of the unwritten rules of the Iowa politics.

Before Christmas, I flew to Sioux City, known by the airport code SUX. Walking through the terminal, I was delighted by the volume of punny swag. Mugs, hats, and T-shirts all reveled in the "Joy of SUX." Some proclaimed "Winter SUX" or "Work SUX." Idly, I wondered if I could find one like "Narrow policy without a cross-cutting strategy SUX," but I suppose it'd be difficult to fit that on a bumper sticker. After the gift shop, I walked by a queue of travelers waiting at the airport's only security checkpoint, then to rental cars desks, and in short order found the exit. I emerged into a blinding winter landscape. Mounds of glistening snow stung my eyes, and the unrelenting wind tore through my travel clothes.

Shivering, I found my car and made my way to the northwest corner of the state. I'd targeted that region because of its strong Republican slant and sparse population. My rationale had been that these precincts would be an unlikely target for fellow Democratic challengers and that the low resident count would make the size of my efforts more manageable. That was the plan, at least.

My first stop was Inwood, a tiny place with fewer than a thousand residents. Later, I realized that Inwood was simply the first in a pattern. All of the little towns I visited seemed to fit a similar mold. I'd be driving down the two-lane highway, with open expanses of snowy farmland stretching out on either side, then all of a sudden, the empty landscape would give way to a small cluster of homes and maybe a gas station, farm store, or fire station. Next, the welcome sign would come into view. Those community placards are noteworthy for the care and wit Iowans put into them. Many of the colorful signs also featured clever taglines, like Rockwell City's "Golden buckle on the corn belt" slogan and Primghar's circular boast of being "The only Primghar in the world."

In Inwood, I went straight to the community center, a multipurpose building that houses the local library, a gym, and meeting space. For that morning, I'd planned for an informal tabling event—that's political lingo for standing behind a table like a Girl Scout selling (election) cookies—and I'd scheduled a town hall for later that evening. My Geek Team arranged advertisements for both events on social media, but according to the analytics, practically no one even saw the ads, let alone clicked on them. Perhaps Facebook and Twitter aren't so popular in rural Iowa. Fortunately, my team had called ahead to the center's manager, so at least one person was there when I arrived. We talked about my presidential campaign, and I told her about my social media flop.

"Oh, you need to go to coffee," she confided. "The ladies meet at 10:00 a.m. at the gas station to the south, and the men meet at 3:00 p.m. at the one up north."

Still midmorning, I had just enough time. I quickly thanked the manager for her tip and then dashed out to meet the ladies. In a town with one main street and no stoplights, the gas station wasn't hard to find. Inside, nearly a dozen women, all well into their retirement years, sat near the back corner. They were chatting with obvious familiarity and sipping from steaming Styrofoam cups. My inner voice immediately revolted, *Am I seriously going to interrupt this group?*

I like to think I'm a sociable person, but I'm far from comfortable when it comes to infringing on people's personal space. *But*, I reasoned as I stared awkwardly in their direction, *I am a campaigning politician, which means it's my job to talk with everyone. Time to work on my candidate skills.* So after a little mental shove, I approached, pausing partway to grab a convenience-store coffee of my own. I smiled at the group. By now, they were surely wondering what this strange woman was doing in their city.

"Hi, I'm JJ, and I'm running for president."

I explained how I'd found my way to the gas station and then asked if I could join their coffee circle. With genuine Midwestern warmth, they encouraged me to take a seat.

"Now why didn't we know you were coming?" a white-haired woman asked as I sat.

"Well, I tried letting people know online, but I'm learning that social media isn't so popular in Inwood," I teased with a little self-deprecation.

The ladies all laughed, and several waved their flip phones. One woman even bemoaned the loss of phone books! After I'd broken the ice, our conversation meandered through my now-well-rehearsed political themes (the things you've read about throughout this book). The women eagerly dove into the political weeds, sharing their own beliefs and concerns. And later that afternoon, I had a similar discussion with the men at their own gas-station gathering. In both cases, the talks enlightened me about Iowa and the residents' local perspectives. Unfortunately, both coffee crews were also entirely comprised of Republican voters, so none of my new acquaintances would be voting in the Democratic primaries.

Later that evening, I held a town hall at the community center. Just one person attended. He was slender and hunched, with thinning grey hair and sun-wrinkled skin. He must have been pushing eighty. We chatted for more than an hour, and he shared a wealth of knowledge on community politics, agriculture, and rural life. For instance, one of his biggest concerns is for family-owned farms and ranches. He worried that those landowners, desperate to hold onto their property, are buying into the propaganda from foreign corporations—mortgaging their croplands piece-by-piece to their questionable interests. He also taught me about hog-confinement stench and why it's important to zone grain elevators near railroads. Despite the low turnout, my town hall fully succeeded in one respect: It helped opened my eyes to the local state of affairs. Thanks, Virgil!

Yet one town and a handful of stories weren't enough. Each day I drove to another village and talked to more Iowans. Between the towns, I crossed seemingly endless acres of sleeping farmland, with only an occasional mailbox or cluster of windmills breaking the monotony. At every stop, my Inwood experience played out again, more or less. Everywhere I traveled, I also always found cliques of citizens eager to chat about governance. In Gowrie, I ran into a data-minded university student debating politics with her dad at the Ole Town Road Pub. In Storm Lake, a handful of seniors at the Amvets Club shared their perspectives on veterans' issues. And in Sioux City, I debated partisanism with a handful of folks at Famous Dave's. With each stop, my mental knowledge bank of Iowa grew.

After a week of exploration, I flew back to Orlando, intent on getting some Christmastime R&R with my family and a few strategy sessions in with my Geek Team. During those campaign meetings, we unpacked what I'd found in Iowa. Everyone agreed we should continue focusing on the Fourth District (that northwest quadrant of the state). We also decided that my haphazard run-into-voters-at-the-library plan was less than ideal. Instead, we got an Iowa Democratic voter list and filtered it by region. There are around fifty thousand Democrats in the northwest quadrant, but only about twelve thousand in the handful of counties we targeted. We looked for the smallest precincts, once again assuming it'd be easier to convince a handful of people in a smaller caucus to go rogue.

Now, you may be wondering, *How did we plan to convince voters? What was our compelling sales pitch to sway them to my camp?* Well, we still hadn't figured that out. There was a lot left to learn.

In early January, I returned to Iowa for a second scouting trip. This time, I'd prepared printed invitations to my town halls. I planned to knock on doors and drop off flyers house by house. After arriving at SUX, I drove to Sioux Center, a moderately sized town by Iowa standards, and found the freshly plowed driveway of Titus and Maggie Landegent, my Airbnb hosts for the evening. I parked precariously by a snowdrift and skidded in my red cowboy boots as I clambered inside.

Their comfortable home made a welcome contrast to the dark and bitter weather. Inside, warm oaken planks covered the walls and floors. Titus and Maggie's two young boys squabbled playfully over a video game in the living room, and the aroma of something delicious wafted from the kitchen where Titus was cooking. Not long after I arrived, we all sat down together for dinner. After a group blessing, bowls of food made the rounds, and we chatted.

"I see you're running for president," Titus observed.

"Oh, you googled me!" I chuckled.

Titus nodded, and we fell into the usual small talk. He and Maggie shared their own backgrounds. He works as a kindergarten teacher and she as a community civil servant. Throughout our conversation, Maggie often framed her thoughtful questions from that local-government lens, and Titus, with his strong Libertarian leanings, frequently examined things from his classically liberal one. Our conversation spilled across topics, progressing quickly from family and careers to the partisan divide, citizens' resistance to change, and (most interesting to me) local political perceptions.

"Tradition and religion are cornerstones here in Iowa," Titus explained. "People will want to know how you'll negotiate the typical Democratic viewpoints on issues like abortion."

This was my kind of small talk!

"What are your plans for overcoming institutional inertia in government?" Maggie chimed in a little later.

And later still, Titus submitted, "I think we should probably reduce the federal government by, like, 90 percent. What do you think about that?"

We talked well into the night, each person making solid points and the others genuinely considering each angle. These are the moments I live for! The opportunity to talk with people, to take the time to share and learn, and to challenge both myself and others. This is the real political discourse—not those media sound bites and online Twitterstorms.

The next morning, Titus and Maggie helped me make some local contacts, including Kim Van Es, deputy chair of the Sioux County Democratic Party, and Laremy De Vries, co-owner of the Fruited Plain Café (*the* place where candidates stump in Sioux Center). Kim and I scheduled a meeting later that day. Meanwhile, hoping to run into Laremy, I headed to the Fruited Plain, a homey downtown coffee joint. I ordered a latte and asked the barista if Laremy was around. As luck would have it, he was standing right there at the coffee bar.

A self-described philosopher-cum-barista, Laremy is a political pillar in the community, and he's hosted events at the café for all of the major candidates over the last several elections. Laremy knows the ropes, which means he also knew how unlikely my campaign was to win, from a conventional perspective. Still I gave him my usual spiel about government, political innovation, and civic responsibility. He listened and ask penetrating questions. Given the opportunity to geek out, my politician persona quickly fell away. Before I realized it, my candidate disguise was replaced by my nerdy truth.

"I'd love to do a whiteboarding session where we all design some government solutions!" I enthused. "Do you think residents around here might be interested?"

"I think so," Laremy considered. "The way I see it, everyone needs to be having those big conversations, especially right now, and with your government angle and alternative approach, you should be part of that dialogue."

Yeah, I thought inwardly, *I may not win an election, but if my voice helps raise the discourse, I can live with that!* So Laremy and I hashed out the details, planning our alternative election event for later that month.

The next day, I moved north to Milford, a lakeside town sitting on the Iowa-Minnesota border. I'd already scheduled a town-hall event and had given two days to hand deliver the flyers for it. But I'd underestimated the practical distance between houses in rural Iowa. On the map, five miles didn't seem so far, but with gusting winds and blankets of snow, that distance might as well have been infinite. As I struggled along the county roads, several lessons came to mind.

If you ever find yourself running for president and canvassing in Iowa, here are a few tips: First, bring Scotch Tape. Most houses don't use mailboxes, and you'll need a way to fasten a flyer to each house's front door. Make sure to use a lot of tape, because the icy wind will rip those puppies away in an instant. Second, wear snow boots. This may seem obvious, but I'd planned poorly and had assumed my cowboy boots would cut it. Stylish footwear is a poor choice for navigating unplowed paths and heaping snowdrifts. Third, while you're navigating those snowy walkways, leave your car door open. Efficiency is key, but more than that, the farmhouse dogs—faithfully protecting their homes from strangers (like you)—may require you to hasten a retreat. The trick is to make it back into the safety of your car quicker than the eager pups can catch you—and to do that without falling on your tuchus. Finally, and most importantly, don't even try to canvass door-to-door in the middle of an Iowan winter. Just send your announcements through the mail. No one wants to talk to an uninvited politician on their ice-covered doorstep, and you definitely don't want to be the one standing there, shivering. It only took two days for me to fully learn those lessons and ditch my original plan. Canvassing SUX.

So what happened to my scheduled town hall? I still held it. (Actually, I held a few, scattered across several small towns.) But since the invitation process was an utter snafu, I didn't get much turnout. Still, like the one-man town hall I'd run in Inwood, my seemingly futile efforts were frequently rewarded with valuable gems of insight.

At the community center in Holstein, for example, I struck up a conversation with the building attendant. He looked to be around twenty-eight years old, with an athletic build and high-and-tight hair.

"So glad you're here!" he welcomed jovially as I entered.

Standing in the entryway, stomping clumps of snow off of my boots, I returned his greeting. Then, with an apologetic expression, I confessed that probably no one else would be joining my event. I explained about the weather, the driving conditions, and other Iowa challenges. He chuckled with understanding, and we struck up a conversation. Given his bearing and style, I was unsurprised to discover his second job is with the National Guard. Eager to talk with someone else who understands politics and defense, we delved into a lengthy chat about the mission of government and changing role of national security.

Around the end of my town-hall time slot, he offered, "You've gotta talk to the head of the local Democrats. She's coming next week to run a mock caucus. I'll give you her number."

I'm not a fan of cold calling, but telemarketing is a critical skill for candidates, right? So I grabbed my phone and dialed. It went to voice mail. I left a message. A half-hour later, Lori Leonard Reyman called back.

"I got your message," Lori greeted with an apparent smile in her voice, "but I'm afraid you were misinformed. I am *not* the head of the Democrats. I'm with the National Federation of Republican Women. Now, to be honest, I'd like to say, 'too bad for you, little lady!' But as a good Holstein girl, I'm gonna help you out. I'll let you know where to find the local Dems."

Then she proceeded to list all of the town's Democrats—not the party leaders or elected officials but the individual Democratic voters, like "the lawyer" and "those folks with the auction company." It wasn't a long list. She was finished in about sixty seconds.

"Wow," I replied. "Not too many Democrats. Is that awkward?" I wondered with a chuckle, "I mean, are they like 'those people' around town?"

"Oh, no!" she replied with mild confusion. "We've all grown up together. At some point, we've watched each other's kids and done business together. We might have different politics, but at the end of the day, we're neighbors first—and you can quote me in that book of yours!" she exclaimed with a laugh. I laughed too.

Before hanging up, we had a wonderful discussion about Holstein life, politics, and government. We closed the call by agreeing on the importance of working together across the partisan aisle. Ultimately, we both acknowledged, our nation depends on it.

May we all follow Lori's "Holstein girl" lead!

Later that January, I returned once again to the frosty Hawkeye State. My first two visits had mainly focused on information-gathering. This time I was determined to be a better candidate. In my earlier visits, I'd found that Iowans take pride in their state's role in the primary process, and as a result, many are civically minded. The residents I met asked good questions and seemed well-read. Many claimed to avoid traditional media, including the debates, preferring instead to hear candidates in person or consult more thoughtful treatments of their positions. That feedback gave me hope: *Perhaps this was a state where my message could be heard—not because I had flashy ads or fancy jingles, but because I had data, a blueprint, and some commonsense strategies worth sharing.*

Another thing that sets Iowa apart is its primary-selection system. Only a handful of states and US territories use caucuses. And for those of us accustomed to voting booths and personal ballots, the caucus process seems a bit unusual. Residents meet at their voting precincts, listen to surrogates advocate for their favored candidates, and then debate each hopeful's merits. After that, everyone votes by moving to a designated spot in the room to stand in clusters of like-minded voters until the final counts are taken. At least, that's the gist of how they work. But I was looking for more than cursory knowledge, so two weeks before the official caucuses, I attended mock caucus (or "mock-us," as they like to call it).

This mock-us was hosted by the Sioux County Democrats, and they hosted it in a large meeting space at Northwestern College library. A podium stood near the front of the room, and several rows of chairs were lined up before it. More than a hundred would-be voters mingled around the room. Travis Andersen, the local Democratic Party chair, called the mock-us to order. He explained its goals (to practice the process so the real caucuses would run smoothly) and rules for the event (no canvassing for real candidates).

Instead of advocating for actual politicians, the mock-us speakers offered a one-minute pitch for their favorite superheroes, including Superman, Captain Planet, and Steve, the local barista and apparent hometown hero. After that, the advocates were positioned around the room, and mock-voters were given ten minutes to assemble with their chosen factions. Meanwhile, based on the total attendance figures, the facilitators calculated the viability number, which is the minimum size a particular group needs to be for its candidate to advance. In our case, for this first round that number was twelve.

After everyone had formed into clusters, the groups with at least twelve supporters signed voting cards. The nonviable groups were disbanded, and their former members had five minutes to join one of the remaining groups. During this second round, pandemonium reigned. Some groups plied would-be supporters with brownies and cookies; others tried to woo new voters with snarky appeals. After everyone had found their second-round homes, the facilitators tallied the group sizes again, voter cards were signed, and delegate awards were announced based on the size of each remaining viable group.

I sided with barista Steve, because who doesn't want to vote for "Coffee for All"? Apparently that was a popular sentiment, because Steve won two out of the five caucus delegates, superhero Malice (who we all know is really a supervillain despite the political spin) also won two delegates, and Captain Planet earned the last one. In a real caucus, the next step would have been to pick someone from each group to physically attend a March meeting in Des Moines, where delegates formally cast their votes for each candidate. What a total contrast to how things work in Florida! Of course, my home state also has its voting quirks—remember hanging chads? (We try to forget them every year.)

Besides attending the mock-us, I organized more campaign events this time around—and I even had a smidge more success. I spoke to a local veterans' club, for example, interviewed a fellow dark-horse candidate running for the Fourth District congressional spot, and I finally held that session at the Fruited Plain. For that coffeehouse town hall, I blanketed the tables with butcher paper and doled out colorful markers. I also handed out copies of the national strategies I'd written. A handful of voters came to the event, and together we discussed, debated, and sketched ideas on the paper table covers—for over three hours.

The room had an atmosphere of open curiosity. Those folks who attended were bemused by my unconventional campaign perspective, but they nonetheless embraced it eagerly. And, as seen throughout my travels, I found that by framing the situation differently, elevating the conversation to a strategic level, and focusing on problem-solving principles (like Rubik's Cube solutions) rather than partisan platforms, the conversation shifted. Those town-hall participates began tackling complex concepts and talking about larger scale issues. In other words, we freed the discussion from the tyranny of the tactical (that *right here, right now*–kind of thinking) and brought the discussion to a higher level.

For me, that town hall in small-town Iowa marked one of the high points of my year. Where before, during my early political exploration and later on my fifty-state tour, I'd been seeking answers, now I finally felt like I had something solid to share. I had started my adventure with a theory (or, perhaps more accurately, a series of hopes) that America has enough ideas, resources, and remarkable citizens to solve our problems. Like so many other moments from my campaign, this little gathering on an icy Midwestern night, reinforced my confidence in the truth of that belief.

The 2020 Iowa Democratic caucuses were held a week later. Just days before, in an eleventh-hour decision, the Democratic party had announced a rule change for the forthcoming New Hampshire debate. Fundraising figures were no longer a requirement.¹ Now, any candidate who earned at least one Iowa delegate could join in. For my campaign, that decision was a potential game changer. My chances of getting onto the national stage jumped from utterly impossible to extremely unlikely. My Geek Team and I decided we'd take those odds!

We doubled down on our Fourth District campaign cramming. We picked the best salespeople from our crew, divvied up the voter contact lists, and devised a makeshift telemarketing strategy. I also contacted all of my new Iowa political pals. Our first goal was to find someone willing to advocate for me in at least one precinct—a thing called "caucusing for someone," which is a critical element in the state's primaries. In addition, we needed to shake loose voters willing to throw their support in my direction, people willing to vote for elevating a rogue candidate's message instead of backing one of the big-name front-runners.

We got to work, and in less than a day, I'd found my advocate. Titus Landegent, staunch Libertarian and my onetime Airbnb host, texted me. "For the first time in history," he wrote, "I've registered as a Democrat so I can caucus for you." Amazing! I felt honored and grateful that someone would dedicate their time (and take on the hassle of voter registration paperwork) for me—or, more accurately, for my message.

Meanwhile, my improvised sales team was hard at work calling Iowa Dems. For voters with unlisted numbers, my Geek Team looked on Facebook and then sent personal messages to voters with public profiles. We wanted to make sure everyone going to the Sioux County caucuses had, at least, heard my name and gotten a hint of my nontraditional message.

Before the big day, I e-mailed some talking points to Titus. We texted back and forth, and he crafted the final pitch in his own words. The night of the caucus, my Geek Team and I hovered eagerly by our phones, wondering how it went. (Candidates aren't allowed into the actual events.) For my own part, I felt like a runner watching the anchor leg of my team's relay race. All I could do was look on from the sidelines, twiddling my thumbs while I awaited my fate.

When my phone finally chimed with a message from Iowa, it wasn't the result I'd hoped for. We hadn't convinced enough voters and hadn't reached the one-delegate mark. But I did hear that Titus gave one heck of a fiery speech! So even though I finished the race in last place, at least I ran it, and at least I crossed that finish line—with spirited enthusiasm, to boot.

One of the many professionals I met during my political journey introduced me to the saying: *Policy doesn't win elections.* That certainly fits my own experiences. The current electoral system isn't designed to favor policymaking performance. Instead, metrics like money and name-recognition rule the day. I'm not naïve to that reality, but even with that knowledge, I couldn't truly convince myself to play the conventional candidates' game. My hard-charging efforts in Iowa were a glaring affirmation that I'm no natural-born politician. I canvass poorly, fundraise terribly, and have an allergy to making backdoor deals for ducats. Even after I tried to shift my focus to winning votes and earning delegates, I still fell back to my comfort zone of ideas—even though I knew my competition was waging a different kind of contest.

After the Iowa caucuses, I formally announced to my small enclave of fans and teammates that I'd be suspending my 2020 presidential bid. Despite my poetic journey and our Hail-Mary attempt at the end, I couldn't sway enough voters to gamble on a no-name candidate running on a platform of problem-solving processes and political innovation. At least, I couldn't convince them in 2020. Stayed tuned. The future—our collective future—is yet unwritten. And winning an election unconventionally isn't the only way to affect change.

CHAPTER TWENTY

Pieces of the Patriotic Puzzle

The 2016 presidential election opened my eyes to the partisan vitriol, absurd election rules, and growing polarization of our nation. More savvy politicos will point out that those undercurrents have been swirling for years and actually date back to some of our earliest presidential races. (I'm looking at you, Rutherford Hayes.) Still, before the 2016 election cycle, I'd been asleep. Sure, I would dutifully vote in the state and federal races, but otherwise I had largely avoided political news, skipped the rallies, and kept my pocketbook far away from those fundraisers. I did my minimum civic duty (or so I had thought) and then got on with my life.

My son's questions in 2016 had planted a seed. They roused me to the election drama, and at first, I found it bemusing: The debate-themed drinking games made me laugh, and it was fun to taunt "fake news" in conversations. But it didn't take long for the humor to sour. The more attention I paid to the political process, the more it chilled me, and that seed of curiosity Mitchell had sown began to feel like a stone of concern. Not unlike my son, I started to wonder, *Are these truly the best people in America? Why is our election process so damaging and illogical? And what in the hell is driving this?* The more I worried at those questions, the more they consumed me—until I decided to do something about it.

My political journey started modestly enough, with reading articles, going to local rallies, and talking to politically active folks. I spent my free time investigating hot button issues and reimagining governmental systems, sometimes under the guise of whiteboard "parties" with my friends. Then I ran my kitchen-table campaign, partially as some good geeky fun and partially to learn the ropes. I launched a blog to sharpen my thinking and even dipped my toe into the icy waters of political social media.

But everywhere I looked—left, right, and center—I saw irrationalities and contradictions, so much so that I began doubting my own perceptions. *Things couldn't really be this bad, right?* I felt like Alice down the rabbit hole, unsure of where to find the terra firma of truth. But I persisted, and gradually, as I developed a sense for the unwritten rules and hidden power dynamics, the invisible logic within the system grew clearer. As it did, I started to feel like I'd swallowed Morpheus's red pill.

The dysfunction seemed more ingrained than I'd anticipated. From what I could tell, federal-level politics is a tight-knit system that's largely controlled by power brokers, sketchy PACs, entrenched incumbents, and the political elite. There's too often a bias toward shorter-term solutions, and there's frequently a focus on retaining power over other concerns. No doubt, many politicos have the best intentions (or at least had them at one time), but the system's structures tend to erode such ideals by incentivizing partisan tactics, hustling for dollars, and questionable influence brokering. Even as an outsider running a largely investigative campaign, I could feel those incentives nipping at my convictions.

The financial drivers are particularly powerful. Chasing greenbacks isn't just a slippery slope for politicians—there's a dang tractor beam at the end. It's been eye-opening. While I wasn't naïve before, I've still been surprised over the last year by the boundless role money plays in federal politics.

It reminds me of a scene from the movie *Black Panther*. T'Challa, the benevolent king, is fighting a bloody duel for the crown against his rival, Erik Killmonger. T'Challa's people watch in horror as their leader gets deposed through an antiquated rite. Afterward, they frown and cry. It's good movie drama. But if Wakanda were a real kingdom, then I'd have to ask, "Why in the hell (as one of the world's most advanced fictional nations) are you still using trial by combat? If you had wanted the noble guy versus the hothead, then maybe pick a different kind of contest." Then again, if you squint your eyes, our own federal system isn't much different. Our electoral structure favors popular names, political connections, and fundraising prowess. It's not exactly trial by combat, but it's more or less trial by currency.

If my yearlong experiment has convinced me of anything, it's that we need to get the money out of politics. Elected office should be something candidates and incumbents apply (versus buy) their way into. But finance reform by itself probably isn't enough. Even if we magically eliminate money's stranglehold in campaigns, then we're still left with a different sort of duel: We'll have swapped Wakanda for Panem. Our major elections (particularly the presidential ones) will still be stuck in the *Hunger Games*. Candidates will still be rewarded for things like on-air zingers, unrelenting self-assurance, and dramatic divisiveness—qualities that often undermine the ability to do good work once in elected office.

When I interviewed innovation expert Jeff Leitner, he'd griped about the presidential selection process with similar incredulity. "We're essentially hiring somebody to run the biggest, most complicated company in America—and we're doing it with a reality show? Shouldn't we be using something more objective?"

If we hope to hire for talent and capability, then Jeff is right: We need to rethink our candidacy system—including, but much broader than, finance reform. It's like Tony Vecchio from the Jacksonville Zoo said about the environment: We can't focus on just one endangered species at a time ("Save the Lions!"). Everything in an ecosystem is interconnected, so we have to think about the bigger picture, look at all of the components, and consider their interplay. If not, when we try to shift one piece at a time, we're likely to have limited success (at best), and we run the risk of unexpected consequences. Plus, without pinpoint planning, there's a good chance the system will simply adapt around a singular change, find another loophole, or grow a scab over the abrasion.

We need that Rubik's Cube thinking again. We need to plan beyond singular solutions (the individual components like campaign finance, primary processes, media bias, voting access, and voter integrity) and start looking at their integrated whole.

At first, as I pondered all of this after my campaign with my rose-colored glasses now removed, the idea of taking a Rubik's Cube approach to federal election reform seemed like cloud-cuckoo-land. *If campaign finance is tough to address,* I brooded, *then comprehensive transformation seems inconceivable.*

There are structural and social incentives that resist change. You'll find similar barriers in most established systems, but in federal politics, they're particularly entrenched. The existing system benefits those already inside it, the elected officials and other power brokers, so the people in the best positions to make systemic changes are also the least incentivized to do so. Plus, the political machine has an indoctrinating effect. Without realizing it, as junior politicians master the game rules, they usually begin operating within them. After all, they can't scuttle those rules if they hope to stick around long enough to have a shot at making an impact. And so, like the proverbial boiling frog, over time many gradually grow comfortable with that warped reality. For those who somehow retain their reformist perspectives, the system produces antibodies against them, like partisan tactics to block mavericks from key positions or that encourage PACs to fund their opponents. These indirect checks-and-balances help the status quo stay afloat, and the Pollyannas who threaten it frequently find themselves stymied or even ejected, as a result.

* * *

For several weeks after the campaign, I let myself wallow in those bitter thoughts, and while I needed to understand the situation, that circular thinking was getting me nowhere. I forced myself to refocus. *What was the real problem I was trying to solve, anyway?* Ultimately, it wasn't politics or government. They're each a means to an end. What really matters are the outcomes they're responsible for, things like securing the nation, spreading quality education, and supporting collective health. So setting aside politics for a satisfying moment, what's the art possible?

That's actually a question I'd been asking throughout my political exploration, and during my campaign tour, I had hoped to find a few pieces of that puzzle. I'd been looking for inspiration and signs of hope outside of the usual political circles. And, oh boy, did I find them! Whether talking to subject-matter experts or citizens on the street, I felt like an archaeologist, digging in the sand of our nation and discovering solutions left and right.

Take the environment: There are so many government programs, legislative committees, and libraries of scientific research. There are impressive nongovernmental groups like the Surfrider Foundation and Sow True Seed, education programs such as the Carolina Raptor Center and Jacksonville Zoo, and crosscutting ones like the Association of Zoos and Aquariums. In other words, there's so much energetic goodness nationwide that it's impossible for me to conclude that we don't have the answers or aren't working hard enough.

I saw similar patterns everywhere. No matter the domain, I consistently found that we have the building blocks—the research, resources, pieces, and parts—to tackle any issue. That doesn't mean I'm blind to our ongoing problems. Rather, I'm simply not convinced that we're lacking the ways and means to solve them. Instead, it's as if we have a glut of individual puzzle pieces strewn across our national table, and we're struggling to put them together. Meanwhile, we're spinning our wheels building new pieces to add to the pile.

As an example, instead of adding to our pile of environmental research, we'd get more bang for the buck making what we already have actionable. We could work toward bridging the "valley of death," overcoming that research-practice gap that Clarke Lethin and the ladies from Worldview Studio discussed. If we shifted some resources from one-off projects and instead invested in translating current research into applied solutions, then we'd multiply those solutions' impacts—and at little-to-no additional cost. Jeff Borden mentioned something similar when he talked about a national-level education architect. Professor Sanjay Mannan highlighted a related need in government-sponsored medical research, and technologist Dean Pianta talked about these themes in the context of cybersecurity.

So when candidates bang their fists on the debate stage and parade their comprehensive new program ideas, it makes me dubious. Those political solutions might be great in sound bites, but they seem out of step with the real world. After exploring our national assets, even on my shoestring budget, I'm convinced that we don't need *more*. We need *different*. In other words, regardless of the topic area—and ideally, even across areas—we already have the puzzle pieces, but we need to think differently about how they're assembled. We need things like big-picture thinking, orchestration, interdisciplinary plans, and practical communication. We need the mortar between the bricks. We need the missing links.

Operating at its best, our federal government could help navigate by applying long-term strategic thinking, fostering a common vision (like a moon shot), and helping to nudge the puzzle pieces into alignment. But in its current state, I worry if government is up to the task. This is another place where those political incentives work against us. Senior elected officials are typically motivated to retain their offices. So they're often lured into chasing nearer-term wins and nominal victories that look good on paper. They're also encouraged to enact solutions based on voting maps rather than best practices. After all, it's easier to spread around tax dollars in key districts than to invest in the hard and unglamorous work of building enduring solutions.

Look at the military's F-35 combat aircraft. It's a notoriously flawed program: over eight years behind schedule, riddled with operational issues, and around $200 billion over budget. But rather than reevaluate or enforce an improvement plan, Congress has continued to flood the program with cash, inserting budgetary earmarks even beyond what the Pentagon has asked for. Why have politicians continued to feed this glutton? In no small part, it's because the F-35 developers cleverly distributed its production across the US, in at least forty-six states.[1] So nearly every legislator who votes against the program would be cutting off millions (or billions) of dollars that are flowing home, and that means they risk irate constituents at the ballot box. The issue isn't really the F-35 or its components. The problem is in the way we've approached the programs and others like it. There's no strategy or long-term design—or more accurately, there is one, but it's focused on political ends.

★ ★ ★

Spreading the tax-dollar love certainly helps politicians build influence, and when that's done at the expense of more careful planning, it can undermine solutions. Yet even more insidious is when politicians (or media) spread outrage and spur hate. Around the political realm, there's an incentive to sell drama and provoke a reaction, which often translates to frustration, fear, and anger.[2] Sensationalism riles the voting base and gets those eyeballs on social channels. Political uproar gets clicks and likes, and it gives people something to fight about. The problem isn't the show, per se, but when political theatrics spill into reality, we need to be concerned. And for the record, I'm alarmed.

Too often, rather than channeling energy toward civic engagement, we're taking aim at each other. The widening span of politicized media and the unchecked use of emotional tactics steadily fuels the escalating partisan divide.[3] I've come to believe that this combination of partisanship and emotionality is among the biggest threats to our country. It undermines trust, foments fear, and builds firewalls against productive problem solving. After all, it's difficult to coordinate solutions and act creatively when you're focused on crushing your opponent.

In my own campground surveys, I talked with irate Democrats eager for the political right to "pay for what they've done," and I found seething Republicans convinced by the propaganda that "the left hates America and is trying to destroy it." Worse, as emotions are wont to do, such feelings often spilled beyond their initial bounds. For example, one gentleman told me about a volunteer project he had tried to organize after a hurricane. He'd struggled to muster enough support, largely because the worst-hit areas voted on the other side of the political aisle from his local community. His neighbors didn't want to sign-up to help people from the so-called opposing team. That story made my stomach turn, and sadly, I heard others like it.

Former Defense Secretary James Mattis seems to have a similar outlook.

He recently remarked, "I'm less concerned right now with foreign enemies than I am with what we're doing to ourselves. We seem to have forgotten that governance takes unity."[4]

Let that sink in. One of the most outspoken warriors of the modern era worries more about national unity than external dangers. Over the last several months (as I write this book in early 2020), Mattis has spoken out regularly about the threat of hyperpolarization, at times referencing Abraham Lincoln's famous Lyceum Address. At a recent conference, for instance, he explained (with some paraphrasing):

> If this country ends, it'll be by suicide. As I look across the scorched political landscape, I think our enemies must be cheering. When we're competing in politics and say "I'm right, and you're wrong. You're dumb." Well, that's OK. It's politics, after all, and we can still work together after the election. But when someone says, "I'm right, and you're evil." There is no room for compromise. If we stick together, no one can take us. Rather, as Abraham Lincoln said, "If this national experiment ends, it'll be by our own authorship."[5]

Mattis is drawing from Lincoln's Civil War–era words. So you might be thinking, *Well, political divisions are nothing new.* Still, there are contemporary trends that make our time distinct. For example, in their book, *The Coddling of the American Mind*, Greg Lukianoff and Jonathan Haidt show how the ebbs and flows of American culture have intersected with the rise of social media to foster three Great Untruths that (among other things) aggravate polarization.[6] The untruths include a perception of fragility that encourages people to censure or shrink away from conflicting views, an "always trust your feelings" mindset that promotes emotional decision making, and a sort of black-and-white thinking that "life is a battle between good people and evil people."

The Coddling book has recommendations on how to confront these untruths, including advice for reducing negative partisanship through open discourse. Along my travels, I found similar recommendations. For instance, Dr. Frederick Lawrence, Secretary and CEO of the Phi Beta Kappa honor society and a civil rights scholar, told me about a concept he calls vigorous civility.

"It's designed to sound like an oxymoron," he explained when I interviewed him. "People think civility means we can only talk about white clouds and doves and, you know, sing 'Kumbaya.' That's not it. Vigorous discussion doesn't mean I'm rude to you. It means that I challenge your ideas, and you challenge mine right back. And vigorous civility means we do that in a context of civility."

"Disagreement is, paradoxically, community building," he later added. "If I disagree with you, that must mean I've heard what you said, and now I'm trying to explain what I think about it. And when I finish talking, I expect you to tell me what you think. If I delegitimize you, though, then you have no place at the table.

Your ideas don't count, and you don't matter. That's destructive to communities, and I would go further: That's antithetical to what the American experiment is all about."

Throughout this book I've preached innovation, and when I interviewed Lloyd Thrall, the former DASD for readiness, he'd called America "the capital of innovation" and maintained that we don't need to invent new solutions. Rather, he'd said, "It's a matter of thinking differently about what we do have." I saw that too. Across all fifty states and threaded through every subject, we have the elements of a solution for nearly every problem—even political ones. *So if there's no straightforward way to evolve our political processes, then maybe some other tactic will work—a way around rather than through the brick wall.*

The political elite comprise only a fraction of our nation. There are hundreds of millions of us outside of that circle. Even if we're lacking money, influence, or the political playbook, we can affect change, but doing so requires active involvement—more than casting a vote, holding a picket sign, or posting angry Facebook rants. In other words, I've come to believe that mobilizing an informed and interdependent citizenry is the first twist of the Rubik's Cube for political change. Together, we can gradually change the zeitgeist of the political ecosystem.

People can get involved in a thousand different ways. You don't have to run for president or even another public office; although that's one place to start. If you're interested in bringing some outside views into the system, then find help learning the game rules from civically minded groups, like She Should Run for women or With Honor Action for military veterans. Be careful of falling into the trap of just being a warm body and be careful whom you listen to inside the political establishment. Don't let your personal *ass*ets get taken for granted.

If running for office isn't your jam, you can help with political campaigns or citizen movements. You can get on open advisory boards or attend government-sponsored workshops. You can become a civil servant, join the military, or participate in programs like the Department of State's Virtual Student Federal Service or the Marine Corps Cyber Auxiliary. There are relevant nongovernmental organizations too, like AmeriCorps or the Service Year Alliance. Or you can write your own adventure, like my friend Banks Helfrich did. He hosts "no assumptions" dance parties where he assembles an audience around two opposing debaters and a fact checker. The panelists discuss things like abortion or entitlements spending with the onlookers, and when things get heated, everyone dances to a live band. Whatever method you choose (or invent), it's all about finding a way into (or, at least, a way to *see* into) governmental structures, creating more political accountability, and contributing your unique talents to our greater community.

Valuing those unique contributions is another twist of the Cube. If we hope to continue to thrive as a healthy nation, then we have to change our collective mindset and, as Frederick suggested, interact with vigorous civility. When we bring all of our different talents together and actively include diverse perspectives, we can overcome any problem we encounter. As an interconnected society, with innovative thoughts, assorted abilities, and so many local solutions, we can resolve anything we turn our collective attention toward.

There are many disconcerting trends that seem to be dividing our nation, but we've faced daunting challenges before, like women's suffrage, the civil rights movement, and the Civil War. The frustrating difference today is that our divisiveness is largely manufactured, even if its results are painfully real. So rather than working hand-in-hand toward a better society, we're too often wasting energy taking political potshots at each other. As retired-General Mattis warned, we're causing injury by our own hands. The silver lining is, at least, that the means of relief is also in our control.

Bridge building isn't just for politicos and govvies. This is something we can all contribute to—if, like Brie and Nancy from Worldview Studio said, we're willing to reach beyond our tribes, beyond our own social and professional communities. That kind of outreach isn't merely a nice thing to have, it's the first step toward helping America build more integrated responses—something we desperately need. It doesn't matter where any one of us sits on the political spectrum; in fact, we need dissenting views from all perspectives. What matters is our shared devotion to society, our willingness to steer clear of emotional partisanism, and our active commitment to bring our puzzle pieces together.

Finally, if there's only one message everyone hears from this book, know this: You're worth more than your vote. What makes this country work isn't the people who sit in the highest offices—it's the citizens that every single day go to work, create new ideas, share their lessons with others, and push themselves to contribute to the invisible web that connects us all. It's our whole-of-nation capabilities and collective ownership of responsibility.

Every single person in this country is tangibly important. This year, I've been fortunate to meet thinkers, doers, dreamers, idea makers, challengers, and observers from all across our nation. I've talked to the helpers and protectors, the builders and fixers, the people who work with their hands and those who work with their voices. So many are striving to connect and strengthen this nation. I hope the anecdotes I've collected from them and the thoughts I've woven throughout this book nudge even a single person to follow in a similar direction. In my wildest dreams, I hope these words might help us to collectively take a small step forward as a nation that embraces our diversity, empowers our collective innovation, and fosters trust among our people. I hope these words inspire a little more strategic and systematic thinking about government, politics, and national solutions. And, finally, I hope they help encourage others to participate more actively in our national story, to be vigorously civil, and to rise above our so-called minimum civic duties. After all, we don't need an act of Congress to fix our nation. We just need a lot of dedicated Americans to work together.

Postscript

In a way, this year of living politically became my citizen-service project, not solely nor even primarily as a way to sate my own curiosity but as a way to volunteer my talents for our society. Across our fifty states, I learned that there's an entire nation of people searching for something similar—searching for how to contribute or where to find answers to our collective challenges. For one reason or another, they don't know how to get involved. I figured if I could break into the hen house and share what I found, maybe that would help blaze some of the trail for others.

On a personal level, I loved parts of my year. Every state is weirdly unique, even all of those little ones in New England and the square ones out west. I loved finding small towns off the beaten path and all of the quirky roadside sculptures. I loved talking to people and hearing their ideas, and I had the exceptional opportunity to live hundreds of funny, touching, and inspiring stories. I found sparks of brilliance across the nation, and everywhere I went, I found interested and knowledgeable citizens. Of course, not everyone is a political scholar (I certainly am not), but just about every person I talked to gives a damn.

I find the audacity and enthusiasm of our next generation enlightening and energizing. I've developed enormous respect for our military service members who, by and large, have shown me genuine courage, an honest focus on completing missions without drama, and an ability to circumvent roadblocks. I've been lifted up by the ingenuity of our people from every walk of life and from all sides of the political spectrum. I'm grateful to those who've encouraged and supported me along this journey. Most importantly, I'm grateful for the countless Americans who recognize the need to act differently, think outside the box, and take action on behalf of our nation. I've been profoundly moved by this experience.

Thank you.

. . . now let's all get to work!

Notes

CHAPTER THREE: IT'S MY POLITICAL PARTY...

1. Aishwarya Kumar, "The Grandmaster Diet: How to Lose Weight While Barely Moving," *ESPN*, September 13, 2019, www.espn.com.

CHAPTER FOUR: ONLY CRAZY PEOPLE RUN...

1. Denise-Marie Ordway and John Wihbey, "Negative political ads and their effect on voters: Updated collection of research," *Journalist's Resource,* September 25, 2016, journalistsresource.org.

   John G. Geer, *In Defense of Negativity: Attack Ads in Presidential Campaigns* (Chicago, IL: University of Chicago Press, 2008).

CHAPTER FIVE: HI, I'M JJ...

1. Kim Parker, "Views of Higher Education Divided by Party," *Pew Research Center,* August 19, 2019, www.pewsocialtrends.org.

2. Klaus Schwab, *The Global Competitiveness Report 2019* (Cologny/Geneva, Switzerland: World Economic Forum, 2019), www.weforum.org/gcr.

   Edward Alden and Rebecca Strauss, *How America stacks up: Economic competitiveness and US policy* (New York, NY: Council on Foreign Relations Press, 2016).

3. Jacob Poushter and Janell Fetterolf, *A Changing World: Global Views on Diversity, Gender Equality, Family Life and the Importance of Religion* (Pew Research Center, April 2019), www.pewresearch.org. The Pew Research Center has published several reports on global diversity. This is just one example.

4. Erik Larson, "New Research: Diversity Inclusion = Better Decision Making At Work," *Forbes,* September 23, 2017, www.forbes.com. Research showing more diverse teams make better business decisions has been published in many venues. This is one example.

5. "Global Innovation Index 2019," World Intellectual Property Organization, accessed October 30, 2019, www.wipo.int/global_innovation_index.

6. *ibid.* See Poushter and Fetterolf, Larson, and the Global Innovation Index, above.

7. Diana I. Dalphonse, Chris Townsend, and Matthew W. Weaver, "Shifting Landscape: The Evolution of By, With, and Through," *The Strategy Bridge,* August 1, 2018, thestrategybridge.org. Note that "by, with, and through" is a military and statecraft phrase. In more recent years, it has been used to emphasize diplomatic collaboration.

CHAPTER EIGHT: MONEY IS THE ROOT...

1. The Center for Responsive Politics, a nonpartisan and nonprofit organization, includes a wealth of information on Political Action Committees. See www.opensecrets.org.

2. Maggie Christ, Brendan Fischer, Meredith McGehee, and William Gray, *All Expenses Paid: How Leadership PACs Became Politicians' Preferred Ticket to Luxury Living*, (Campaign Legal Center and Issue One, July 2018), www.issueone.org. Politicians have few restrictions on how they spend their Leadership PAC resources. Issue One, a nonpartisan and nonprofit organization, has completed several reports on PACs.

3. The FEC lists contribution limits at www.fec.gov.

4. Michael Beckel and Amisa Ratliff, *Leadership PACs, Inc.: How Washington power players use leadership PACS to buy access and influence* (Issue One, October 2018), www.issueone.org. Historically, many politicians have use their Leadership PACs to pay for influence.

5. Peter Schweizer, *Extortion: How Politicians Extract Your Money, Buy Votes, and Line Their Own Pockets* (New York: Houghton Mifflin Harcourt, 2013).

6. Ballotpedia, a nonpartisan and nonprofit organization, maintains detailed records of ballot access requirements. See ballotpedia.org.

7. *60 Minutes*, "Dialing for Dollars," correspondent Norah O'Donnell and producers Patricia Shevlin and Miles Doran, aired April 24, 2016, on CBS, www.cbsnews.com. Note that Representative David Jolly served in the US House from 2014–2017. During his tenure there, he attempted to expose and address fundraising conflicts of interest, including through this documentary.

8. Kendall Karson, Adam Kelsey, and John Verhovek, "Here's How the First 2020 Democratic Presidential Debates Work," *ABC News*, June 25, 2019, abcnews.go.com. The Democratic Party clearly outlined the qualifications necessary to participate in the debates. This ABC News article summarizes those requirements.

CHAPTER NINE: AT LEAST I CAN HANDLE...

1. Andrew M. Davenport, "A New Civil War Museum Speaks Truths in the Former Capital of the Confederacy," *Smithsonian Magazine*, May 2, 2019, www.smithsonianmag.com.

2. Julie Jennings and Jared C. Nagel, *Federal Workforce Statistics Sources: OPM and OMB* (Congressional Research Service, R43590, October 24, 2019), https://crsreports.congress.gov. This report discusses the size of the federal workforce.

3. David M. Cohen, *Amateur Government: When Political Appointees Manage the Federal Bureaucracy* (The Brookings Institution, CPM Working Paper 96-1, February 1, 1996), www.brookings.edu. This report offers an in-depth and rather snarky discussion on political appointees. Although decades old now, its sentiments still ring true.

4. Scott Limbocker, "Partisanship and Politics in the US Civil Service" (PhD diss., Vanderbilt University, 2018), etd.library.vanderbilt.edu. This dissertation offers a detailed treatment of many political appointee issues, including turnover.

5. Gary E. Hollibaugh, "Oxford Research Encyclopedia of Politics," in *Oxford Research Encyclopedia of Politics*, September 2019, 10.1093/acrefore/9780190228637.013.1395. This is one more reference on political appointees, just for good measure. It has similar themes to David Cohen's report (cited above) but captures more timely data.

CHAPTER TEN: THE GREAT AMERICAN...

1. The National Park Service employs around sixteen-thousand regular personnel as well as several thousand addition seasonal workers. For comparison, *Fortune* lists the size of Fortune 500 companies at fortune.com/fortune500.

2. Ken Chamberlain, "Lt. Gen. Jay Silveria: Diversity Is a 'Force Multiplier'," *Air Force Times,* February 14, 2018, www.airforcetimes.com.

CHAPTER ELEVEN: NEITHER HEALTHY...

1. For a real-time list of endangered and threatened species refer to the International Union for Conservation of Nature's Red List of Threatened Species, available at www.iucnredlist.org. The statistics used in this chapter were retrieved from the "Stats" section of the site in December 2019.

    Noah Greenwald, Brett Hartl, Loyal Mehrhoff, and Jamie Pang, "Shortchanged: Funding Needed to Save America's Most Endangered Species," (Tucson, AZ: Center for Biological Diversity, 2016), www.biologicaldiversity.org/publications/papers. This report discusses funding for endangered species—particularly the ugly ones.

2. Wallace J. Nichols, *Blue Mind: The Surprising Science That Shows How Being Near, In, On, or under Water Can Make You Happier, Healthier, More Connected, and Better at What You Do* (Little, Brown, 2014).

3. "Veterans Health Administration," US Department of Veterans Affairs, last modified July 14, 2019, www.va.gov/health.

4. United States Interagency Council on Homelessness, *US Government Report: Homelessness in America: Focus on Veterans* (Washington, DC: Interagency Council on Homelessness, 2018), www.usich.gov.

5. For information on Veterans Affairs Telehealth Services, see telehealth.va.gov.

6. "Fact Sheet: Telehealth," American Hospital Association, dated February 2019, www.aha.org.

7. Arthur Allen, "A Hospital Without Patients," *The Agenda,* November 08, 2017, www.politico.com/agenda.

8. "National Health Expenditure (NHE) Fact Sheet," *US Centers for Medicare & Medicaid Services,* revised December 5, 2019, www.cms.gov.

CHAPTER FOURTEEN: MORE THAN A FASTER...

1. JJ Walcutt and Sae Schatz, eds. *Modernizing Learning: Building the Future Learning Ecosystem* (Washington, DC: Government Publishing Office, 2019).

2. John D. Bransford, Ann L. Brown, and Rodney R. Cocking, eds., with additional material from M. Suzanne Donovan, John D. Brandsford, and James W. Pellegrino, eds., *How People Learn: Brain, Mind, Experience, and School* (Washington, DC: National Academy Press, 2000).

   National Academies of Sciences, Engineering, and Medicine, *How People Learn II: Learners, Contexts, and Cultures* (Washington, DC: National Academies Press, 2018).

3. Xinhua, "China's Spending on Education in 2018 Increases," *China Daily,* May 5, 2019, www.chinadaily.com.cn.

4. Laurie Chen, "Chinese Parents Spend Up to US$43,500 a Year on After-School Classes for Their Children," *South China Morning Post,* December 4, 2018, www.scmp.com.

5. *China Power: Unpacking the Complexity of China's Rise,* Center for Strategic and International Studies, August 6, 2019, chinapower.csis.org/military-spending.

6. Patrick Vlaskovits, "Henry Ford, Innovation, and That 'Faster Horse' Quote," *Harvard Business Review,* August 29, 2011, hbr.org. According to Vlaskovits, there's no evidence Ford ever uttered the famous adage. Still, it's routinely attributed to him.

CHAPTER FIFTEEN: 'OHANA

1. The Church publishes its teaching online, including guidance on moms working:

   The Church of Jesus Christ of Latter-Day Saints, "Mothers' Employment Outside the Home," in *Preparing for an Eternal Marriage* (Salt Lake City, UT: The Church of Jesus Christ of Latter-day Saints, 2001), 237–240, www.churchofjesuschrist.org.

   ... and the roles of husbands and wives:

   "The Family: A Proclamation to the World," The Church of Jesus Christ of Latter-Day Saints, accessed January 29, 2020, www.churchofjesuschrist.org. This web page lists the proclamation read by President Gordon B. Hinckley as part of his message at the General Relief Society Meeting on September 23, 1995, in Salt Lake City, UT.

CHAPTER SIXTEEN: A DUMMY'S GUIDE...

1. Bruce Ackerman and Ian Ayres, *Voting with Dollars: A New Paradigm for Campaign Finance* (New Haven, CT: Yale University Press, 2008).

Voting with Dollars refers to Ackerman and Ayres's book, which outlines a campaign reform agenda where each citizen would have $50 "patriot dollars" to spend on candidates each year, and all campaign contributions would be made anonymous and untraceable by the FEC.

Also, Clean Elections is a type of publicly funded election currently used in some states, such as Arizona. Qualified candidates who agree to forgo special interest and high-dollar contributions in exchange receive a sizable chunk of funding from the state. See, for example, www.azcleanelections.gov.

CHAPTER SEVENTEEN: HOW ARE WE STILL TALKING . . .

1. Peter M. Lee, "Lies, Damned Lies and Statistics," The University of York, Mathematics Department, revised July, 19 2012, www.york.ac.uk/depts/maths.

    The phrase "lies, damn lies, and statistics" was popularized by Mark Twain but its origin remains unknown. This post offers a summary of its possible sources.

2. Don Wallace, "Who Owns Oʻahu? Mystery Buyers, High Fliers and All Those LLCs—We Take a Look at Who's Claiming Stakes on Oʻahu." *Honolulu-Magazine.* May 18, 2015, www.honolulumagazine.com.

3. Danny Buerkli, "'What Gets Measured Gets Managed'—It's Wrong and Drucker Never Said It," *Centre for Public Impact,* dated April 8, 2019, www.medium.com/centre-for-public-impact.

    Simon Caulkin, "The Rule is Simple: Be Careful What You Measure," *The Guardian,* February 9, 2008, www.theguardian.com.

    The quote "what gets measured gets managed" is often attributed to Peter Drucker, but it has questionable origins, as Buerkli points out. More importantly, it's often misunderstood. As Caulkin writes, "The full proposition is: 'What gets measured gets managed—even when it's pointless to measure and manage it, and even if it harms the purpose of the organization to do so.'" He goes on to highlight lethal pitfalls in that way of thinking, including the "implication that management is only about measuring . . . [which] is often misunderstood, with disastrous consequences."

CHAPTER EIGHTEEN: BLACK SWANS . . .

1. JJ Walcutt, *Innovating Government: Re-designing the Executive Branch* (Washington, DC: Office of the Under Secretary of Defense for Personnel and Readiness, Work number HQ0642812453, 2020).

2. Oklahoma City National Memorial Museum, *Revitalization of the City,* September 2019, www.memorialmuseum.com.

3. Asher Kohn, "The French Quarter's Not-So-Secret Slaving History," *Timeline,* February 9, 2016, www.timeline.com.

4. CNN Library, "Hurricane Katrina Statistics Fast Facts," *CNN,* updated October 30, 2019, www.cnn.com.

5. John Schwartz And Mark Schleifstein, Fortified but Still in Peril, New Orleans Braces for its Future, *The New York Times,* February 24, 2018, www.nytimes.com.

   NOVA, "The Man Who Predicted Katrina," *PBS,* www.pbs.org.

6. Nassim Nicholas Taleb, *The Black Swan: The Impact of the Highly Improbable* (London: Penguin, 2007).

CHAPTER NINETEEN: THE LAST MILE

1. Maggie Astor, "Democrats Can Qualify for the Next Debate by Winning a Single Delegate in Iowa," *The New York Times,* January 17, 2020, www.nytimes.com.

CHAPTER TWENTY: PIECES . . .

1. Sean Kennedy, "Congress is Ultimately to Blame for F-35 Fiasco" (opinion), *Air Force Times,* March 2, 2020, www.airforcetimes.com.

   Jeremy Bender, Armin Rosen, and Skye Gould, "This Map Explains the F-35 Fiasco," *Business Insider,* August 20, 2014, www.businessinsider.com.

2. Pew Research Center, "Partisanship and Political Animosity in 2016," *Pew Research Center,* June 22, 2016, www.people-press.org.

   Dan Balz, "Americans Hate All the Partisanship, but They're Also More Partisan Than They Were," *The Washington Post,* October 26, 2019, www.washingtonpost.com.

3. Carroll Doherty, "7 Things to Know about Polarization in America," *Pew Research Center,* June 12, 2014, www.pewresearch.org.

   Ezra Klein, *Why We're Polarized* (United States: Avid Reader Press / Simon & Schuster, 2020).

4. "Mattis: 'We seem to have forgotten that governance takes unity'" (video), *NBC News,* December 13, 2019, www.msn.com.

5. Quote captured extemporaneously during NS2 NOW Security and Innovation Summit, October 30, 2019, McLean, VA.

6. Jonathan Haidt and Greg Lukianoff, *The Coddling of the American Mind: How Good Intentions and Bad Ideas Are Setting Up a Generation for Failure* (United States: Penguin Publishing Group, 2018).

CPSIA information can be obtained
at www.ICGtesting.com
Printed in the USA
FSHW020903130620
71001FS